Trauma Culture

The Politics of Terror and Loss in Media and Literature

E. Ann Kaplan

Rutgers University Press
New Brunswick, New Jersey, and London

Library of Congress Cataloging-in-Publication Data

aplan, E. Ann.
Trauma culture : the politics of terror and loss in media and literature / E. Ann
lan.
p. cm.
cludes bibliographical references (p.) and index.
3N 0–8135–3590–5 (alk. paper) — ISBN 0–8135–3591–3 (pbk. : alk. paper)
errorism in motion pictures. 2. Disaster films—History and criticism. 3. Psychic
n motion pictures. 4. Psychic trauma in literature. 5. Literature, Modern—20th
–History and criticism. I. Title.
)5.9.T46K37 2005
6552—dc22 2004023482

Cataloging-in-Publication record for this book is available from the British Library.

Manufactured in the United States of America

Contents

ACKNOWLEDGMENTS

AS USUAL, there are many people to thank for help in writing this book. To start with, I want to thank my erstwhile Stony Brook colleague, Ban Wang, with whom I taught the first course on trauma at Stony Brook in 1997. Ban's quick intelligence and critical appreciation of trauma studies, then just emerging, resulted in spirited interchanges over time that were invaluable as my ideas developed.

I also learned a great deal from the various students in courses I taught over many years on different aspects of trauma studies. Their questions and insights, in conjunction with my writing lectures, enabled me to formulate my ideas.

Graduate students in the Humanities Institute helped me with my research in between their other jobs, getting books for me or undertaking the onerous work of seeking images on the Internet. Thanks especially to Craig Peariso, Chad Laird, and Niharika Dinkar.

Beverly Haviland read drafts of two chapters and gave me useful feedback. I very much appreciated her support. Patrice Petro provided an insightful response to my manuscript, with useful suggestions. But my husband, Martin Hoffman, bore the brunt of my struggles to get the book finished. He patiently helped edit some sections of the book, and was always there to offer advice and support. In addition, I learned from, and was able to make use of, some of his research in chapter 4. Our discussions encouraged me to think more about the many levels of the human organism involved in responding to trauma.

I want to thank the Humanities Research Center at Australian National University, Canberra, for providing a visiting fellowship in spring 2000, during which I did the research for chapter 5, and Green College, University of British Columbia, for a visiting professorship. While at Green College, I worked on conceptualizing "trauma cinema" and the politics and aesthetics of trauma.

The introduction to this book, " 9/11 and 'Disturbing Remains,'" contains material that was published as "A Camera and a Catastrophe," in *Trauma at Home: After 9/11,* edited by Judith Greenberg (University of Nebraska Press, 2003). However, my own photos now accompany the piece, and the chapter contains new material.

Some of the films analyzed in Chapter 5 were discussed in an essay, "Traumatic Contact Zones and Embodied Translators," in my coedited book, *Trauma and*

Cinema: Cross-Cultural Explorations (Hong Kong University Press, 2004), but the framing of the essay here is quite different.

Adrienne Munich gave me excellent advice about images for the cover, and in searching her files, came up with Kate Millett's sculpture (photographed by Chie Nishio) that was finally agreed upon for the book. I very much appreciated this help.

I want to thank Rutgers University Press editors Leslie Mitchner and Marilyn Campbell, for their patience during the exacting final stages of preparing the manuscript for press. Mary Cicora did thorough copy-editing work for the book, and kept me busy with necessary questions.

I am delighted that the book is finished and I look forward to continuing the conversations about trauma started here.

E. Ann Kaplan
December 2004

Trauma Culture

INTRODUCTION

9/11 and "Disturbing Remains"

THIS BOOK is about the impact of trauma both on individuals and on entire cultures or nations, and about the need to share and "translate" such traumatic impact. My study of trauma and its cultural politics opens with reference to 9/11 because the catastrophe offers insight into some of the book's main themes, namely that trauma produces new subjects, that the political-ideological context within which traumatic events occur shapes their impact, and that it is hard to separate individual and collective trauma. The experience of 9/11 also demonstrates the difficulties of generalizing about trauma and its impact, for, as Freud pointed out long ago, how one reacts to a traumatic event depends on one's individual psychic history, on memories inevitably mixed with fantasies of prior catastrophes, and on the particular cultural and political context within which a catastrophe takes place, especially how it is "managed" by institutional forces.

Also important about trauma is how one defines it. Trauma studies originated in the context of research about the Holocaust. This event was of such a magnitude as to warrant the use of trauma in its historical (one might say "classical") form. Some of the films and other texts I study deal with World War II and the Holocaust, but the narratives involve not internees or soldiers but relatives of internees or women and children living in terror because of World War II. Other films are about descendants of indigenous peoples in postcolonial contexts, who are also living in terror still after centuries of displacement and attempted annihilation. Such daily experience of terror may not take the shape of classic trauma suffered by victims or survivors, but to deny these experiences as traumatic would be a mistake. Instead, I extend the concept of trauma to include suffering terror. This should not make the term meaningless. Rather, one recognizes degrees and kinds of trauma. The impact of a major public event on relatives indirectly involved in terror I call "family" or "quiet trauma," following other scholars. Retaining the concept in this broader way allows work like my own to be linked with work that favors a more narrow definition. The word "trauma" gestures toward a sphere of knowledge or a terrain that my book contributes to. I contribute precisely by addressing problems of definition and in distinguishing different types of trauma, and analyzing different ways people relate to traumatic events.

Equally important about trauma is one's specific positioning vis-à-vis an event. For this reason, it is necessary to distinguish the different positions and contexts of encounters with trauma.[1] At one extreme there is the direct trauma victim while at the other we find a person geographically far away, having no personal connection to the victim. In between are a series of positions: for example, there's the relative of trauma victims or the position of workers coming in after a catastrophe, those who encounter trauma through accounts they hear, or clinicians who may be vicariously traumatized now that increasingly counseling is offered to people who survive catastrophes.[2] People encounter trauma by being a bystander, by living near to where a catastrophe happened, or by hearing about a crisis from a friend. But most people encounter trauma through the media, which is why focusing on so-called mediatized trauma is important.

The phenomenon of 9/11 was perhaps the supreme example of a catastrophe that was experienced globally via digital technologies (Internet, cell phone) as well as by television and radio, and responded to in a myriad of ways depending on peoples' national and local contexts. In what follows, I offer a personal account of experiencing 9/11 that will illustrate the complexity of a catastrophe as registered through one consciousness, with its unconscious substrates. The events radically altered my relationship to New York, to the United States qua nation, and produced a new personal identity. In my account, the difficulty of fully distinguishing trauma from vicarious trauma emerges; one can see the way that symptoms of prior traumatic events are triggered by new ones or glimpse how the political-ideological shaping of 9/11 through the United States media emerges in my being "hailed" by dominant images and discourses. I became dimly aware of this by encountering other discourses on the New York streets. One finds the complex interconnections between individual and cultural trauma—such that, indeed, where the "self" begins and cultural reactions end may seem impossible to determine. One can also find the single hopeful thread of a catastrophe, namely the perhaps short-lived but real creation of new public-sphere communities as specific crises are "translated" from group to group.

SEPTEMBER 11, 2001 AND AFTER

In the shocked days after the Twin Towers collapsed and thousands of people died in unimaginable ways, I wandered around my neighborhood between Union Square and SoHo, trying to absorb what had happened. My camera was my only companion. I snapped pictures (sometimes feeling guilty—was I invading people's privacy?) in an attempt, I think, to make "real" what I could barely comprehend. My immediate physical world had changed dramatically with the disappearance of the Twin Towers from my daily visual landscape at the end of Broadway and their reduction to a mountain of smoking wreckage sending

1. English children sitting on rubble from bombing of London (National Archives and Records Administration)

acrid air into our apartment. My relation to the public sphere was also changed since New York City, and the United States as nation, both were destabilized as concepts. But my inner world was even more changed; not only did the catastrophe reactivate my old traumatic symptoms from World War II England but it also brought about surprising new crises to do with my professional and political identifications—or rather with my political *identity* itself. This resulted in unexpected ruptures with colleagues I had earlier always agreed with.

Ever since experiencing World War II as a small child in war-torn England, I have been ready to jump at any unexpected sound. Every time I hear a police siren it recalls the warnings of an impending air-raid attack. Various phobias—fears of elevators, tunnels, small spaces—have been hard to shake over the years. Nightmares of being abandoned during an air-raid attack, of losing my parents, of suffocating in my gas mask, of being unable to escape from an underground shelter, or of being chased by Hitler (who assumed in my infant consciousness a kind of monster form) had pursued me from time to time in my teenage years, but much less so since coming to the United States to study in the 1960s. When the Towers were struck, some of these muted symptoms returned. My childhood sense of extreme vulnerability returned, as if our very New York apartment building might not continue to stand; changes in the acrid smells made me

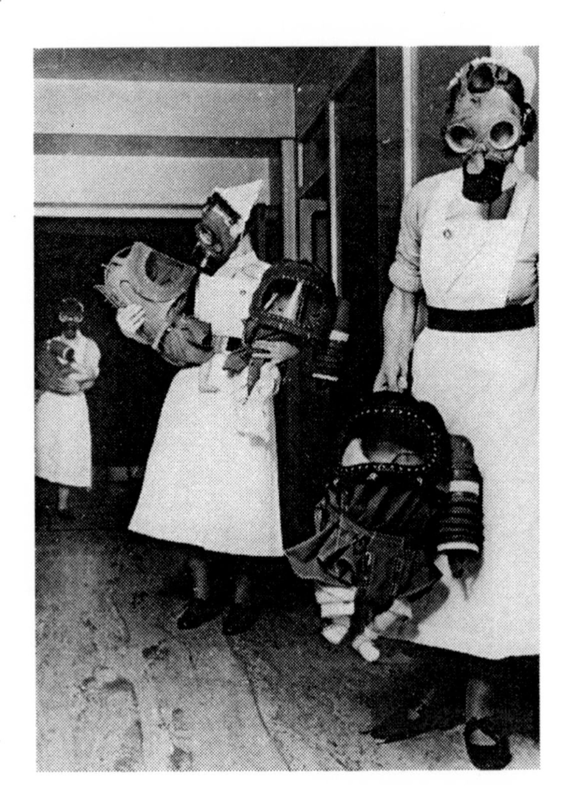

2. Nurses with gas masks carrying babies also protected against gas: Drill in war-torn England (EarthStation 1 Multimedia)

think our building was on fire; I hardly dared take the subways, since even in normal conditions as a result of war trauma I often had panic attacks when a subway train was stalled in the tunnel. Now, I seemed to fear an attack whenever I was on a train. In other words, the new traumatic event merged with the childhood events, so that history and memory, time and space collapsed into one present time of terror; 9/11 produced a new subjectivity.

Because of this merging of traumatic experiences, it is hard to say whether I was experiencing direct or secondary trauma. The positions seemed to collapse into one another. On the one hand, I had not been in the Towers when they were destroyed, I was not a worker called in to deal with the catastrophe, and I did not personally know anyone killed in the attacks. Yet, the event had taken place very close to where I lived, it had a big impact on my daily life, and it triggered what had been a direct, earlier trauma. It is also clear that another person might not have been traumatized either by my relatively minor World War II experiences or by the impact of the Towers' collapse on our neighborhood and daily life. Individual psychic organization makes a difference, as Freud knew.

My experience in World War II England was not just about family; it was an experience of the violence of the political and military cataclysms that Julia Kristeva talks about in her psychoanalytically oriented volume *Black Sun*. She

3. Wartime English poster about children and London (Earth-Station 1 Multimedia)

argues that "the shattering of psychic identity" that accompanies even the periphery of such events has an intensity no less violent than war itself, but that it is hard to perceive (222). Possibly I suffered some of that kind of shattering in both the war and 9/11. Kristeva links the two kinds of trauma—the military/political and the personal—and claims that both do damage "to our systems of perception and representation." This is important because there are some who want to reserve the concept of trauma only for large public events, like the Holocaust.

In my case, in regard to 9/11, identities other than my psychic one were also threatened, as, for example, my certainty, as a film scholar, that I could easily analyze media manipulations. At first, that was not the case. I would be swept up in certain live reporting, such as the National Service of Mourning or even George Bush's speech to the entire assembled Congress. It was only as I wandered about Union Square and the streets around my apartment with my camera that I was gradually able to attain a perspective on the media reporting, and to distinguish the different levels through which the catastrophe was being "managed."

4. Union Square Park: The War Memorial plastered with images of missing people, the Twin Towers, and appeals for love and unity (Courtesy of the author)

5. Informal shrine in Union Square with candles to honor the dead and to assert ongoing strength (Courtesy of the author)

THE STREET AND LOCAL COLLECTIVE TRAUMA

There was, then, the street level. Looking through the pictures I took brings those days back as if they were now. The first pictures are of the memorials in Union Square and of the posters stuck all over the streets near me, especially along Tenth and Twelfth Streets, outside the New School and the various fire and police stations in the area (figs. 4–7). These rows of images of lost people overwhelmed me (fig. 6). They hung there as appeals, as desires that the one imaged not be dead, that he or she turn up having escaped. They made visible the need for closure, the awfulness of not knowing if a loved one is dead, and if dead, if one would ever have a body to mourn over.

I hardly dared move further downtown for weeks. But there is a second group of photos from Ground Zero, when finally I felt brave enough to go and look as closely as people were allowed to. National Guard soldiers in their khakis stood at the barriers, their gear reminding me of World War II. The crush of people pressing around me made me feel as claustrophobic as did the crowds jamming into the underground shelters during my childhood. We all reached

6. Images of missing people on the Church Street Post Office wall (Courtesy of the author)

7. Images hung outside police precinct (Courtesy of the author)

over the Ground Zero barriers to take photos. The smoke from the long smoldering buildings is visible in the photos, insistently snarling into the air. The carcass of one tower loomed. Huge chunks of twisted metal jutted out from buildings still standing. I tried to snap the shop windows with objects inside covered in layers of ash. Buildings we passed were still covered in ash. Ground Zero was a huge crematorium.

A final batch of photos was taken later when I was getting used to the changed worlds. I found myself snapping all the odd places flags popped up. I had grown used to the flags on cars, especially those flying from radio antennas, but they were also squeezed into shop doorframes or added into window displays in creative ways (figs. 8–10). A Radio Shack store juxtaposed three carefully arranged flags in the window on one side with an image of lovers (selling a cell phone) on the other. But sitting in the doorway was a homeless man covered by an umbrella and cardboard boxes, while trash sat on the pavement awaiting pick up. That is, response to 9/11 is added onto normal New York life. A flag perched high up on the scaffolding of New York University's new Student Union was perhaps most eye-catching of all.

But what did all this flag flying really mean? Certainly, on one level the flags represented a newly engaged patriotism (a patriotism increasingly problematic for me), echoing sentiments written on memorials in the park and on the walls and around fire stations and police precincts, such as "United We Stand: God Bless America," "We Love America," and so on. But (at least in New York around where the catastrophe had happened) the flags were also a way to indicate empathy for those who had lost relatives and friends, and a shared trauma about the shock to the United States. The inconspicuous nature of the displays supports this view. Some messages in Union Square suggested what I read into flag displays, such as "The Terrorists thought that they can tear us apart. But it brought us together," or "We Are Not Broken," or (one in French), "Aimez Votre Frères Parce-Que Demain Matin Ils Ne Seront Pas." Messages about peace—such as "2001 Years of Violence: What Have We Learned?" or "United We Stand: Violence Creates Violence" or even just "Love One Another"—were more common than saber rattling (fig. 11).

Perhaps because I had not lost anyone I knew personally, wandering around I began to understand in ways I had only theorized before what collective trauma felt like. Everyone was in shock: people did not laugh out loud in the streets or in the Square; voices were muted. People's expressions were somber. I felt a connection to strangers that I had never felt before. On the subway too, we looked at each other as if understanding what we all were facing. For at any moment, it seemed, another attack could take place, the subway could be blown up, gas might fill the tunnels. . . . Nowhere was safe, just as nothing had been safe in wartime England. And we were in this together.

I felt the togetherness especially walking around Union Square, which

8. Flag in watch shop window, Greenwich Village (Courtesy of the author)

9. Flags and models in Ann Taylor Loft window (Courtesy of the author)

10. Flags in Radio Shack window with homeless man on doorstep (Courtesy of the author)

11. Messages about peace and unity abounded (Courtesy of the author)

instantly became a huge, makeshift memorial and also a site for posting images of people still lost. On those bright sunny September afternoons, the Square was crowded with mourners and with people like myself needing to share in the grief and loss we all experienced, even if one had not personally lost a loved one. I snapped pictures of a diverse array of spontaneous, rough drawings and writings. I watched as a huge roll of paper was brought into the Square, gradually unfurling as more and more people knelt down and drew or wrote on the spur of the moment. It became one vast communal outpouring of emotion and thought. The candles and the flowers took on many different forms, reminding one partly of 1960s protest culture, partly of memorials produced when Princess Diana died. And yet this was so different; this was personal and political in new ways. Different religions were represented. But despite all the differences in perspective that the artifacts showed, an apparent commonality reigned in the form of a respect for differences within a whole (the events) that we shared.

The gap where the Twin Towers had stood in the weeks that followed became a space full of horror but also of heroism. Their visual absence was traumatic: That is, it was impossible to comprehend that they were gone—that I no longer found the Towers in their place. Psychoanalytically, this gap or lack can be read in many ways—as Lacan's *petit objet 'a,'* castration (the Towers were huge, phallic), the infant's loss of the mother, a loss standing in for death, abandonment, and abjection. But while these underlying infantile emotions may have been unconsciously evoked, the gap was phenomenological as well as symbolic.

12. Images of the Twin Towers atop flowers in Union Square (Courtesy of the author)

On the other hand, the "gap" was filled with other images—of burning people jumping out of the Towers, of firemen rushing up to rescue people and being crushed when the buildings collapsed, of the huge cloud of smoke pursuing fleeing people like a cement roller or like the giant marshmallow of the movie *Ghostbusters*. People tried to fill in or recover the absence of the Towers by creating images of them (fig. 12). The *New Yorker* created an unforgettable front page that was apparently totally black, but within whose dim darkness one could glimpse shadows or the ghosts of the Towers haunting the city. One or two art stores in Greenwich Village filled their windows with different sizes of beautiful framed color photographs of the Towers in the city landscape (figs. 13–14). Did we hope that pictures of the Towers would undo the trauma of their collapse? Or that they would write over the haunting, unforgettable scenes of the plane driving straight into the second Tower, and of the bright flames that burst forth into the pure blue sky that have returned again and again in nightmares? The images were part of the traumatic symptom already evident in the media's constant repetition of the Towers being struck. Given trauma's peculiar visuality as a psychic disorder, this event seemed to feed trauma by being so highly visual in its happening. The images haunted one waking and dreaming. American culture was visually haunted by the repeated still unbelievable shots of a huge plane full of people plunging into a seemingly impenetrable tower, and bursting into fabulous orange flames.

Level of the Media and Discursive Formations

It was through wandering around the streets with my camera that I began to understand the differences between the media, reporting more or less national (or at least "official" positions), and what I was witnessing myself. It gradually became clear that national ideology was hard at work shaping how the traumatic event was to be perceived. The best that can be said is that the media had to tread a difficult line. In the shaky days following the attacks, reporters presumably felt they had to stick to what United States and other leaders were doing and saying as they tried to calm and to unify the nation as they desperately figured out how to respond. The world was watching. Osama Bin Laden and Al Qaeda were watching. The media aided the attempt to present a united American front. But this proved to be a fiction—a construction of a consensus in a Eurocentric and largely masculine form.

On the streets, by contrast, I experienced the multiple, spontaneous activities from multiple perspectives, genders, races, and religions or nonreligions. Things were not shaped for a specific effect, nor apparently controlled by one entity. By contrast with what I witnessed locally, the male leaders on television presented a stiff, rigid, controlling, and increasingly vengeful response—a response I only gradually understood as actually about humiliation. While a "disciplining" and homogenizing of United States response was at work

13 and 14. Images of the New York skyline with the Towers in Art Shops (Courtesy of the author)

through the media, on the streets something fluid, personal, and varied was taking place.

LEVEL OF POLITICAL IDENTITY AND RUPTURES

One of the unexpected aspects of the catastrophe was the rupture in my political persona: Since the 1960s, I have always (if loosely) identified with left positions, which I shared with my colleagues and friends. But after 9/11 I found myself taking different positions than some of my colleagues or friends in response to the attacks. I have always been critical of the international policies of the United States, of the United States as the latest imperial nation, of its insidious role in postmodern, postcolonial global capitalism. But to my mind these past actions did not "cause" the terrorist attacks nor justify them, as some colleagues argued. America has gotten what it deserves, they said. But the United States was attacked. This was a separate event—in the here and now of 9/11—that needed to be dealt with in its specificity. Linking the attacks to the past actions of the United States was to collapse incommensurable levels of happenings and thought. It reminds me of a colleague who, when I arrived at the university on September 11 about three hours after the attacks, said: "What about Hiroshima? Didn't we do that?" Yes, indeed, and it was horrendous. But to evoke Hiroshima at this moment indicated an intellectualizing of present, highly emotional happenings—a distancing and displacement characteristic of some political scholars. As leftists and political people, I asked, can't we also live in the present and relate to present emotions?

Part of the problem lay in people's different standpoints vis-à-vis the attacks, and their literal closeness or distance from Ground Zero. Some European scholars immediately took a very abstract and theoretical approach. An example of the broad generalizations that arrived promptly via the Internet was Slavoj Žižek's essay "Welcome to the Desert of the Real" (echoing the words that end the celebrated movie *The Matrix*). While Žižek's article overstated the political/psychic symbolism of the attacks, looking at the event from a distant intellectual perspective, I did agree that the attacks broke through an illusory haze in which many Americans may have been living. I appreciated Žižek's argument that in some ways the United States had already anticipated the event in the many movies about uncannily similar catastrophes—as if unconsciously aware of the illusion citizens were living, of the repressed knowledge that now emerged in film fantasies.

But this thesis does not exhaust or actually get close to the specificity of the event for those of us living close by. It is possible that the Towers represented to the terrorists (perhaps schooled in American movies) postmodernity, technology, the city, architectural brilliance, urban landscape, the future high-tech, globalized world. But for those nearby, they functioned phenomenologically as part of people's spatial universe, in and of themselves, not especially representing

American capitalism or American might. The discourse of the United States and "the desert of the real" are orthogonal to the experience of those of us close to the attacks. Both levels need taking into account. The different standpoints of some European and American scholars was evident in a heated debate in the letters section of the *London Review* between scholars in Europe and America. Many Europeans saw the international policies of the United States as leading to hatred intense enough to bring about such terrorism, while American scholars saw a need to deal with the horror of the attacks as a specific set of events. This is not to say that the United States did not have our own writers—like Susan Sontag—taking strong positions close to those of Europeans. Like Žižek, Sontag saw the event as "a monstrous dose of reality" and the public response as "self-righteous drivel being peddled by public figures and TV commentators." She claimed that politics was being replaced by psychotherapy (*New Yorker* 32). But was the therapy discourse really that inappropriate? Mightn't therapy talk be viewed as usefully included in public discussion in times like this? It is true that the media found it easier to relate to the events through a therapy lens (I have a large number of clippings about post-traumatic stress disorder), but isn't it interesting to see psychological issues being taken seriously by a press that has traditionally scorned such perspectives? Political public discussion of 9/11 has been, and still is (despite the remarkable 2004 9/11 Report) inadequate because of the unfortunate limits being set on what can and cannot be debated. But why must confrontational, thorough, and critical political debate be opposed to a discourse including empathy for those who suffer trauma and hurt? Can't we have substantial political analyses that criticize the actions of the United States in the past and present, and yet welcome public discussion about trauma, post-traumatic stress disorder, vicarious traumatization, and ways to help those suffering these disorders?

The United States has been humiliated by the brilliance of the terrorists' imaginations, and their ability to make happen what they had imagined (or perhaps what we had also imagined at least in our movies). And yet, once the event happened as lived experience it still felt "unimaginable." It was also humiliating because the terrorists produced the seemingly impossible by taking advantage of the United States' own open society. The United States' deep humiliation is another way of framing the current situation from the standpoint of theories about the nation descending into the abyss of the "Real."

MARCH 11, 2002 AND AFTER

By March 11, 2002, I had collected piles and piles of newspaper clippings. I had obsessively saved every article about 9/11 that came my way, every mention in the newspapers of all kinds—an activity I now see as partly a symptom of the trauma, as perhaps was also my obsessive taking of photographs. Then all the books began to appear. Amazon.com's array of 9/11 texts was daunting. I thought

I should buy everything there, but ultimately settled for buying just several books. I was going to bring all of this together in some great synthesis or even thesis! But the more I strove to arrive at a synthesis, the more fragmented my thoughts became. I was overwhelmed with data.

Part of the problem in writing about 9/11 at this (relatively) late date, is indeed that so much has been written, so many books published, so much visual art—films, photographs, and videos, like the remarkable documentaries from people happening to be at Ground Zero at the time of the collapse of the Towers, or the huge Reuters photos shown at the New-York Historical Society—so many dramas, speeches, psychological studies, and endless debates in magazines, that one is exhausted simply attending to these things. What new could there possibly be to say?

But it was also worrisome *that* so much was being said, written, and shown. Were people indeed beginning to exploit the event as traumatic effects waned? Was the event being fixed within certain tropes of patriotism and male heroism that began to pall with distance? Was the "realness" of 9/11 being gelled into stock images, stock forms that would forever limit its meanings? Hearing that the scroll of paper that finally wound its way around Union Square was to be displayed in an upcoming museum exhibition, I felt conflicted. How could that scroll on display in a museum mean what it had meant being spontaneously written on in those warm September evenings in the days after the attacks? New York University's La Maison Française held a one-day symposium on "Rupture de l'Ordre Symbolique" (with Paul Ricoeur and Jacques Rancière, among others) debating Žižek's earlier point about the United States being plummeted finally into a harsh reality from an illusory (and exceptional) security. How could we keep the event open, fluid, specific?

I also now understood, of course, that we really had not been "together," as my notes from the time assumed. Many Arab and Muslim individuals have been (and continue to be) arrested or interrogated. There is an entire spectrum of responses to the attacks, a diversity of interpretations. It has become its own phenomenon, with circles spreading out like those from a stone thrown into a pond. I sometimes no longer know what "my" response really is: So I was happy to return to my photos taken at the time and to notes written immediately following the catastrophe, and forget any (in any case impossible) "synthesis."

March 11, 2002 was a difficult day. It brought back vivid memories of September 11. I watched the Ground Zero memorial service for the families of the victims, and was moved. America has learned to mourn and to respect mourning, and that's a good thing. I liked the Twin Towers of Light that were turned on that day. They seemed a gesture that was strong yet peaceful, as against the violence that has characterized much of the response of the United States. Watching the huge blue beams of light from Fifth Avenue (Broadway is too well lit for them to show where they really should have been seen), I felt the gap restored to

15. Images of black smoke emerging from the Towers as people swarmed over the Brooklyn Bridge (Mike Schade)

my visual landscape—or at least there was something there that could not be knocked down. I recalled my last view of the Twin Towers from the Long Island Railroad as I was on my way to work on 9/11. Once out of the tunnel, I turned and saw the two towers still standing, but with great swaths of black smoke pouring from both (fig. 15). The smoke was like an enormous black roll, spreading miles along the sky, following the train to Long Island.

I still have all the front pages of the *New York Times*'s special section, "A Nation Challenged" (I had appreciated this term as much more helpful than CNN's hysterical "America under Attack," and later their even worse, "America at War"). Our nation really was and in 2004 still is "challenged" by the attacks. They are a challenge to us in the sense that the United States has had to respond, to deal with the situation. Their (our?) difficulty has to do so with little tradition to rely on, since these attacks are only the second of their kind in the short history of the United States. At first I thought we had learned from Vietnam, but as time went on that did not seem to be the case. By the end of March 2002, it looked less and less possible that our leaders would rise to the occasion rather than lapsing into isolationist, "go it alone," or revenge tactics. Subsequent events—the invasion of Iraq in March 2003—proved my fears only too warranted.

I pick up the thread of 9/11 again, and continue its/my story in the epilogue on "Wounded New York: 9/11 Memorials." But in between I take up a number of different theoretical issues and case studies. The book examines how subjects are formed through the shocks of modernity and colonialism—a process complicated by the fact that trauma conflates or blurs the boundaries between the individual and the collective as seen in the case of 9/11. I show the increasing importance of "translating" trauma—that is, of finding ways to make meaning out of, and to communicate, catastrophes that happen to others as well as to oneself. Art, perhaps paradoxically, is one such way, as my book shows.[3] Trauma can never be "healed" in the sense of a return to how things were before a catastrophe took place, or before one witnessed a catastrophe; but if the wound of trauma remains open, its pain may be worked through in the process of its being "translated" via art.

The book moves between a focus on the formation of specific traumatized subjects, such as Sigmund Freud, Marguerite Duras, and Sarah Kofman in wartime Austria and France, and a focus on specific collective traumas (such as 9/11, World War II, and colonialism). While in each case it is hard to separate individual from collective experience, the emphasis differs in each chapter. I have deliberately selected varied traumatic situations so as to explore each one's specificity and the particular way it is communicated—in the case of film and literature, its aesthetics—while, by the end of the book, also still arguing that the impact of trauma can be (indeed must be) usefully translated across these specificities. I have also chosen to focus not on the huge catastrophes that others have written about so eloquently—the Holocaust, Hiroshima, the Chinese Revolution—but on what I call "family" trauma, that is traumas of loss, abandonment, rejection, betrayal. These traumas, similar to what T. M. Luhrman has called "quiet traumas" (158), or what Deidre Barrett calls "common traumas" (5), warrant study.[4] Their neglect is partly due to the implicit gendering of trauma studies, such that traumas of (and perpetrated by) men have been a main focus.[5] The gendering of trauma as it arises from its interesting theoretical history is taken up in chapter 1.

Chapter 1 provides a brief overview for readers unfamiliar with Freud's trauma theories, which were developed as the modern industrial nation-state came to fruition and Western imperialism was reaching its peak. Freud only belatedly became engaged in discussion of war trauma because he was studying sexuality and how unconscious motivation produced neurotic symptoms. I then look at how trauma studies developed particularly in the humanities disciplines in the 1990s. As Deidre Barrett points out, in general "the psychology of trauma received remarkably little attention, with only minor renewal of interest following each war as society was challenged to integrate the survivors" (2). Like Judith Herman and Barrett, I also see "the modern study of psychological trauma" emerging from the dual 1970s events of Vietnam War veterans returning with severe post-traumatic stress disorder, and feminists demanding that domestic abuse of children and women be taken more seriously. In presenting my own interests, I discuss recent developments in contemporary neuroscience that enabled researchers to show what happens in the brain during trauma—circuitry that

Freud anticipated long before researchers had the technical means to prove his ideas. I also discuss how the phenomenon of "secondary" or "vicarious" trauma may be especially common in women. Women in the past did not participate centrally in national catastrophes such as war, and may thus have avoided the direct trauma of such situations. However, they did participate *vicariously* in their many roles as nurses at home, in the field, as trackers for the air force, factory workers, as mothers of wounded sons, and as wives or daughters of men captured or sent to camps. They were therefore subject to vicarious traumatization.

Chapter 2 introduces case studies that pick up on my earlier discussion of 9/11 as a paradigmatic recent example of a national trauma that was at the same time deeply personal and individual. Through brief discussion of my own experiences of the attacks on New York, I showed first how such catastrophes produce new subjectivities through the shocks, disruptions and confusions that accompany them, and second, how a new catastrophe reactivates emotions associated with prior ones in both the individual and the nation. Case studies in chapter 2 continue the focus on World War II, only now starting from the position of the subject as part of the collective. The chapter addresses the vicissitudes of traumatic memory (see Walker, "The Vicissitudes of Traumatic Memory"), and what Michael Roth and George Salas have poignantly called "disturbing remains," through studying written memoirs of traumatic events by survivors. The painful personal memories explored expose the complex interrelatedness of the subject with the powerful and inevitable historical and political forces in which she is inescapably caught up. The chapter discusses three autobiographical memoirs, all dealing with World War II. In order to compare and contrast the different ways in which men and women may negotiate the personal and public spheres in the context of trauma, I juxtapose Freud's *Moses and Monotheism* with memoirs by Sarah Kofman and Marguerite Duras. Freud, a Jew, writing in the late 1930s as the Nazis began their anti-Semitic program, arguably displaced his current fears about Nazism and aging into a narrative about Moses. But Kofman, also a Jew, recalls in midlife in powerfully simple language memories of her traumatic childhood situation in France once the Nazis began deporting Jews; she barely survived as a child in Nazi-occupied Paris; Marguerite Duras, meanwhile, a non-Jew born in Indochina but living in Paris as a young adult, writes about her agonizing wait for her husband's return from a concentration camp in the wake of her experiences as a resistance fighter. These victims of parallel but different traumatic situations put their experiences in writing, I believe, for several reasons: to organize pain into a narrative that gives it shape for the purposes of self-understanding (working their trauma through), or with the aim of being heard, that is, constructing a witness where there was none before. The "disturbing remains" of history, inscribed in the memories of these writers, show the effects of social disaster on the individual.

In this chapter, I develop an aesthetics and politics of trauma. Each text evidences different literary techniques used to produce in the reader the impact of a traumatic situation, that is, to "translate" the trauma as personal and political happening for the reader.

Chapter 3, also about World War II, focuses on the ways in which the United States, as a modern nation-state, worked to dissociate the national trauma of World War II, while indirectly alluding to it. Here comparison with the nation's more direct response to 9/11 reveals important cultural/social changes in regard to awareness and self-consciousness about traumatic impacts since the 1940s and 1950s.[6] While film (the medium I deal most with in the book), is apparently unique and individualistic, it is deeply communal in its implications. In this and other chapters, I rely on film theory, revisited through the lens of trauma studies and taken in new directions. While I restore a phenomenological dimension to film analysis, this is not to replace psychoanalysis but to complement it.

Taking Alfred Hitchcock's 1946 postwar melodrama *Spellbound* as my case study, I argue that like the culture at large, the film splits off the catastrophe of World War II, displacing it into the hero's childhood crisis. The film might have followed Freud and showed how a new traumatic happening, such as experiences in war, could trigger a prior childhood trauma, but this would have required directly confronting the war and its horrors. Instead, we are shown trauma as dissociation or "splitting" on the national level, a phenomenon that allows sentimentality and a focus on individual suffering to stand in for an uncompromising look at national catastrophe and at its political causes. "Sentiment" can be an ideological response, consciously or unconsciously geared to mobilize the public through arousing certain kinds of emotion. It stands in contrast to the stark language of trauma used by Duras and Kofman, and by the artists studied in the rest of the book.

Chapter 4, "Vicarious Trauma and 'Empty' Empathy," looks at media images of Rwanda and Iraq, and continues discussion of emotions as manipulated in trauma culture. I coin the term "empty empathy" in analyzing the function of war photographs in relations to viewers. The chapter makes an original contribution in bringing to bear on cinema and trauma data collected in interviews with trauma therapists. Here I address the complex issue of vicarious traumatization and its relevance to being a spectator of traumatic events shown in popular media. I argue that viewers of the media, like therapists working with trauma victims, are often vicariously traumatized. I explore the degree to which this vicarious experience of trauma can be pro-social, and the degree to which it may turn viewers away from the suffering of others. I note the vicissitudes of translating trauma when journalists, therapists, and film viewers may be vicariously traumatized. Vicarious traumatization may be an inevitable part of sharing what others have suffered, but it too can have socially productive aspects in specific contexts.

In addition, I compare sensationalized reporting, with what I call its fragments of "empty" empathy, to reporting that tries to avoid sensationalism. I heed the dangers, pointed out by Lauren Berlant and Wendy Brown (among others), of a culture of sentimentality and addiction to "wounded attachments," which arguably is especially prevalent in the United States. However, it would be wrong to rule out the importance of empathy and sharing trauma just because United States media exploit catastrophe. In fact, understanding how media sensationalizes and specularizes trauma is part of overcoming negative aspects of popular culture. To argue against sentimentality usefully corrects how emotion is exploited for political and other ideological ends—often to mask underlying political agendas powerful forces wish to conceal. And yet, to assume from the "therapy" culture of the United States that all discussion of emotion is part of the same negative sentimentality would be a mistake. My discussion will highlight the different modalities within which trauma is addressed, showing that sentimentality is one kind of process, but by no means the only one. In these studies, I show how thin the line is between sensationalism and "objective" reporting or listening.

Chapter 5, "'Translating' Trauma in Postcolonial Contact Zones," sets the stage for the larger question of an ethics of sharing within postmodernism. Throughout, I attempt to bridge local and global perspectives, as well as individual and collective experience. This chapter links European trauma to the trauma of indigenous peoples through the "translations" of artists and critics. Sharing of trauma in this context includes Europeans "translating" the traumas of others as part of incorporating this suffering into their own guilt at its being caused by their European leaders. My case studies juxtapose films by indigenous artists with those of postcolonial directors, so as to highlight the complex postmodern situation where self-consciousness of crimes committed in the past motivates white artists in ways that are often problematic. Meanwhile, indigenous directors increasingly narrate their own experiences in powerful ways. My case studies come from select Australian, United States, First Nations, and Native American films dealing with diverse traumas experienced by indigenous peoples. Once again, the powerful concept of "disturbing remains" takes on an uncanny literal resonance in images of corporations seeking to disturb sacred sites where ancient historical Aboriginal "remains" live.

Chapter 6 moves beyond the concept of sharing to consider the ethical requirement for "witnessing" as part of reconciliation; I explore how people can move beyond sharing trauma and engage in witnessing, which is a new level of responsibility. It differs from vicarious trauma, from voyeurism/sensationalism, and from melodramatic attempts to close the wound as in Hollywood treatments of historical trauma. Rather, I suggest that "witnessing" happens when a text aims to move the viewer emotionally but without sensationalizing or overwhelming her with feeling that makes understanding impossible. "Witnessing" involves not just empathy and motivation to help, but understanding the structure of injustice—that an injustice has taken place—rather than focusing on a specific case. Once this happens one may feel obligated to take responsibility for specific injustices. Art that invites us to bear witness to injustice goes beyond moving us to identify with and help a specific individual, and prepares us to take responsibility for preventing future occurrence.

"Witnessing" thus involves a stance that has public meaning or importance and transcends individual empathic or vicarious suffering to produce community. My two dramatically different examples—Maya Deren's 1947 *Meshes of an Afternoon* and a short film, *Night Cries,* by the Australian Aboriginal artist Tracey Moffatt—refer back to themes discussed earlier so as to underscore the points made in the book.

The book ends with an epilogue, "Wounded New York: Rebuilding and Memorials to 9/11," which returns the reader briefly to 9/11. I analyze the still continuing struggle in New York City to determine appropriate buildings for the site where the Twin Towers once stood, as well as a fitting memorial for the three thousand victims. In going over the many articles and discussions about buildings and memorial space, it appears that residues of the trauma are preventing any easy moving forward with rebuilding. So many different interests are involved (relatives of victims, real estate interests, city residents, economic entrepreneurs) each standing in varying positions vis-à-vis the catastrophe, and so many powerful emotions are at stake that consensus appears to be an impossible ideal. But there are many admirable aspects to the process that the city has initiated—a process that aims to be communal, to involve the collectivity of the city, and that has produced a new kind of collectivity. In that I think the process has succeeded. The catastrophe may have forever changed New York City qua city, and New Yorkers as well. The trauma produced a new collective subject within the city; it created a kind of togetherness such as perhaps the city had never experienced before. It changed my personal relationship to the city, as a new subjectivity as a *New Yorker* emerged from the ruins.

A premise of this book is that catastrophic events (like 9/11) remind us of the urgency for a focus on transnational conflict with a view to developing understanding among people. There is a need to transfer difference into something other than trauma. The disturbing material remains of the Towers embody the forces that pull things apart. The "remains" (in the form of the ashes of three thousand bodies) in Ground Zero will forever mark the historical forces and human will that brought about the catastrophe.

Chapter 1

"Why Trauma Now?"

Freud and Trauma Studies

Trauma is often seen as inherently linked to modernity. Kevin Newmark, for instance, drawing upon Walter Benjamin's groundbreaking work, stresses the break in consciousness that modernity represents, as "it occurred historically to interrupt once and for all the unified structure of what we continue to call 'traditional' experience" (238). Modernity, deeply intertwined with imperialism, consumerism, and Fascism, as Paul Gilroy has so lucidly shown in *Against Race,* is seen to produce basic twentieth-century experiences, such as the catastrophic event and global cross-cultural conflict. Indeed, it is partly because of accumulated twentieth-century traumatic events that psychologists, sociologists, and humanists are investigating trauma. Among art forms, cinema is singled out by scholars like Tom Gunning, Wolfgang Schivelbusch, and Lynne Kirby as involving a special relationship to trauma in the "shock" experience of modernity, especially as cinema disoriented traditional, primarily literary cultures. Others importantly focus on the cinema as a cultural institution in which, in Miriam Hansen's words, "the effects of modernization on human experience could be acknowledged, recognized, negotiated, and perhaps reconfigured and transformed" (ix).

It is precisely such possibilities of transformation that are central to my concerns in this book. While modernity may have ceded to postmodernism and postcolonialism—paradigms that, as Michael Hardt and Antonio Negri have argued, are themselves transitional to something else they call "Empire" (9–21, 137–159)—the remembering of recent catastrophes implicates us back into the trauma of industrial warfare, totalitarian atrocities, and the annihilating speed of modernization that, along with imperial invasion and colonial subjugation, demolished traditional cultures. Here, the borders between modernity, postmodernity, and Hardt/Negri's "Empire" seem porous: For this reason, I focus later on traumas of postcolonialism, immigration, and diaspora, as well as those of the world wars, as they have an impact on women, children, and families.

In this chapter, for readers new to trauma studies, I first provide a brief overview of different phases of Freud's ideas about trauma, as these emerged in the late nineteenth century from the influence of French clinicians, and in his work with Josef Breuer; gradually developed at the end of World War I as Freud's interests shifted to the traumatic impact of war injuries; and finally as they were revisited by Freud in *Beyond the Pleasure Principle* and in his last work on Moses. I then explore three distinct phases of renewed interest in trauma from the 1980s to the present: 1) the 1980s wave of books (some popular) by psychologists (some feminists), responding (as did Freud) to war injuries (this time however to the Vietnam War) and to increased awareness of child sexual abuse;[1] 2) the unexpected turn of humanists to trauma in the late 1980s (and increasingly from then on), perhaps because trauma theory provided a welcome bridge back to social and political concerns in an era when high theory had become abstract; and 3) the reaction to what rapidly was seen as a kind of "faddish" interest in trauma, or a collapsing of everything into trauma. My interest in trauma developed in between and in the midst of these three phases, and the rest of the chapter consists of my responses to all three levels of development.

Freud and Trauma

It all begins with Freud, of course. And the more I read of contemporary trauma theories, the more I believe that Freud had already said a great deal.[2] At least, along with Freud's contemporaries and the pioneering clinicians who preceded him, nineteenth- and early twentieth-century thinkers had discovered the basic phenomena and structures of trauma. It took the more sophisticated scientific technologies of the late twentieth century to prove what these pioneers could only theorize about brain circuitry and mechanisms, sometimes, though, at the cost of Freud's insistence on unconscious fantasy as also involved in traumatic effects.

The phenomena of trauma, particularly hysteria, that interested clinicians did not arise in a vacuum. The phenomena were closely linked to modernity, especially to the industrial revolution and its dangerous new machines (the railway, the factory), as well as to the linked growth of the bourgeois family. This family became the site for female hysteria (caused partly by that family's patriarchal and puritanical codes), while industrialization (that required the bourgeois class and was, circularly, produced by that class) provided the social conditions for the train and machine accidents, and for large-scale wars. These in turn prompted attention to the traumatic symptoms such accidents and wars produced in men.[3]

What's interesting is that unlike psychologists and others writing today, Freud and his peers did not set out to write a *theory* of trauma. The concept of trauma emerges in their work on hysteria as if already assumed. It is used to explain processes in hysteria, rather than as a concept that has itself to be theorized. French clinicians, mainly J. M. Charcot and his student Pierre Janet, pioneered research on hysteria and hypnosis. Charcot's research in neuropathology at his Salpètrière clinic (significantly, most of the patients were women, although Charcot argued that men also suffered from hysteria) produced students such as Janet whose case studies were central to ideas of hysteria at the time. Charcot and Janet inspired Freud and Breuer, who visited the Salpètrière in 1890 (see Freud's 1893 moving obituary to Charcot who died soon after), although Breuer, a noted Viennese physician, had already begun research on hysteria in his treatment of Fräulein Anna O. Following the practices developed by Charcot and Janet, Freud and Breuer used hypnosis in their work with their hysterical patients, although shortly thereafter Freud began to experiment with his "talking cure," and in many ways was already moving beyond Charcot.

The influence of French theories and experiments is cited in an essay, "On the Psychical Mechanism of Hysterical Phenomena," written in collaboration with Breuer and published in their joint volume, *Studies in Hysteria*.[4] Here the clinicians distinguish between ordinary hysteria and traumatic neuroses, and introduce the concept of "traumatic hysteria." Already the doctors understand that whether a person experiencing a distressing affect "of fright, shame or psychical pain" will be traumatized depends on the particular sensitivity of the person—something even now not sufficiently recognized. In addition, they hint at the belatedness of the onset of symptoms, attributing this to the fact that traumatic memories are not available to the patient in the way his commonplace ones are, but act "as a kind of foreign body" in the psyche, "an affective agent in the present even long after it first penetrated" (6). The famous statement that "hysterics suffer mainly from reminiscences" appears in this essay.

In this work, Freud and Breuer specifically note that the symptoms of hysteria are the result of trauma. The physical phenomena they cite, including what happens to memory in trauma, anticipate by many years the now so familiar litany of effects labeled in American Psychiatric Association's *Diagnostic and Statistical Manual of Mental Disorders: III-R* as Post-Traumatic Stress Disorder (or PTSD). In the same essay in *Studies in Hysteria,* the clinicians note the way in which other ideas including fantasies get attached to the traumatic event. "A memory," they say," of such a trauma . . . enter[s] the great complex of associations, it comes alongside other experiences, which may contradict it, and is subjected to rectification by other ideas" (9). They note that after an accident, memory of the danger and repetition of the fright "becomes associated with the memory of what happened afterwards—rescue and the consciousness of present safety."

Freud and Breuer implicitly gender trauma in accordance with the way the bourgeois family in Europe was organized in their day: Males largely have traumatic effects from accidents, women from watching by the bedside of sick parents or children, or (at first only implied) from extreme sexual repression. The three early case studies published in *Studies in Hysteria*—those of Anna O. (Breuer), Emily von N. (Freud), and Miss Lucy (Freud)—set the stage for Freud's later case studies while still revealing the legacy of Charcot (especially in Breuer's text) in focusing on detailed descriptions of the women's physical symptoms and treatments with massage, hydrotherapy, and electrotherapy, and in insisting on dissociation as a major symptom. Freud does indicate traumatic sexual origins for the hysteria in his cases, but it was not until the Dora case history that Freud provided a detailed investigation into female hysteria and its traumatic symptoms as occasioned by sexual incidents in an environment of rigid sexual repression such as characterized Freud's nineteenth-century Austria.[5] In the case of Dora, Freud concludes that the hysteria was due to shame triggered by her arousal in response to inappropriate advances of a friend of her father, and further stimulation by attraction to, including sexual discussion with, this man's wife. In Dora's case, hysterical phenomena result from both "seduction" and fantasies.

In their essay introducing *Studies in Hysteria,* Freud and Breuer only mention sexuality as a precipitating cause for traumatic hysteria, asserting that "the determining causes which lead to the *acquisition* of neuroses, their aetiology . . . is to be looked for in *sexual* factors" (257). But a few years later in several papers written in 1894 and 1896 Freud baldly states that sexual abuse lies behind female hysteria. In his paper on "Heredity and the Aetiology of the Neuroses," Freud is fully aware that his audience would find this provocative.[6] He argues that hysteria comes from "memory relating to a sexual life," stating further that "the subject has retained an unconscious memory of *a precocious experience of sexual relations with actual excitement of the genitals, resulting from sexual abuse committed by another person; and the period of life* at which this fatal event takes place is *earliest youth*—the years up to the age of eight to ten, before the child has reached sexual maturity" (154, italics in original).

While these early essays deal mainly with trauma's processes and symptoms rather than their causes, and often imply female patients and situations, they sometimes include examples of male trauma but not hysteria. In "Heredity and the Aetiology of the Neuroses," Freud suggests why women resort to hysteria while men manifest obsessional neuroses by distinguishing the kinds of infantile sexual abuse boys and girls receive (women receive it "passively," males "actively"). Yet he does not realize the implicit acceptance of prevailing concepts of gender in this statement. That is, Freud does not go on to ask how cultural, political, and social roles laid down for men and women produce different neuroses in the case of sexual trauma. Indeed, Freud and others of his time rarely ask if trauma impacts differently on males and females. When the war neuroses force attention to male hysteria, as we'll see, clinicians do not ask if hysteria in men and women is the same. Yet, how the contrasting positions for men and women within national imaginaries result in different traumatic syndromes is important. These are questions I return to throughout this volume.

Trauma, then, was at first closely linked to the sexual experiences of young women within a close-knit bourgeois family and circle of friends such as was common at the turn of the nineteenth century. However, Freud soon questioned the degree to which the trauma depended on actual sexual abuse (not necessarily out of fear of offending his male friends and colleagues whose children he was treating, as is often assumed),[7] and theorized that fantasies of forbidden sexual desires could produce the same symptoms.[8]

Freud moved on to develop other aspects of his psychoanalytic theories, and when he returned to trauma, it was now in relation to the symptoms of soldiers in World War I. At this point, interest in trauma focused on men involved in public catastrophes, such as defending the nation at war. A great deal of research and debate in Europe followed the increasing number of soldiers reporting paralysis and other hysterical symptoms preventing them from fighting. Doctors in England, France, and Germany studied these symptoms of soldiers unable to continue in battle (they were often termed "malingerers"). Articles published in the *Lancet,* a British medical journal, between 1895 and 1915 amply reveal the different hypotheses advanced about the soldiers' symptoms, and show how debates drew upon research carried out earlier in regard to industrial accidents and factory workers also described as malingerers.[9]

British doctors faced with traumatized soldiers, apparently applied theories of female hysteria caused by sexual trauma to battle trauma.[10] It is unclear whether they arrived independently at their conclusions about war trauma as hysteria or simply did not mention Freud's views on hysteria because it would require discussion of female sexuality. Elaine Showalter quotes W. H. Rivers in 1917, also in the *Lancet,* noting the "correspondence between Freudian theory and his [Rivers's] clinical practice, and especially the ideas of the unconscious." Rivers concluded that "the advent of the war presented psychiatry with an extraordinary demonstration of the validity of Freudian theory in general" (Showalter, *The Female Malady* 188–189).[11]

It is significant that Freud's development of his ideas about trauma was only belatedly prompted by what happened to soldiers in World War I. His first writings on World War I, namely "Thoughts for the Times on War and Death" and "Why War?", deal with man's binary instincts for love and hate. It is not surprising that both essays reflect the broader cultural and social thinking that Freud developed in his 1920 *Civilization and Its Discontents,* rather than relating to his clinical and more technical research. The essays were written for a broad audience, after all, and one of them was directly addressed to Albert Einstein. Freud often implicitly (if not explicitly) relates his patients' symptoms to the larger cultural (implicitly ideological) thinking that these general essays reveal. Such insights appear in short parentheses (such as reference to the social repression of sexuality). But Freud was wary of mentioning the codes of his social, medical, and political milieu, not wanting to hamper acceptance of his theories by challenging social mores of the day.

Toward the end of World War I Freud and his colleagues published papers that Sandor Ferenczi, Karl Abraham, and Ernst Simmel had presented on war neuroses at the proceedings of the Fifth International Psycho-Analytical Congress, held in Budapest on September 28 and 29, 1918, with an introduction by Freud. The congress was concerned about the treatment of soldiers and, not knowing the war was about to end, wanted to set up special psychoanalytically oriented clinics for traumatized men.

In his short introduction to the volume, Freud observes what essays in the *Lancet* had already observed, namely that war conditions had "an important influence on the spread of psycho-analysis." Freud goes on to note that "medical men who had hitherto held back from any approach to psychoanalytic theories were brought into closer contact with them when, in the course of their duties as army doctors, they were obliged to deal with war neuroses" (Freud, Standard Edition 17: 207). Indeed, Freud takes the opportunity to communicate his irritation with doctors (he may well have some of those in the *Lancet* in mind) who are only ready to use psychoanalysis when it is a matter of the war neuroses, which do not (at least obviously) involve sexuality. In his words, war neuroses do not appear to involve "the conflict between the ego and the sexual instincts which it repudiates" that Freud has been arguing is the basis of "the ordinary neuroses of peace-time" (208).

In the rest of the essay, Freud is at pains to find a link between the traumatic neuroses of war and of peacetime (also termed transference neuroses), which he does by arguing that in both cases there is a conflict in the ego. In the case of war, it is between the soldier's "old peaceful ego and his new warlike one, and it becomes acute as soon as the peace-ego realizes what danger it runs of losing its life owing to the rashness of its newly formed, parasitic double" (209). But Freud does not want to relinquish the possibility that even war trauma has something to do with sexuality, while at the same time fully understanding that he does not have evidence yet of "the relations which undoubtedly exist between fright, anxiety and narcissistic libido" (210).[12] He tantalizingly ends his essay by asserting that, in the case of both the war and peacetime neuroses, "what is feared is nevertheless an internal enemy" (210). He asserts that it is possible that repression underlies all reaction to trauma, whether sexual or external.

Freud's statements here are "tantalizing" in that he begs the question of whether there is any difference between ordinary neurosis and trauma—a difference that involves the difference between neurotic repression and traumatic dissociation that has plagued recent trauma theorists. But these same comments by Freud are important in linking so-called peacetime neuroses and war neuroses, and in challenging his theory of female hysteria as about repressed fantasies, not *memories*. If hysteria is the result of *fantasies*, then it cannot be the same phenomenon as war trauma, which has a clear external cause. War trauma seemed to be of an entirely different order than female hysteria—closer to the delayed impact of train accidents Freud was later to theorize, and not involving fantasies as such. Yet Freud's early theory that hysterical women suffered from memories of sexual abuse (not fantasies as he later claimed) did match the traumatic phenomenon of soldiers, namely that they too suffered from memories of an overwhelming event that they had been unable to cognitively register at the time it happened.[13]

Freud cannot in the short space of such an introduction go further into the complexities of his thought about links between the peacetime and war neuroses, neatly gendered as they are in Freud's account. There is no evidence that Freud had ever treated any patients suffering from war neuroses (as had Simmel and the others contributing full papers to the volume), but he was nevertheless called upon to be an "Expert Witness" about such neuroses at the investigation of his renowned colleague, Professor Wagner-Jauregg (at the time of the investigation director of the clinic at the Allgemeine Krankenhaus in Vienna).[14] This investigation came about as a result of allegations in a newspaper, *Der Freie Soldat,* about military abuses as World War I came to an end. A commission, presided over by Professor Lofler, was set up to investigate neglect of military duty during the war. Several articles accused the medical profession of "knowingly supporting the army's harsh and inhumane treatment of soldiers during the war" (Eissler 14). Extracts from a diary by Walter Kauders, who was treated by Wagner-Jauregg, had been published, and an investigation began.

Freud's 1915 essay "Thoughts for the Times on War and Death," perhaps, taken together with the introduction discussed above and his status as the "inventor" of psychoanalysis, evidently was seen to qualify him to be an "Expert Witness" in this case. But Freud was in a delicate position in testifying since he could not say anything that would harm the career of this renowned medical man, and yet he also could not agree with the nonpsychoanalytic treatment (usually electrical charges and isolation) that Wagner-Jauregg (like most of his colleagues) used for traumatized soldiers. Freud's "Memorandum on the Electrical Treatment of War Neurotics," submitted to Professor Lofler, allows us to see Freud treading elegantly around similar issues to those that had preoccupied the doctors writing in the *Lancet.* The debate was over whether the soldier's symptoms resulted from organic injuries to the nervous system or were caused by psychic changes such as we understand happens in trauma. Freud comes down clearly on the latter side, noting that "what is known as the psychoanalytic school of psychiatry, which was brought into being by me, had taught for the last twenty-five years that the neuroses of peace could be traced back to disturbances of emotional life. . . . It was therefore easy to infer that the immediate cause of all war neuroses was an unconscious inclination in the soldier to withdraw from the demands, dangerous or outrageous to his feelings, made upon him by active service" (Freud in Eissler 24–25). Freud insists, against claims by Wagner-Jauregg, that only a very small proportion of soldiers with traumatic symptoms were "malingerers." He is careful to note that the physician had a conflict, namely between his duty as a medical man and his military duty to get the soldiers back on the front line, in giving electrical treatment for a "fast fix," as we might say. "Medicine," says Freud, "was serving purposes foreign to its essence" (27). Deaths resulted from the treatment, although Freud will not say that Wagner-Jauregg's clinic used dangerous levels of electrical current. He concludes by referring to Ernst Simmel's success with psychotherapeutic methods ("introduced by me," Freud has to add) in treating war neuroses.

Significantly, Freud found himself returning to the issue of war neuroses in the year following his appearance as an Expert Witness in the Wagner-Jauregg investigation as he was writing *Beyond the Pleasure Principle*. In attempting to understand how the mental apparatus produces pleasure and unpleasure, he began to distinguish between unpleasure from the pressure of internal unsatisfied instincts and unpleasure from an external perception recognized by the mental apparatus as a danger (*Beyond* 28). This leads him to mention the "mechanical concussions, railway disasters and other accidents involving risk to life," that have been given the name of "traumatic neurosis" (28). But his thought immediately turns to the war, as he notes, "The terrible war that has just ended gave rise to a great number of illnesses of this kind," and he footnotes the introduction noted above. Freud continues to reflect on similarities between the traumatic neurosis of war and that of hysteria, as if he continues to be puzzled by these similarities. Referring back to his earliest work with Breuer on female hysteria, Freud notes that war neurotics too "suffer mainly from reminiscences" (29).

But at this point he makes a sharp break to discuss child's play and the famous *fort-da* game of his grandson. However, he returns later in the volume to the issue of internal versus external assault on the ego that had led him to the war neuroses in the first place. He is still trying to understand the different kinds of unpleasure involved in the different contexts, only now he theorizes that trauma results from a breach in a protective shield that the mental apparatus sets up to ward against overviolent stimuli. It seems throughout this discussion (52–61) that he has in mind the situation of war for the external assault on the mental apparatus and hysteria for the internal "assault" being theorized. This assumption seems to be valid since Freud refers explicitly again to the war neuroses and to his idea in the 1919 introduction that war neuroses result from a conflict in the ego, as much as from fear or, as he now notes is a more correct term "fright" (62).[15]

But Freud's most significant, and most complete discussion of trauma occurs, not incidentally, at the end of his life, in *Moses and Monotheism,* when Freud was forced to leave his homeland and take up exile in England. At the end of *Moses,* Freud repeats his well-known theories about the etiology of the neuroses, only now in a way never quite articulated before he specifically includes the issue of trauma. He likens the latency of the man who walks away from the train accident apparently unharmed, only later to develop psychical and motor symptoms, to the "forgetting" of monotheism in the Jewish religion, only to have it return later as something insistent. But more importantly, he links common infant traumata to the latency phenomenon. He summarizes: "These three points—early happenings, within the first five years of life, the forgetting, and the characteristic of sexuality and aggressiveness—belong close together. The traumata are either bodily experiences or perceptions, especially those heard or seen." But not everyone responds in the same way to similar experiences, so Freud conceives of a sliding scale and slow series of developments that result in trauma symptoms.[16] It is not too much to infer from what Freud says here that the difference in how soldiers react to similar war traumas may depend on how far the war situation triggered prior psychic conflicts. In war, such internal conflicts, together with intense fear for his life or that of close ones, threatened the soldier's identity and hence the dizzy panic or paralysis that followed, and that is described by many treating such neuroses.

Central to this Freudian theory of trauma is a motivated unconscious. In this case, the traumatic event may trigger early traumatic happenings, already perhaps mingled with fantasy, and shape how the current event is experienced. There may, for instance, in the case of battle trauma, be unconscious guilt at surviving an attack; or events in battle may unconsciously recall childhood violence where the victim wished for a sibling's death, etc. The events may in this case fall into the arena of repression and be recoverable in therapy.[17]

Thus, Freud's ideas about trauma gradually grew in complexity and preciseness from the early *Studies on Hysteria* to *Moses and Monotheism,* the latter work bringing together finally the long nurturing of his early concepts into a theory that anticipates much that clinicians working on combat fatigue and PTSD are now researching. We see Freud, especially in *Beyond the Pleasure Principle,* struggling to develop models of the brain that neuroscientists have only recently been able to produce through new technologies and lab experiments unavailable in Freud's day. Indeed, I have discussed Freud's ideas at such length because they seem to me to still be valuable for the work in this book. The specific complexities of brain circuitry, discussed below in the context of vicarious trauma, Freud could not know, since it has taken intricate modern neuroscience research to determine such circuitry. But he anticipated such circuits without the knowledge new technologies have made possible.

Late Twentieth-Century Interest in Trauma

In the wake of the Vietnam War, as they confronted symptoms presented by returning Veterans, clinical psychologists became newly engaged with thinking about trauma. However, their research was not widely distributed until the mid-1990s—an attention marked by Denise Grady's *New York Times* article (December 16, 1997), "War Memories May Harm Health." Inspired by Joseph Boscarino's book about Vietnam War veterans' Post-Traumatic Stress Disorder (PTSD)—then a relatively new term, replacing "shell shock" or "combat fatigue"—the article argued that PTSD was scientifically valid. Studies had shown the ways in which stress affects the brain, which in turn impacts on other human systems, like the immune system. PTSD had been introduced in 1984 by the American Psychological Association in their *Diagnostic Manual.* Meanwhile, feminist psychologists, like Judith Herman and Laura S. Brown, began to confront what they ironically saw as the implicit male bias in defining PTSD (ironic because traumatic hysteria was first diagnosed as a female disorder, only belatedly being applied to males). The American Psychiatric Association had not recognized that PTSD could be related to symptoms of female hysteria analyzed by Freud, perhaps because "hysteria" as a medical term had fallen out of fashion. Psychologists' worries arose from female patients increasingly presenting symptoms of child sexual abuse, as well as from treating more battered women who were now willing to come forward. Herman's book on *Trauma and Recovery* (1992) quickly became a best seller and was reprinted in 1997, while Laura S. Brown's 1995 article pointing out the gender biases in the 1984 PTSD formulation had an influence beyond its small scope (Brown,"Not Outside the Range" 100–112).

A veritable flood of media attention and printed books followed in the 1990s, bringing along with them intense debates among psychologists, especially in regard to recovered memories of child sexual abuse.[18] In a perhaps ironic twist, the sufferings of ordinary, now aging Jewish victims of the Holocaust—long enduring their symptoms quietly and without due attention—finally found a voice in the remarkable Fortunoff Video Archive Project, headed by Dori Laub and Geoffrey Hartman at Yale University. A new psychological dimension was added to Holocaust studies through the interviews videotaped.

The new dimension is reflected in Dori Laub's contributions to his volume, *Testimony,* coedited with Shoshana Felman in 1992. This volume, together with Cathy Caruth's earlier *Unclaimed Experience* (1986) and her edited volume, *Trauma: Explorations in Memory* (1995) initiated what has become a growing field in the humanities. Books by Geoffrey Hartman (1994, 1996), Dominick La Capra (1994, 1998) and Michael Rothberg (2000) proved influential in deepening and furthering humanities Holocaust research. Memoirs, like those of Charlotte Delbo, published in French in the 1970s but not given much attention, now translated find a new wide audience in the United States and beyond. New memoirs like that of Ruth Kluger (1994) were written and form the basis of extended commentaries.

But trauma theory quickly extended beyond Holocaust studies in the humanities, especially in the wake of increasing revelations about child abuse in the 1990s. Books like Janet Freyd's *Betrayal Trauma: The Logic of Forgetting Childhood Abuse* (1996) in turn influenced film scholars, like Janet Walker, who was one of the first to use trauma theory explicitly in studying cinema (Walker,"The Traumatic Paradox"), although Kaja Silverman had implicitly theorized cultural trauma as early as 1992 in her work on the war film in *Male Subjectivity at the Margins.*[19]

But what "theory" were many of these humanities scholars using? Understandably, not being psychologists, humanists turned to the official definition of trauma that could be found in the American Psychiatric Association's *Diagnostic Manual.* This manual, especially in the 1994 revised edition, stressed the phenomenon of dissociation in trauma, already discussed years earlier by Pierre Janet, Josef Breuer, and Freud. Bessel O. van der Kolk stressed dissociation in his 1987 *Psychological Trauma,* and he repeatedly wrote about it in many subsequent articles, some cowritten (1989, 1991, 1994). Such theories apparently influenced Cathy Caruth, whose acceptance of dissociation as central in trauma is evident in her by now famous definition of trauma as "a response, sometimes delayed, to an overwhelming event or set of events, which takes the form of repeated, intrusive hallucinations, dreams, thoughts or behaviors stemming from the event." The pathology, she notes, consists "solely in the *structure of the experience* or reception: the event is not assimilated or experienced fully at the time, but only belatedly in its repeated *possession* of the one who experiences it" (Caruth, *Trauma* 4–5).

Not surprisingly, the most vivid description of trauma as dissociation in Caruth's volume is found in van der Kolk's essay, cowritten with Otto van der Hart. These psychiatrists—sometimes seen as antipsychoanalytic—worked with neuroscientists to show brain mechanisms that support the thesis of trauma producing dissociated selves. In arguing that trauma is a special form of memory, they stated that in trauma the event has affect only, not meaning. It produces emotions—terror, fear, shock—but perhaps above all disruption of the normal feeling of comfort. Only the sensation sector of the brain—the amygdala—is active during the trauma. The meaning-making one (in the sense of rational thought, cognitive processing), namely, the cerebral cortex, remains shut down because the affect is too much to be registered cognitively in the brain. (Pierre Janet and Freud grasped this process intuitively but could not prove it without the tools of postmodern science.)[20] Caruth, taking these theories for granted, argued that just because the traumatic experience has not been given meaning, the subject is continually haunted by it in dreams, flashbacks, and hallucinations.[21]

This narrow focus on dissociation, together with what seemed increasingly like a "faddish" aspect to humanities trauma research soon produced strong objections from some literary and film scholars in the late 1990s. As Michael Roth first argued in an essay, "Why Trauma Now?" (1999), it is significant that it was Paul De Man's students at Yale (Caruth, Felman) who first turned to trauma.[22] Deconstruction scholars focus on language as primary, and accept Lacan's concept of affect and the unconscious split off from linguistic signifiers, which obscures emotion. Roth asks: "Was theory's continued insistence on unmasking truth claims, realism, and intentionality merely a screen to conceal its own inability to engage the world?" (Roth, "Why Trauma Now?" 16).[23] And I might add: Was deconstruction a screen that masked emotion and the body—aspects of life that trauma theory hoped to reintroduce?[24]

This is an important point, and bears dwelling on for a moment. Theories are symptomatic, partly, and come to the fore when a particular intellectual climate is appropriate. By the late 1990s, critical theory had, indeed, through the influence of Lacan and poststructuralism more generally, become very abstract. Critics tended to be wary of falling back into an insufficiently theorized Marxism, on the one hand, or into an insufficiently theorized concept of the body and the subject, on the other. In addition, Felman and Caruth were at Yale where Laub and Hartman had begun to interview Holocaust victims in a climate where renewed interest in World War II and its sociopolitical meanings and personal sufferings was on the rise. Addressing the phenomena of trauma must have seemed one way for critics to begin to link high theory with specific material events that were both personal and which implicated history, memory, and culture generally. To this extent, the turn was productive; suggesting reasons for it should not detract from the importance of the intervention. Giving reasons for the turn says more about the state of theory before trauma became of interest than offering a critique of the turn.

Other critiques were less sympathetic than Roth's. Elaine Showalter spearheaded hostile tendencies about trauma studies in her book, *Hystories* (1997). Here she argued that the rash of child abuse cases, among other cultural phenomena, manifested itself in a hysterical "victim" culture in the United States. Susannah Radstone, somewhat influenced it seems by Showalter's work, in turn objected to trauma theory: for psychoanalysis, she argued, "memory is the outcome of complex processes of revision shaped by promptings from the present, whereas trauma theory posits the linear registration of events as they happen, albeit such registrations may be secreted away through dissociation." She further claims that "trauma theory exorcises . . . psychoanalysis' later insistence on the agency of the unconscious in the formation of memories" (Radstone, "Screening Trauma" 109). In short, she argues that humanists are drawn to the concept of post-traumatic stress disorder because it avoids the complexities of dealing with the unconscious: In Radstone's words, "At stake . . . is the issue of the inner world's *mediation* [*sic*] of the external world, a mediation which is foregrounded by psychoanalytic theory and minimised by trauma theory" (89). It seems paradoxically that the deconstructionists who turned to trauma fell from the frying pan into the fire: that is, in trying to bring the body and the social back into their research, they overlooked the unconscious implicit in their prior theories. As Radstone summarizes it, "Trauma theorists associate trauma not with the effects of triggered associations but with the ontologically unbearable nature of the event itself" (89).

Here, readers will notice, Radstone is basically following the lead Freud set: Freud had insisted from the start on the presence of fantasy, the unconscious and present conditions as inevitably implicated in traumatic memories. So Radstone's critique was a welcome reminder that a certain overly narrow focus (perhaps inspired by psychiatrists like van der Kolk) had become entrenched in trauma studies.

Meanwhile, in a carefully researched and detailed examination of the uses of trauma theory in Freud and other clinicians in her *Trauma: A Genealogy* (2000), Ruth Leys aimed to lay bare impossible inherent contradictions in Freud's own ideas about trauma as well as in all subsequent theorizing. By implication, these contradictions rendered the theory inoperable. It seemed for a while as if humanist scholars had been called to task, and that trauma theory had led them up untenable paths.[25]

But this is not the message that I take from these challenging responses to the growing humanities interest in crises and their aftermath. Rather, these objections pushed me to develop a more complex and malleable theoretical system in working on the impact of trauma, the subjects it produces, its implication in ideology, and in searching for ways in which trauma can be "translated."

My intersection with trauma theory was propitious: I had been living with certain trauma symptoms when, in 1995, I read Cathy Caruth's edited collection on trauma. The theory, in this case, put words to what I had already experienced. A Foucauldian reading, perhaps, would argue that the discourse found me, and constituted my experiences retrospectively, perhaps with a view to enabling a certain conformity to social norms (getting rid of my "symptoms"). But such a view ignores the reasons one allows oneself to be "taken up by a discourse," if one agrees to a Foucauldian reading in the first place. One grabs the discourse, as it were, because it helps or benefits one. The difference is between those assuming a discourse is forced upon a subject, and my view, which is increasingly that one can (even in non-privileged situations) choose a discourse. This is not to say that certain ideological processes (à la Althusser) do not also interpellate subjects in the aftermath of trauma. These are unavoidable, but can be analyzed as one feels oneself "hailed," if one can but get some distance (perhaps through writing) on what is going on in one's culture.

Having actively chosen this discourse, then, it brought me closer to the sufferings of others, which had already been a scholarly focus—but from a certain distance.[26] Trauma theory bridged the gap and enabled me to approach the political/national structures that produce catastrophe while at the same time shaping its impact according to prevailing ideological and other discourses. But it soon became clear that a more complex model than that of Caruth and many psychologists was needed. Radstone is absolutely right to say that individual trauma certainly should not be viewed as a linear registration of an event that avoids the unconscious, especially if we follow Freud and recent brain research rather than van der Kolk. Ruth Leys usefully points to confusions within trauma discussions, such as the lumping together of "truly horrible events" and the dubious harm of Paula Jones's sexual harassment (Leys, *Trauma* 2). But her challenge to some humanists' claims—such as those by Cathy Caruth—seems in its turn tendentious if often more in keeping with the model I will develop here (Leys, *Trauma* 266–297), partly because Leys does not offer anything in place of the theories she attacks.

I understand and appreciate the criticism of Caruth's insistence on the "unspeakability" and "unrepresentability" of trauma: I will argue that telling stories about trauma, even though the story can never actually repeat or represent what happened, may partly achieve a certain "working through" for the victim. It may also (my main concern in this book) permit a kind of empathic "sharing" that moves us forward, if only by inches.[27] What seems wrong in the way criticisms have been formulated is the apparent dismissal of the phenomena of both dissociation and generational transmission of trauma. Many have written movingly about the experience of dissociation (once they became aware that such a splitting had occurred) as well as about intergenerational transmission of trauma.[28] A more complex model could hopefully accommodate both my sense that the phenomena I was interested in were "real" and important, and take into account the persuasive criticisms about the predominant ways in which trauma has been theorized.

In order to develop this model, I need to return to how the brain functions in trauma. Earlier, we saw that literary scholars have been fascinated by the phenomenon of dissociation, which psychiatrists working with neuroscientists (like van der Kolk and van der Hart) had shown to be a key indicator of PTSD. But how complete are van der Kolk's theories? Toward the end of a paper on vicarious trauma, Martin L. Hoffman touches upon the work that neuroscientists have done in relation to the neural substrates of trauma and vicarious trauma (Hoffman, forthcoming). Building on his schema might resolve some of the controversies in humanities trauma research, and aid in developing a more complex model. Relying on work by Joseph LeDoux, Hoffman explains that trauma is "a powerful unconditioned stimulus that bombards the brain's amygdala with electrical and chemical signals" (15). These signals, he goes on to show, "are linked synaptically to sensory images (e.g. sounds, sights, smells of blood in battle) that reach the amygdala about the same time . . . because these images are salient and powerful enough to bypass the cortex and take a quick route through the thalamus." As a result, Hoffman says (still relying on LeDoux), "the sensory images become the conditioned stimulus (CS) component of a powerful CS-Thalamus-Amygdala circuit." Hoffman means by this that the overwhelming sensations of the traumatic event become through association linked to terror and panic. Encountering such sensory images may trigger feelings of terror, as a result: LeDoux, then, suggests that this CS-Thalamus-Amygdala circuit may be the neural basis of PTSD. LeDoux agrees that trauma involves emotional as against a "conscious" memory that requires cortical processing (15).

But, unlike van der Kolk and van der Hart, LeDoux also argues (extrapolating from his lab studies with rats) that in some human cases, as with victims of battle trauma showing symptoms of PTSD, the victim is conscious of the trauma. In this case, in a sense, two circuits happen at the same time: a circuit as described above, where the cortex is bypassed; and a circuit that includes the cortex, so that the trauma does find its way into memory. So we can distinguish three possible kinds of brain function in firsthand trauma: first, the dissociation function (which so attracted humanists) in which the trauma is not accessible to cognition or memory, and where the event is understood to come from outside, not mediated by the unconscious; second, the circuitry just referred to, which involves both dissociation and cognition, thus allowing for the trauma to be in conscious memory; and finally, a function not discussed by neuroscientists and which goes back to Freud's "seduction theory" where the victim of trauma involving perpetrators and their victims partly identifies with the aggressor. In this way, the victim is implicated in the traumatic situation. The new situation may in addition trigger earlier memories or unconscious fantasies.

Suggesting that there is not just one set of brain processes relevant to every subject confronting a traumatic situation, but rather at least three possible processes, enables me to see that each of the theories discussed earlier has some validity. None has to be ruled out. If Caruth overstresses the role of dissociation and does not pay enough attention to unconscious processes, Radstone overstresses the role of the unconscious and does not give enough attention to the realities of neuroscience discoveries of brain circuitry. Each theorist presents one psychic mechanism as defining what happens in trauma, whereas it seems to me that things are more complex. How a victim will respond depends on the particular situation, on an individual's specific psychic history and formation, and on the context for the event. Each of the three possible processes might come into play, and more than one might be involved.[29]

As this book goes to press, experimental and cognitive psychologists are increasingly entering into debates about trauma. Richard McNally's exhaustive review of studies he and others have conducted to test the validity of the American Psychiatric Association's diagnosis of PTSD appeared in 2000, and is gaining increasing attention.[30] In addition, McNally and others are mainly concerned about claims for "recovered memories" of supposed victims of child abuse. These cases led, in the 1980s, to a frenzy of media attention to court cases in which child-care workers, accused of abuse by small children, were sometimes put in jail. The real-life impact of therapists' testimonies about their patients' abuse partly accounts for the attacks on psychoanalysis. Other kinds of trauma do not necessarily involve dissociated memories, so that McNally's experiments showing that trauma victims always recall their experiences do not per se invalidate trauma phenomena such as I study in this book. In any case, McNally does not dispute the presence of post-traumatic symptoms in his concern to prove that traumatic events can be remembered.

Meanwhile, David Becker (2001) usefully warns us of the dangers of too readily universalizing the term "trauma" and its experience as has become common in international agencies sending trauma workers all over the world (and, I might add, in much trauma studies as well). "Trauma can only be understood," he says, "with reference to the specific contexts in which it occurs," including cultural norms, political context, the nature of the event, the organization of the community, and so forth (*Conflict Transformation* 1). Becker also argues that instead of speaking about trauma per se, we should talk of the "traumatic situation," since that phrasing implies that one is not just looking at an individual who has suffered but at what surrounds that person's suffering—his or her environment, specific institutions involved, the state of her community, its politics. Becker suggests, therefore, "that in each different social context people should create their own definition of trauma within a framework, in which the basic focus is not so much on the symptoms of a person but on the sequential development of the traumatic situation" (*Conflict Transformation* 7).

Becker's intervention takes place within his specific context as a psychologist and a therapist, a consultant for development agencies, and a person who has worked as a member of different teams all over the world helping victims of political persecution. This introduces a main problem in trauma studies, which is distinguishing different domains within which people work or relate to trauma. A basic distinction is that between the trauma victim and her work with a clinician (itself a contested site), and the work of scholars studying trauma (also a contested site). A second distinction is that between the many varied scholarly discourses about trauma—be these psychological, psychoanalytic, political, philosophical, sociological, or historical—and images of trauma in film and popular culture studied mainly by literary and media scholars.[31] In practice, there is slippage between these arenas, but each discourse makes its own contribution. Each contributor needs to specify the terrain of her research so as to avoid speaking across, rather than to, one another.

In concluding this chapter, I will look briefly at a phenomenon not discussed much if at all in humanities trauma research, namely vicarious trauma. In chapters that follow, I'll argue that the reader or viewer of stories or films about traumatic situations may be constituted through vicarious or secondary trauma. Indeed, most of us most of the time experience trauma in the "secondary" rather than direct position, for good or ill. In the absence of much attention to or concrete research about vicarious trauma in the humanities, work by clinicians may offer some insight.[32] While Freud himself and many clinicians following him never isolated or named vicarious or secondary trauma, vicarious trauma has been recognized by clinicians in recent years, to the extent that there is now a substantial literature on the subject.[33] Martin Hoffman neatly summarizes the now largely accepted definition of the phenomenon in a paper reporting findings of in-depth interviews with clinicians that he conducted together with Tatiana Friedman:

> Pearlman & Saakvitne (1995) define vicarious traumatization as the deleterious effects of trauma therapy on the therapist. It is a process of change in the therapist's inner experiences—the normal and understandable by-product of personal engagement with clients' trauma memories and narrative descriptions. Pearlman and Saakvitne's questionnaire survey which asked 188 therapists about their exposure to clients' trauma material as well as their own psychological well-being indicated that trauma therapists are negatively affected by their work with patients. They often reported intrusive thoughts, efforts to avoid thinking about their patients' traumas, somatic symptoms such as headaches, nausea, sleeplessness, intrusive imagery triggered by something innocent at home like a child sobbing; also increased feelings of personal vulnerability, difficulty trusting others, emotional numbing and flooding, sexual difficulties, irritability, alienation, changes in their beliefs about themselves and others, progressive loss of energy and idealism. Saakvitne and Pearlman's (1996) summary of the signs and symptoms of VT include: social withdrawal, increased sensitivity to violence, cynicism, generalized despair and hopelessness, and nightmares. Also changes in identity, world view, or spirituality; intrusive imagery, dissociation, and depersonalization.[34]

Charles Figley had suggested that clinicians' empathy plays a role in the impact of working with victims, but Hoffman, whose research on empathy is well known, goes on to cast vicarious trauma "within a comprehensive theory of empathy-based pro-social behavior" (2), so as to explore in depth its relevance to therapists' motivation to help their trauma patients, as well as detailing what aspects of patients' behavior trigger the painful effects of empathic distress. He uses this theory to analyze trauma clinicians' detailed answers to questions about their immediate and long-term reactions—thoughts, feelings, images—to patients' accounts of their traumas. The empathic emotion in question is empathic distress: There is evidence that trauma therapists, more than other professionals, are vulnerable to an extremely painful form of empathic distress that Hoffman calls "empathic over-arousal" (EOA). An example is the male clinician treating a Vietnam veteran who said, "I think I'm getting secondary wounding," and later, "I've had dreams about blood, dead bodies, and body bags." When patients' trauma narratives are vivid enough empathic clinicians may experience painful images of what happened to the patient and imagine the same thing happening to themselves ("I tasted things she described tasting"). Empathic overarousal not only produces nightmares, flashbacks, and "psychic numbing" but also physical symptoms such as heavy breathing, gasping for air, heart rate acceleration, body shaking, dizziness, fatigue, neck tautness, hairs on back of neck standing up, stomach pain, and tears. It can also hinder treatment by interfering with clinicians' cognitive functioning: "I felt the sadness re-surge and envelope me . . . at this point it was very difficult to concentrate and attend properly" (Hoffman 11–15).

Hoffman's respondents also provide evidence of certain nonempathic emotions—feelings of helplessness, incompetence, being weighed down by the burden of being the patient's only hope. This can be intensely painful because such emotions threaten the individual's professional identity and self-concept.[35] He or she may have cynical, paranoid-like feelings about the world, due to frequent exposure to abused and tortured patients, fear of a patient's harming oneself or someone else, or of becoming involved in litigation.[36]

While the phenomena of vicarious trauma are amply evidenced by the responses from clinicians that Hoffman and Friedman obtained from their broad-ranging questionnaire—evidence that is supported by the findings of Pearlman and Saakvitne among others—the question remains as to the differential impacts depending on clinicians' prior life experiences (which Hoffman addresses), their capacities for empathy (this varies from individual to individual), and by the clinician's own support system. All these have bearing on how severe a clinician's vicarious trauma may be. Symptoms range from quite mild to severe, according to Hoffman's data. Nevertheless, the transfer of symptoms to enough clinicians is sufficient to warrant establishing vicarious trauma as a factor of clinical work with victims of catastrophes and physical abuse.

While clinicians have described and theorized vicarious trauma, why has the distinction between traumatic situations per se and vicarious ones not been written about much in literary or cultural studies?[37] Why has the fact that most of us encounter vicarious, rather than direct, trauma not received more attention? Perhaps literary and film scholars were distracted from studying the reader or viewer position by focusing on events within a fictional or documentary text and studying the representation of trauma in terms of protagonists. In chapters that follow, I explore in more depth than humanities scholars have hitherto done the way trauma impacts on readers and viewers. In particular, I make distinctions between direct and vicarious trauma, analyze the cultural politics of each type of trauma, and explore the aesthetics of catastrophe in a range of different media.

CHAPTER 2

Memory as Testimony in World War II

FREUD, DURAS, AND KOFMAN

I HAVE ARGUED that the model of trauma as dissociation in individuals involves too rigid a view of what happens to memory in extreme situations. Research by scholars working on memory has been helpful in foregrounding the dangers of holding too inflexibly to one version of brain circuitry as regards what happens to memory in trauma. For the idea that a traumatic event overwhelms the cortex and thus is not cognitively processed would mean that the event is completely unavailable to memory. This does not seem to be verified by how people experience trauma; frequently the subject does have memories, or partial memories, of what happened. But at the same time, what one remembers may be influenced by fantasies and desires, or by a wish that things had been different.[1] Subsequent events may subtly have an impact on a traumatic memory. One may hear of things that happened to others in a similar situation and these images may become mixed in with one's own experiences. As Janet Walker explains, "With regard to truth, traumatic memory is paradoxical. . . . Such memories may be even *more* veridical than memories for everyday events when it comes to the 'gist' of the memory" (Walker, "Vicissitudes" 136). But Walker warns that "it is also true that real catastrophes can disturb memory processing" (136). Pumla Gobodo-Madikizela, a psychologist working with victims and perpetrators during South Africa's Truth and Reconciliation Trials, notes that "when the rupture of one's sense is a daily occurrence, as in South Africa's violent past, old memories fuse with new ones. The narratives of trauma told by victims and survivors are not simply about facts. They are primarily about the impact of those facts on victims' lives and about the painful continuities created by violence in their lives" (Gobodo-Madikizela 86).[2]

In studying memoirs of traumatic situations, then, one has to bear in mind the vicissitudes of memory, to borrow Janet Walker's term, and the workings of the unconscious, the imaginary.[3] Walker points out that the "traumatic paradox" has to do with the ways in which "a common response to real trauma is fantasy" (Walker, "Traumatic Paradox" 809). She goes on to argue that the most effective films and videos about trauma are "those that figure the traumatic past as meaningful yet as fragmentary, virtually unspeakable, and striated with fantasy constructions" (809).[4] Yet such memoirs are not "fiction" in the usual meaning of that term. The writer is struggling to communicate something powerful that happened in the past, something that the writer remembers (in the senses given above), but which we are not to read as a literal rendering of "truth" as in the case of a witness in a court of law (even then, I doubt that most witnesses can remember in ways other than what I outlined above, but at least there is the effort and the legal requirement to "tell the truth").

In a memoir, then, "truth" in regard to events is not, per se, at issue. The main thing about a memoir is the emotions that are remembered and the ways in which the writer expresses them. Also important are the ways in which national/social codes and discourses shape both the impact of the trauma on the individual and how it is remembered. A possible difference between memoirs by male and by female writers may emerge here because social codes of male and female behavior differ. While no generalization will hold, arguably authors of female memoirs locate themselves within emotional relationships at stake in the past, while male writers may focus more on institutional, historical, or sociopolitical contexts. Yet, in both cases, personal and sociopolitical elements are involved. It is a matter of what the writer chooses to emphasize.

I will make a tentative gesture toward consideration of gender difference in memoirs by contrasting the construction of traumatic memory in three texts dealing with memories about World War II, namely Freud's *Moses and Monotheism,* Marguerite Duras's *La Douleur,* and Sarah Kofman's moving short memoir, *Rue Ordener, Rue Labat.* In the two texts by Kofman and Duras, how the writer feels is a main theme. Relationships and their symbolic importance are central to the underlying project of working through that perhaps motivates women to write memoirs. Freud on the other hand displaces his actual emotions about what is happening in the Nazi Germany where he starts writing into a struggle to understand the biblical Moses and to question his purported Jewishness. In addition Freud is unable to address directly his implied concerns about aging.

All three memoirs offer examples of what Freud named *Nachträglichkeit,* "belatedness," which I want to distinguish from dissociation.[5] In all three texts I am interested in differences in what I call an aesthetics of trauma, as it embodies belatedness. Freud's own "belatedness" is clear in *Moses,* a text he had always meant to write and which he leaves until nearly the end of his life when he is in a dire situation; Kofman arrives at writing about her emotions and childhood relations with her parents in Nazi-occupied Paris only at middle age, even though she suggests that all her prior philosophical and other writings about art have lead up to writing her memoir. Duras, meanwhile, evidently wrote *La Douleur* in the white heat of her traumatic experiences working with the French Resistance and caring for her very sick husband on his return near death from a concentration camp. Yet she pushed the material away and didn't even recall writing it when she discovered the manuscript also in midlife.[6] Arguably, each work reflects the project of "working through" as motivating the memoir.[7] Like Leigh Gilmore, I honor as an achievement "the ability to write beyond the silencing meted out by trauma" (Gilmore 24). The memoirs may reflect another motive, namely that of seeking a witness where there was none before (see Laub,"An Event" 75–92, and later discussions).[8]

FREUD'S *MOSES AND MONOTHEISM*

Freud's *Moses* shows less a case of dissociation than of "belatedness." But readers may be surprised to find that I am calling Freud's *Moses and Monotheism* a *memoir.* I will show that that term can apply, but I will also explore the ways in which Freud's own theory of trauma, further developed in the text, itself illuminates *Moses.* In addition, I look at how the text inscribes traumatic symptoms. How far are the text's traumatic symptoms linked to exile and cultural loss? How far is Freud's focus on the figure of Moses as an Egyptian a symptom of traumatic memory of anti-Semitism? In what ways is the trauma of aging (also evident in *Moses*) manifestly "male"?

In relation to exile, why is it at this moment in his life—the work was begun in 1936 as Hitler rose to power, and the first two parts published in *American Imago* in 1937—that Freud tries to argue that Moses was not Jewish but an Egyptian? Several hypotheses come to mind, hypotheses that the text itself could not "know." First, perhaps unconsciously terrified that anti-Semitism might impact seriously on him and his family, Freud thinks of showing that Jews are linked to non-Jews through his thesis about Moses—succumbing, then, to a kind of reaction formation. Second, perhaps Freud suffered the not unusual phenomenon of accommodation to the oppressor—partly disowning his own Jewishness in the context of Nazi oppression.[9] Third, Freud may have overidentified with Moses—whether a Jew or an Egyptian—in terms of Moses' alienation from his nation, his giving the Jews a new religion, and his being forced into exile. Freud like Moses was contemplating forced exile by the Nazis, leading a people not necessarily his own to the new practice and theory of psychoanalysis (a new religion, some would say).

The text reveals exile as a situation par excellence of loss of identity—without all the usual familiar surroundings with their strong affect, and without the discursive supports, including language, that reminded Freud of who he was, he may have lost his sense of himself. The many false starts to the work (even in 1937) and Freud's doubts that he can prove his argument, are symptoms of trauma: the style of the work embodies Freud's traumatized consciousness as he writes. Traumatic markers dog the book throughout, not only in the many false starts, but in the repetitions, the constant return to past arguments, and the weaving in and out of positions vis-à-vis Moses.[10] These reveal Freud's anxiety and his already threatened sense of identity, so it is not surprising that at the end of the volume he rehearses his trauma theories developed over the course of his career, and takes them further into the cultural realm. His traumatized state is dramatized as he resumes his delayed text in March 1938 while the family was still tenuously in Vienna, and continues with it in the safer climate of London in June 1938.[11]

The first mention of trauma in *Moses* comes when Freud is contemplating the two Moses, only one of which, he says, having to go into exile "passed through what may properly be termed a traumatic experience which the other was spared" (64–65). By 1939, he has himself passed through traumatic exile. "The exceptionally great difficulties [note the hyperbole signifying distress] which have weighed on me during the composition of this essay dealing with Moses' inner misgivings as well as external hindrances, are the reasons why this third and final part comes with different prefaces which contradict, indeed, even cancel, each other," Freud says. He continues: "For in the short interval between writing the two prefaces the outer conditions of the author have radically changed. . . . In the certainty of persecution—now not only because of my work [psychoanalysis], but also because of my 'race' [he puts this in quotes, interestingly]—I left, with many friends, the city which from early childhood through seventy-eight years, had been a home to me" (70).

This sentence, laden with intense feeling and unspoken pain, is Freud's testimony to a trauma that he could barely speak. He notes his continuing uneasiness with his work—something I will return to—but when he speaks of "missing the consciousness of unity and intimacy that should exist between the author and his work" (70), he may have in mind missing his home, his surroundings, his sense of himself in that place, his identity, in a way. "To my critical faculties," he says, "this treatise proceeding from a study of the man Moses, seems like a dancer balancing on one toe" (71). Yet because he finds analytic support in the exposure myth and in a historian's research, he pushes on.

This pushing on, repeating yet again in the manner of a traumatic symptom the history of Moses (now in abbreviated form) shows the work assuming more clearly the shape of trauma—that is, the compulsion to repeat reveals Freud's uncertainty about what he is writing and his fears about his personal situation. His mind is able to argue brilliantly and logically in specific places, but the book is like a series of fragments spliced together. It is as if Freud forgets that he has already stated an argument because he is distracted by fears for his family and himself. In addition, anxiety about aging breaks through the text: After repeating the publishing history of the work, including, "in March 1938 . . . the unexpected German invasion" that forced him from his home, he concludes that "the creative power of an author does not, alas, always follow his goodwill."

Freud's trauma of aging is very much there, if subliminally, and is evident in his uncertain identity throughout the volume. While aging is rarely linked to trauma (largely because said to be a "common" or "quiet" crisis), I have elsewhere made the case for aging as traumatic in the sense of the elderly being as vulnerable to identity crises as are adolescents (Kaplan, "Trauma, Aging, and Melodrama"). For women, identity crises hover around bodily changes in a culture obsessed with normative ideas of feminine beauty. The core of feminine subjectivity is threatened. For men, aging identity-crises involve loss of power and prestige. Freud's hesitancies and self-doubts throughout *Moses* manifest his fears of losing the power and authority he relied on for his identity within the psychoanalytic circles in which he had already become legendary. Only in part 3 however does Freud address aging directly: He notes that his earlier reference to failing powers referred to age. "I was of course referring to the weakening of the creative faculties which accompanies old age" (66). But there is an interesting footnote to Bernard Shaw, where Freud expresses strong disagreement with Shaw that men could only achieve worthwhile things if they could live to the age of three hundred years. "With the mere lengthening of the period of life nothing would be gained unless much in the conditions of life were radically changed as well," he says.

But the doubts reflect not only his anxiety about illness and aging but the special anxiety about being Jewish caused by the rise of Nazism. While Freud's sense of exile, aging, and loss haunt this text, such themes are also evident in the letters written in the years before leaving Vienna and once in London. Freud's letters support this reading of the subliminal influence worked through the narration in *Moses* and in the text's very aesthetic form. His trauma of exile (an external trauma) triggers prior inner psychic conflicts we can deduce from what we know of his childhood, together with his somewhat displaced cultural knowledge of anti-Semitism.[12]

Freud's book circles back to his opening comments about heroic myths and the slaying of the father in the primal horde central to the development of (male) religion and culture. Here Freud elaborates his prior trauma theories by introducing the concept of cultural trauma. He links what happens in individual trauma to what happens in cultures. The belatedness common in individuals, he argues, may also be seen in cultures. The trauma of the overthrowing of Moses, and the rejection of monotheism, is split off, not remembered until the memory resurfaces in a later generation. Cultural trauma functions as a symptom that is "forgotten" but repeated historically.[13]

But what about gender in Freud's very male story? Freud notes the replacement of a matriarchal social structure by a patriarchal one (*Moses* 145), but (I assume in unquestioning rapport with standard androcentric anthropology of his time) he argues, "This turning away from the mother to the father . . . signifies . . . a victory of spirituality over the senses, that is to say, a step forward in culture, since maternity is proved by the senses whereas paternity is a surmise based on a deduction and a premises" (146). We know that partly for this reason of paternal uncertainty Jewishness is passed down through the mother, apparently making her theoretically important if culturally marginalized. So what about women in the primal horde? What about women in developing religions? What about traumas specific to females? Since Freud's text leaves such issues aside, I turn to two very different memoirs written by women about the same war, but in contexts completely different from that of Freud's writing of *Moses*. Both offer female-centered perspectives, and both importantly focus on relationships as central.

Marguerite Duras's *La Douleur*

Marguerite Duras, well-known writer, filmmaker, and activist, tells the reader in a short text at the start of *La Douleur* (literally, "The Sorrow," but translated in the 1986 English version as *The War*), that she "found this diary in a couple of exercise books in the blue cupboards at Neauphle-le-Chateau," and that "I have no recollection of having written it."[14] While she knows she did write it, recognizes her handwriting and details of the story, she "can't see herself writing the diary." She can, however, see the place central to the narrative, namely the Gare d'Orsay, and the various comings and goings described. She understands (and so does the reader) that she could not have written the account while she was waiting for Robert L.'s (her husband, Robert Antelme's) return, yet she wonders, "How could I have written this thing I still can't put a name to, and that appalls me when I reread it?" (Duras, *The War* 4). She only thought about the text when asked for something she had written when young. She agrees, "*The War* is one of the most important things in my life. It can't really be called 'writing' . . . I found myself confronted with a tremendous chaos of thought and feeling that I couldn't bring myself to tamper with, and beside which literature was something of which I felt ashamed" (4).

I have quoted this passage at length because there is much to discuss. First, there is the obvious amnesia—something quite common in trauma. If we are to believe Duras (and I can see no reason not to), she wrote this at a time close enough to the events so that the white heat of the more or less prolonged panic attack was still alive, able to be recalled and put down. Perhaps it was written as soon as Robert L. was well enough to be on his own; perhaps guilt at divorcing her husband so soon after his return created inner turbulence which, added to the trauma itself, resulted in Duras simply dissociating the events and her account, splitting them off as she renewed her life. It's interesting that Duras does not say that she cannot remember the events she reads in her account, but that she cannot see herself *writing* the diary. So, the amnesia seems to be more about the writing than the events themselves, although clearly she endured something very traumatic in the waiting and then arrival of Robert L. The writing style itself amply communicates the panic state Duras endured for weeks on end. (Strangely, Duras tells us that she found herself "looking at pages regularly filled with small, calm, extraordinarily even handwriting," when you might expect a handwriting that would reveal the panic being relived as she wrote.) But why was the *writing* about the events itself so traumatic?

Let me leave this question for now, and say something about Duras's comment that she couldn't bring herself to tamper with the text, partly because of the extreme emotions reading it produced, but also because such "tampering" would involve making the text into "literature," something she now feels ashamed of. What can she mean here? Why ashamed? Is it that literature seems too self-conscious, too worked on, too studied, and thus too removed from the horror and violence surrounding Nazism and concentration camps? Perhaps too removed in general from the horror and violence of life in the twentieth century? Is it that words pushed out in extreme situations are not really "literature" but something else? Could it be that Duras has in mind the difference between narrative and "witnessing" that interests me? Putting forth testimony about something horrific should be a genre of its own. Duras suggests as much in calling what she has produced "this thing," something that she can't put a name to and that defies literary genres as we know them. In this sense, her text anticipates debates about trauma, about dissociation, and about the vexed question of "literature" dealing with trauma, especially in regard to the Holocaust. Let me provide a reading of the text before returning to these evocative questions.

The text consists of about eleven entries in April 1945 (indicated on p. 30), the month Paris was finally liberated, followed by a few entries in April 1946 ("the first summer of the peace"). The final ones are presumably in June or July 1946. Some of the entries just say "April," while others have specific dates, up to April 28, 1945. The last pages consist of very short notes, without dates, but clearly dating from summer 1946, after the war ended. Perhaps the "genre," if there is one, is indeed "the diary," despite the subtitle in the translation of "A Memoir," but on the other hand, "diary" suggests a sort of casual recording of a day's events, not the kind of panic-ridden writing of *La Douleur.* The specificity of the dates makes one wonder if indeed the text wasn't written as Duras was enduring the crisis, perhaps in those dark evenings when she was taking medications for her fragile emotional state, or in a state of utter sleepless exhaustion.

However that may be, the text perfectly expresses a phenomenological consciousness of panic attacks. Perhaps more than any other text, *La Douleur* illustrates how trauma produces a new subjectivity. The narrator is in a state of high alert as the text opens, waiting for a phone call to announce her husband's (Robert L.'s) release from the camp, or, better still, his sudden appearance at the door.[15] She is living utterly in the present moment, aware only of objects close to her that are relevant to her vigil—the phone next to the fireplace where she is sitting, then the door and the passage that leads to the front door; the phone may ring to announce Robert L.; he may arrive at the front door. Her heightened vigilance creates fantasies in rapid succession, as the speaker imagines her husband's arrival and their greeting one another, or his voice at the end of the phone line. The words on the page take us inside the speaker's consciousness, her inner thoughts, her fantasies about what might happen. "There wouldn't be any warning. He'd phone. He'd arrive. Such things are possible. He's coming back anyway. He'd ring. 'Who's there?' 'Me.' Lots of other things like this do happen" (5). We see here the speaker's split consciousness—split between fear Robert L. will not return, and conviction that he will return. She tries to convince herself of the latter, while fearing increasingly, as the days go on, the former.

The phone rings, but it's a neighbor, trying to see if Duras has heard anything. The neighbor tells her Belsen was liberated, which she didn't know before. She's torn between wanting to go and read the lists of names and not wanting to: "I must go down and buy a paper and read the list. No. I can hear a throbbing in my temples getting louder and louder. For one thing, I've been trying lists for three weeks, and that's not the way" (6). Here the reader learns the extent of time the speaker has been waiting, the better to understand the extreme crisis she now seems to be enduring.

The speaker tries to hold on to reality by deliberately noting things in her environment but she is unable to stop her mind darting forward in fantasies: "It's time to move. Get up. Take a few steps, go to the window. The medical school is still there. And the people going by—they'll be walking by when I hear he's never coming back. A notification of death. They've started sending them out recently" (6). We see how the speaker cannot keep focused; she tries to grasp reality, but then moves immediately to the fantasy of being notified of her husband's death when the outside world would go on as before, but her world would stop.

The thought of Robert L.'s death brings more panic: "The throbbing in my head is still there. I must stop it. His death is in me, beating in my head. No mistake about it. I must stop the throbbing, stop my heart, calm it down—I must help it, it will never calm down on its own. I must stop my reason from flying off at a tangent, out of my head" (6–7). Shortly after this, she goes outside, but feels like "a sleepwalker." Soon, reflecting on the march of the Allies through Germany, her thoughts suddenly begin to fantasize Robert L.'s death. "In a ditch, face down, legs drawn up, arms outstretched, he's dying, Dead. Beyond the skeletons of Buchenwald, his. It's shot all over Europe. The advancing Allied armies march past him. He's been dead for three weeks. Yes, that's what happened. I'm certain of it, I walk faster. His mouth is half open, It's evening. He thought of me before he died. The pain is so great I can't breathe, it gasps for air. Pain needs room. There are far too many people in the streets, I wish I were on a great plain all alone. Just before he died he must have spoken my name" (7).

We see here how close to stream of consciousness this writing is. Duras manages to record a mind in such a state of crisis that thought is disordered. One thought is associated with another, with perceptions of her environment occasionally breaking through and then setting up more associations. Realizing that she's on the street, she thinks of people, especially the young, somewhere in Paris laughing. She notes that she on the other hand only has enemies. Then her thoughts go to Robert L.: "Over there it's evening too. It's getting darker in the ditch, his mouth is in darkness now. A slow red sun over Paris. Six years of war ending. Nazi Germany is crushed. So is he, in the ditch. . . . Nothing in the world belongs to me now except that corpse in the ditch. It's a red evening. The end of the world. My death's not directed against anyone. . . . When I die, I won't rejoin him. I'll just stop waiting for him. I'll tell D., 'It's best to die—what good would I be to you?'" (8).

In this very casual way, the speaker's current lover, D. (Dionys Mascolo), a friend of her husband, enters the text. And the text from now on keeps him present. It's also shortly after this, as the speaker urges D. to reassure her about Robert's return, that the reader learns for sure for the first time that Robert L. is returning from a concentration camp. We have been able to deduce it before, but this is the first time that the words are actually put down. The speaker still cannot keep her thoughts in order. Going to make dinner, and (perhaps significantly) with the only sound that of the gas stove, Duras's fantasy again turns to Robert in the ditch. Her imagination is very vivid, as it always is in panic attacks: "Fourteen days, fourteen nights, abandoned in a ditch. The soles of his feet exposed. With the rain, the sun, the dust of the victorious armies falling all around him. His hands are open. Each hand dearer than my life. Known to me. Known like that to me alone. I cry out. Slow footsteps in the sitting room. D. comes in. I feel two strong gentle hands around my shoulders" (10). Sitting down to eat, the speaker becomes nauseous. Her bread is bread her husband hasn't eaten, and for lack of which he died, she thinks. The section ends with Duras saying: "I fall asleep beside him every night, in the black ditch, beside him as he lies dead" (10).

The second entry deals with the speaker's attempts to find out where Robert L. is by forcing her way into the Gare D'Orsay where all the returning prisoners are being processed. The people in charge, de Gaulle's police and agents, are hostile and cold to the speaker, as she tries to set up a table for her newspaper's tracking service. But there are no deportees yet, just prisoners. The people in charge are only interested in finding out about Nazi atrocities rather than in getting the people back to their families, it seems. The prose here is less filled with traumatic signs; Duras has things to do and authorities to work around, and her left-wing politics keeps her thoughts away from Robert L. (that is, she is taken up with criticizing the authorities whom D. characterizes as "the Right. . . . What you see is the Gaullist staff taking up its position. The Right found a niche in Gaullism during the war. You'll see—they'll be against any resistance movement that isn't directly Gaullist" (14). The police try to remove her group from the site, but they persist in taking down names and getting what information they can from the prisoners. She keeps asking about the deportees, but to no avail. Finally, some deportees arrive but Robert L. is not among them.

The text returns to the speaker's inner thoughts and state of being. She can't wait to leave the Gare D'Orsay and "shut myself up with the telephone, be back again in the black ditch" (22). She describes her grimy state and her permanent fever before suddenly turning on herself as a coward: "This evening I think about myself. I've never met a woman more cowardly than I am. I go over in my mind other women who are waiting like me—no, none is as cowardly as that." She recalls D.'s words, saying that she is sick, mad, destroying herself: "Look at yourself—you look like nothing on earth" (22). At this point, Duras interrupts the text for the only time, with the following sentence, in brackets: "[Even now, transcribing these things from my youth, I can't understand the meaning of those expressions.]" This is an odd sentence. Which expressions? The ones that people said to her about being crazy and sick, and destroying herself? Why can't she relate to these words in the present of her typing (as I assume she is) the handwritten text?

The next section begins with Duras's disjunctive information about what's happening in regard to the Allies moving into Germany, and the Germans shooting the Jews before the Allies arrive. In such sections, the reader gets a very good sense of the period of the war's end, the liberation of the camps, and the return of the prisoners and deportees. Many pieces of information are inserted in between other bits of the speaker's stream of consciousness. Elements of the confused transition from war to liberation emerge between other thoughts, fantasies, and memories of the narrator. She has a double image of a German killing Robert L. and of Robert L. exposed to the gun. She feels her head against the cold glass of the apartment. "I can't hold my head up any more; my legs and arms are heavy, but not so heavy as my head. It's not a head anymore, it's an abscess. The glass is cool. D. will be here in an hour. I shut my eyes. If he comes back, we'll go to the seaside, that's what he likes best. I think I shall die anyway" (28). Then she returns to the opening fantasies of Robert L. ringing at the door. "'Who is it?' 'It's me, Robert L.'—all I'd be able to do is open the door and die" (28).

The next section, dated April 22, 1945, continues with a similar mixture of news about the ending of the war, Duras's continuing illness, and her incoherent stream-of-consciousness observations about herself, D., and her neighbors who are also waiting for loved ones to arrive. Just before the end of this section, Duras describes what is definitely one of the consequences of prolonged trauma like hers: Thinking of her friend, she says: "In her head, as in mine, there are upheavals without substance, lapses and collapses of what we know not what, distances, seeming to open toward a way out, then disappearing, shrinking almost unto death. . . . That's why thought can't function. It's not part of the chaos, it's constantly being supplanted by it, helpless against it" (36).

The section that follows, just headed "April—Sunday," offers perhaps the most vivid account of a traumatic attack: The speaker describes losing touch with reality: "All of a sudden I had looked up and the apartment had changed. So had the light from the lamp, it was suddenly yellow. And suddenly certainty, certainty burst in: he's dead. Dead. Dead. . . . It had happened in the space of a second. No more throbbing in my head. Not Now. My face falls apart, changes. I fall apart, come undone, change. There's no one in the room where I am. I can't feel my heart any more. Horror mounts in a slow flood. I'm drowning" (37).[16] She no longer knows who she is, who Robert L. is, or who D. is. It seems that she stands outside herself, looking at herself, as in the dissociation that often happens in traumatic situations. She runs to find D. to regain reality, and the episode ends.

Somehow, mysteriously, this falling apart presages news of Robert L. The phone rings. A deportee has reported seeing Robert L. alive. D. and Duras rush to talk to the man. The text bustles now with movement, haste, and anxiety to know. But because there is such a long delay after this, the following sections, both from Friday, April 27, find the speaker moribund, unable to get out of bed. A friend who is waiting to hear about a daughter looks after Duras. Duras tells the woman's story, in plain words. The speaker continues to be deeply depressed: "Nothing. The black hole. No light thrown. I go over the sequence of days, but there's a void, a gulf, between the time when Phillipe didn't hear a shot and the station, where no one saw Robert" (45). D. insists on taking her out to eat, but she is nauseated by other people eating. "I want to die. I'm cut off from the rest of the world by a razor; even from D. The hellish calculation: If I don't have any news by tonight, he's dead" (45). Her thoughts are again interwoven with bits of news about the Allies, news that's coming out about German atrocities, about de Gaulle's coming to power in a way that terrifies the speaker. She identifies herself with the "suspense, as old as time, that of women always, everywhere, waiting for the men to come home from the war" (46). Her thoughts move to the larger picture of Europe, where these horrendous things happened, and a sort of traumatic guilt or shame envelops her, creating a new subjectivity through her realization of a certain complicity: "We belong to the part of the world where the dead pile up hugger-mugger in charnel houses. It's in Europe that this happens. That they burn Jews by the million. That they mourn them. America watches in amazement as the smoke rises from the crematoriums of Europe" (46).[17] She continues to associate herself, as a European, with the crimes: "We are of the same race as those who are burned in the crematoriums, those who were gassed at Maidenek; and we're also of the same race as the Nazis. . . . We have a share in those graves; those strangely identical skeletons belong to one

European family" (47). These things have happened on the soil of Europe, right where she is. The skeletons of the German Communists are in "the great European grave, too—with every Jew, every one, the idea of God."

In the section dated April 28, Duras is still waiting for Robert, but now disgusted at how quickly France is "forgetting"—just as American culture tried to "forget" the war as well: "Peace is visible already. It's like a great darkness falling, it's the beginning of forgetting. Paris is lit up at night. . . . I went out, peace seemed imminent. I hurried back home, pursued by peace. There's no room for me here anywhere. I'm not here, I'm there with him in that region no one can reach, no one else can know where there's burning and killing" (48). In the following entry of the same date Duras is awed by the number of Jews exterminated as more and more knowledge of the camps emerges. "Seven million Jews have been exterminated—transported in cattle cars, then gassed in especially built gas chambers, then burned in specially built ovens" (49). She comments again on the forgetting: "In Paris, people don't talk about the Jews yet. Their infants were handed over to female officials responsible for strangling of Jewish babies and experts in the art of killing by applying pressure on the carotid arteries. . . . How can anyone still be a German?" she asks. But then, in the same difficult move as before, Duras argues that Nazi crime cannot just be considered a German problem. To do so, is to reduce the brave resisting people to only regional dimensions. "The only possible answer to this crime is to turn it into a crime committed by everyone, to share it. Just like the idea of equality and fraternity. In order to bear it, to tolerate the idea of it, we must share the crime" (50).[18] I will return to this difficult idea in concluding.

Immediately after this, news comes from François Mitterrand (Morland in the text) that Robert is alive. He and D. immediately go to retrieve Robert. D. calls Duras to warn her of Robert's condition, which is very close to death. He also describes how Robert speaks unceasingly as they bring him home, with words pouring out uncontrollably after so much silent suffering, but how after that, he went silent again.

After all that waiting, Duras's first sight of Robert is traumatic: He is changed, reduced, a walking corpse. Duras shrieks and doesn't want to look; she runs away. "The war emerged in my shrieks. Six years without uttering a cry" (54). Finally, she's able to look at him, but she doesn't recognize him. "There's a supernatural weariness in his smile, weariness from having managed to live till this moment. It's from his smile that I suddenly recognize him, but from a great distance. . . . And then the smile fades, and he becomes a stranger again" (54). But there is great relief as well: "But the knowledge is still here, that this stranger is he, Robert L., totally" (54).

After this climactic moment, the tone of the entries changes. Panic text is replaced by calm, detailed, and devastating descriptions of Robert L.'s body, of his uncanny corpse-like shape, and of the strange excrement emerging from his

16. Buchenwald survivors (EarthStation I Multimedia)

body, symbolizing the dark night from which he was slowly emerging. It is a fight with death, and the doctor who saved Robert is coming every day. Slowly his fever subsides and is replaced by an awesome hunger. Duras tells us that Robert has gone and hunger has come in his place. "He is giving to the void, filling what was emptied: those wasted bowels. That's what he's doing. Obeying, serving, ministering to a mysterious duty" (61). Duras starts to eat and sleep as well for the first time in seventeen days. But she still suffers PTSD, being hypervigilant, waking in terror that Robert died while she slept. As he gains strength slowly, they begin to give him sad news, that his sister died, and then, finally—in a sentence that shocks the reader, since we are unprepared—Duras tells Robert that "we had to get a divorce" (63). The reader comes across this statement with great surprise, all the more because of the casual way that Duras introduces it: "Another day I told him we had to get a divorce, that I wanted a child by D., that it was because of the name the child would bear. He asked if one day we might get together again. I said no, that I hadn't changed my mind

17. Lager-Norhaus survivors (EarthStation I Multimedia)

since two years ago, since I'd met D. I said that even if D. hadn't existed I wouldn't have lived with him again. He didn't ask me my reasons for leaving. I didn't tell him what they were" (64).

It's a strange paragraph, full of unanswered questions for the reader. How could Duras want to leave Robert after having shown so great a love in waiting for him to come home and in bringing him back to life? It's inexplicable. And we too, as readers, are not given the reasons. The statement about the child and its name is inexplicable. What's the meaning in regard to the name? And that alone? We just don't know.

As the text nears its end, the speaker continues to manifest great love for Robert L. Duras mentions the powerful (and influential) book, *L'Espèce Humaine* (The Human Race), that Robert Antelme later wrote about his experience in the camps, but again, there's an odd phrasing. Duras says, "He wrote a book about what he thought he had experienced in Germany" (65). Why "what he *thought* he had experienced"? Does the narrator not think Robert could tell what happened? Or is the statement a recognition about the general vicissitudes of memory discussed earlier? Is Duras suggesting that her writing may also have fallen prey to such vicissitudes? We are left to infer what we can, and also to note that this comment must have been inserted as Duras typed up her "forgotten" manuscript, since Antelme only wrote the book when fully recovered.[19]

The last section deals with a hot summer day when Duras, Robert, and friends are at the beach. Duras describes the beauty of the scene, the sea, the mountains behind, and the villages up the hill. People are playing and laughing, but she says, "We can still hear the players. But Robert L.—we still can't hear him. It's in that silence that the war's still there, flowing across the sand and through the wind" (67). She surmises that it was Robert L.'s "peculiar grace which carried him through the camps—the intelligence, the love, the reading, the politics and all the inexpressible things of all the days. That grace peculiar to him but made up equally of the despair of all" (68). Could it be that despair that made it essential for Duras to divorce him? We don't know.

The text ends with tenderness; Duras and Robert L. are by the sea together. "I came near the edge. I looked at him. He saw me looking. . . . And I knew he knew, knew that every hour of every day I was thinking, 'He didn't die in the concentration camp'" (68).

Going over this text so closely, it became clear that the mental state of traumatic panic that it details so clearly is reworked in many of Duras's later texts, such as *Monsieur Andesmas, La Maladie de la Mer, Yann Andrea,* or *C'est Tout,* her very last piece of writing. It is not that Duras understood the genesis of the state of consciousness that these texts reveal, for Duras writes beyond (outside of?) the psychoanalytic system, for reasons that I speculate on below. Understanding her own state of consciousness or that of her characters is not what interests Duras; precise description of such states is her gift, her genius. But to this reader, it seems that the war and perhaps the specific experience of waiting for Robert L. while betraying him with his friend, produced a complex of contradictory emotions—of guilt, love divided, horror of the Holocaust and Nazism, despair at human nature's capacity for evil—and all of these states of being pervade her writing.[20] The works share the style of *La Douleur,* perhaps paradoxically given what Duras said in the preface to the text about being "disgusted" with literature. All Duras's texts are characterized by similar short abrupt sentences, the sense of total aloneness, the impossibility of love, with predominant themes of betrayal, of rupture, and of not being in touch with reality. Paradoxically, even *La Douleur* may be "literature," despite Duras's denial. And it is literature because of its power to propel readers into a traumatic situation and make it come alive for us. Perhaps, if we had to place it in a genre, "testimony" would be appropriate. The text reveals the paradox that trauma is unrepresentable and yet must be represented. It also illuminates the other paradox about dissociation and memory—namely that if the trauma is dissociated, it cannot be recalled. Whatever her state of mind, Duras apparently was able to write her traumatic experience; she subsequently suffered amnesia about that writing, but not about the events. As she reads the text after discovering it years later, she remembers the events but not the process of writing. In this case, the writing itself proved overwhelming. The text consists of phenomenological descriptions rather than interpretations that writing with more self-consciousness, with distance or within a psychoanalytic system would evoke: the descriptions characterize of the literalness of the traumatic state. Hence the text's oblique relation to psychoanalysis makes sense.

It is possible that Duras's characteristic panic and depression may have been a result of her problematic relationship with her mother. Growing up in Indochina, then a colony of France, poor (once her father died), her mother scraping a living together, Duras in addition suffered incredible jealousy of her mother's special love for Duras's violent older brother (who evidently exploited this love) and intense love for her sick younger brother. Her premature and passionate love affair at a young age with a much older man (fictionalized in *L'Amant*) suggests a search for the father or for both parents. And perhaps, in her last young lover, Yann Andrea, Duras found a place for herself as the mother she never really had.

In a sense, the young Duras seems to have been an orphan, running wild in the French colony, desperately seeking love. It's no wonder that once in France she quickly linked up with the radical movement, including the Communist left. These young intellectuals were bonded by their orphan-like status, throwing off their bourgeois parents, very much as many also did as members of United States 1960s movements like Students for a Democratic Society. Duras tries to replace the mother through her various lovers, none of whom, however, ever satisfy, or ever manage to fill the hole left by her loveless childhood. D. in *La Douleur* is alternately father (his stern voice telling her to pull herself together) and mother (his kind voice urging her to eat, to sleep, or his strong arms comforting her).

Duras never seemed interested in psychoanalytic approaches to consciousness. Perhaps it is this deliberate turning away from psychoanalytic thought, so much a part of intellectual life in 1960s Paris, that annoyed Julia Kristeva about Duras. In Kristeva's essay on Duras, "The Malady of Grief" (1989), one can see Kristeva's distaste for the kind of moves Duras is making in her art. She calls Duras's texts "morbid" and leading to madness. The two make an interesting contrast in ways of dealing with the new social, political and aesthetic realities of the late twentieth century that they both respond to: Kristeva looks for spiritual hope, for moving beyond despair; Duras, on the contrary, prefers to look directly at loss, without blinkers—something that must threaten Kristeva. In taking Duras for one of her case studies in *Black Sun*, Kristeva sees Duras as an example of "the malady of grief" that haunts so many and that, for Kristeva, "deprives literature of opening out onto music," leaving it rather to "illogicality and silence."

This is not quite how I see Duras: I do not agree that Duras's concern with loss reflects what Kristeva calls the dangerous "seduction" of Duras's writing and vision. I rather appreciate Duras's bravery in looking squarely at trauma, at the loss of the object (in this case her mother), at the violence and hatred she knows about through her elder brother, and finally at death. Duras seems a paradigmatic case of a traumatized person, seeking her own distance from trauma. She does this by creating a gap between the trauma and the present lived moment through writing, which she could not live without. Kristeva misses the political commitment that is so obvious in *La Douleur*—the commitment to justice and human rights, and the disgust at racism and arrogance such as the Germans and many French revealed during the Nazi occupation of Paris.

SARAH KOFMAN'S *RUE ORDENER, RUE LABAT*

Sarah Kofman, younger than Duras but living in Paris during the same years as Duras, surely knew Duras and certainly knew her work as well as that of Duras's husband, Robert Antelme, so prominent in *La Douleur.*[21] However, Kofman experienced the period in a remarkably different manner, partly due to her situation as a young Jewish child, but also due to her vastly different personality and sensibility. In some ways, Kofman is much closer to Freud (and not only because as an adult she studied and wrote about Freud, whom she considered a mentor). Her sensibility led her to psychoanalysis and to finding meaning in the psychoanalytic system so alien to Duras. What Duras and Kofman do perhaps have in common is the link between trauma and subsequent writing. And Robert Antelme provides another link through the impact on Kofman of Antelme's book, *L'Espèce humaine,* about his experiences in German concentration camps.[22] In a sense, the two memoirs function like mirror-images of one another. For Duras, language flows in an hallucinatory state as she waits for Antelme; for Kofman, who feels close to Antelme because his experience in the camps, described so vividly in his book, must have reminded Kofman of what her father went through and perhaps inspired the writing of *Rue Ordener, Rue Labat,* writing has to force its way out of a silence brought on by deep pain. Kofman dedicates *Paroles Suffoqées* (her book about the Holocaust) to Antelme as well as to Blanchot, whose influence can also be strongly felt.

As a well-known philosopher, a Jew, and a successful scholar, with many books behind her, Kofman found herself, at middle age, impelled to write an account of her terrifying childhood in Nazi-occupied Paris. What precisely occasioned the piece in 1993 we cannot know. But in speeches in honor of Kofman, gathered into a volume of *Les Cahiers du Grif* in 1997, some colleagues speculated about links between her philosophy and her life. Jean-Luc Nancy, for instance, suggests reading Sarah Kofman's opus in the same manner that she read male philosophers, namely in terms of what a work brings to the life. Nancy quotes Kofman saying, "It is . . . a certain relationship of system to life which interests me: to see, not what the work *owes* to life but what the work *brings* to life; to grasp how a philosophical system can take the place of *délire*" (see Jean-Luc Nancy in Deutscher and Oliver viii). Other articles in both *Les Cahiers du Grif* and the anthology coedited by Penelope Deutscher and Kelly Oliver (1999) also illuminate links between Kofman's writings and her own struggles. That is, they show how Kofman's choice of texts to write about (such as Oscar Wilde's *Dorian Gray* or a staging of Sophocles' *Antigone*) reverberates with aspects of her life—or rather, bring certain aspects of her to life, as it were.

In writing *Rue Ordener, Rue Labat* it is also possible that Kofman was searching for a witness in her readers where there was none before, much as the Holocaust survivors Dori Laub interviewed at Yale also sought a witness. Kofman (like Freud and others) had apparently "forgotten" her terrifying and dangerous wartime situation until her middle years. Tragically for Kofman, as for many survivors, the remembering may have been too much, for Kofman committed suicide in 1994. This fact adds to the poignancy of the description of a childhood filled with mother-daughter conflicts intensified and magnified by the drastic situation of a Jewish family trying to survive virulent anti-Semitism and Nazi annihilation. The two streets in the title of the memoir suggest a series of doubles that pervade the volume. The names embody two vastly differing "homes," one organized according to Jewish ritual (Rue Ordener, Kofman's original home), the other organized according to Christian and local French culture (Rue Labat, the street where Kofman's family hid out to avoid deportation).

The memoir opens with Kofman's reference to her father's pen, which she used throughout her schooling and which still sits, patched up, in front of her on her desk, making her "write, write." She then adds, significantly: "Maybe all my books have been detours required to bring me to write about 'that'" (Kofman, *Rue Ordener* 3). The topic is evidently still too painful to name, even as Kofman readies herself to "remember." Expanding her brief comment about all her books being detours leading to this one, could one say that writing over the years with her father's pen, or with it in view, unconsciously reminded Kofman of what she finally had to write about, perhaps not knowing its cost, perhaps knowing it full well?[23]

The entire memoir is written in the sort of direct, clear language, freed from self-consciousness or any artfulness that one perhaps becomes capable of only when writing "too close to the bone" (in Allon White's words), or, as White put it as well, "Like beginning to write at twilight with no lamp as the darkness falls" (White 26). This aesthetic differs markedly from that explored in Freud's *Moses,* where the writer remains unaware of his trauma, so that the marks of it appear in the fragmented thinking, the moving backwards and forwards, the repetitions, the doubts about what he is doing, and so on. It also differs from Duras's text, where the speaker writes in the first person and in the present tense, as if in the midst of the panic, putting down observations and reactions along with insistent fantasies or hallucinations of what she dreads. By contrast, Kofman, like Allon White, is writing at a moment of sudden lucidity about the trauma that has marked her life as it had White's. There is a focus and an intensity that seems impossible until one has reached back into the trauma and accepted the necessity (or inevitability) of death because trauma's pain is too much.[24] We have then an acceptance of death instead of, as in both Freud and Duras, I think, a fear of death that produces the fragmented, disjointed text. Kofman's and White's prose on the brink of a death that is, however, accepted, may be a very rare, and special, occurrence.[25]

The first part of the memoir focuses on Kofman's close bonding with, and love for, her father. Kofman recalls first the trauma of the night her father was "picked up," linking her own and her siblings' wailing to the lament in a Greek tragedy, "Oh papa, papa, papa" (7). She recalls the card her father sent from the camp—the only news the family ever received after his being taken away—and her unsuccessful search for it when her mother died. "It was as if I had lost my father a second time," she says. (Puzzling is the following comment, that "from then on nothing was left," since Kofman still had the pen. But perhaps she meant nothing that came from his last abode, namely the camp.) There follow happy memories of religious rituals that Kofman loved, linked as they were to her father's position as a rabbi. She treasured the walks back from the synagogue holding her father's hand. Some of the rituals were scary for a child as sensitive and fearful as Kofman clearly already was. She associated the special razor with which her father slaughtered chickens on Friday evening with Abraham's knife, "and the gutteral sounds of the Shofar with cries from the chickens' severed throats" (14).

It is only gradually that the reader learns of Kofman's dependency on her mother—a dependency (her internal infantile trauma) already unusually strong before the crisis but no doubt heightened because of the terrors of her father's deportation and her own and her family's constant fear of being caught by the Nazis (the triggering external event). Chapter 8 begins: "The real danger: separation from my mother" and goes on to recount Kofman's extreme anxiety when sent at age three and a half with her older sister to summer camp. Eventually getting sick, she returns home: "The Gare du Nord: glued to the train window, I watch for my parents and at last catch sight of my father's smile. I am saved" (27). But after that, Kofman says, she changed, becoming irritable and whiny. This memory emerges in the course of detailing the many attempts of Kofman's mother to hide the children safely (which meant separation), one of which was putting them with a Jewish Communist family on a farm. But Kofman cannot bear to be apart from her mother, and keeps on devising strategies, including vomiting and falling sick, to get back to her.

The family's most frequent haven, we learn, was "the lady on the Rue Labat." This lady had been mentioned just once before, in passing, but as the memoir proceeds, she becomes a central figure, known as Mémé. It is the troubled triangular relationship among Mémé, Kofman, and her mother that develops into a main theme. Kofman is pulled in two diametrically opposed ways by her two "mother" figures, to the extent that, being already psychically vulnerable, a traumatic split seems to occur. It is this traumatic split, recalled by Kofman in middle-age, that I want briefly to focus on in the remaining section of this chapter.

The split takes many forms: Mémé, a Christian, has tastes in food, dress, and deportment quite the opposite of Kofman's Jewish mother. Kofman describes how she is gradually "made over" into a little Christian girl, right under her mother's nose. Mémé is also more emotionally expressive than had been the custom in Kofman's family, and this is exciting and alluring to the child. As a sexually active woman, Mémé sleeps weekly with a friend with whom she owns a small press. On those days, she makes herself up in a way Kofman has not seen before. Temperamentally quite different from Kofman's mother (who, by the way, is never given a name, a point I will return to), Mémé is calm and gentle, while her mother is loud, easily hysterical, and always nervous (obviously, the difference in their situations has something to do with this, but Mémé is risking a great deal in harboring Kofman and her mother). Further, Mémé likes to read and has many books in the house: she introduces Kofman to philosophy, to the Larousse Dictionary, and to medical books. It is from Mémé's lips that she hears (in the context of Mémé's ambivalent attitudes toward Jews) the names of Spinoza, Bergson, Einstein, and Marx.

As she recalls the splitting of her subjectivity between the two women, Kofman presents little of her mother's painful experience of "losing" her child to the woman who is saving their lives, although she does recall "forgetting" everything about her heritage and her family, including her father. It is as if even in midlife, Kofman cannot bring herself to identify with her mother's experiences. Perhaps she is still unconsciously tied symbiotically to her mother so that she cannot grasp the distance necessary to put herself in her mother's place, thus feeling what life must have been like for her. She rarely thinks about her mother, living alone more or less secluded in a room in Mémé's house, unable to do anything about the bonding between Kofman and Mémé for fear of being discovered (the child has a much easier time "passing" on the streets than would the mother). Not giving her mother any name suggests either symbiosis on Kofman's part (not really understanding her mother as a separate entity), underlying anger at her mother's attempts to send her away to safety, or perhaps oedipal rivalry over her beloved father. It's hard to know. Yet this split is deeply embedded in Kofman, only fully reemerging as she writes the memoir.[26]

The struggle continues after the liberation of Paris and the end of the war, since Mémé wants to keep Sarah with her. There is an ugly court case, in which the beatings of Kofman by her mother come to light; Mémé is awarded custody, but Kofman feels guilty, and is "deep down" relieved when her mother forcibly seizes her back from Mémé (61). This relief, I think, supports an analysis of Kofman's ongoing symbiotic relationship to her mother, suggesting a pre-oedipal attachment that is never overcome, awkwardly combined with the oedipal jealousy noted above. In turning to the philosophical fathers, then, Kofman is seeking relief from her suffocating pre-oedipal symbiosis, as she also sought it, perhaps in Mémé during her childhood. She is claiming closeness to her father at the same time.

This brings the reader to the end of the flashback section of the memoir. With chapter 18, there is a break. We are back in the present of Kofman's writing the memoir—a present only infrequently included. In this and the next chapter, Kofman offers what insight she has into the split that has so troubled her as she presents the reader with two powerful mother images in art. Both seem to be signifiers for what she has experienced. One is the famous Leonardo da Vinci portrait of *The Madonna and Child with Saint Anne*; the other is a scene from Hitchcock's *The Lady Vanishes*. Kofman's identification with both images is strong. In the first, the Leonardo da Vinci portrait, Kofman quotes Freud's analysis of the complex family relationships that must have inspired da Vinci's images. For the first time, at least implicitly in quoting Freud's perspective, Kofman permits herself to identify more strongly with the (her) birth-mother than with the second mother (in her case, Mémé). For Freud, Kofman thinks, seems to sympathize more with Leonardo's birth-mother, Caterina, than with his young stepmother, Donna Albiera. Freud, she says, analyzes the "blissful smile of Saint Anne" (standing in for Caterina, he thinks) disavowing and cloaking "the envy which the unfortunate woman felt when she was forced to give up her son to her better born rival, as she had once given up his father as well" (64).

In this case, both mothers seem to be basically good, although Leonardo's father prefers the higher-born woman to his first wife, Caterina. In her second textual example, Hitchcock's film *The Lady Vanishes* (cited as "one of her favorites"), Kofman discusses "the visceral anguish" she experiences in the film when "the nice little old lady, Miss Froy, seated in the train opposite the sleeping heroine (a young Englishwoman named Iris), vanishes" (65). But the part that terrifies her even more is when the heroine returns to the compartment to find that there is a lady with a "hard, shifty face" sitting there in Miss Froy's clothes. Kofman says, "Just when one was expecting to see the good old lady's sweet smiling face, instead, there it is—menacing and false" (66).[27] In this second case, the mothers are split between a good and a bad mother.

If the first image suggested Kofman's perception of her two mothers during the war, the second one refers, perhaps, to her perceptions after the war: Kofman actually experienced at that point, as we learn in the next chapter, a sort of Hitchcockian substitution of one (good) mother for another (harsh) one. While her birthmother tried to keep Mémé and Sarah separate, in the mother's absence they reunite. However, one evening, expecting the smiling, warm Mémé to pick her up from school, instead Sarah finds her harsh mother. She is not allowed to return to Rue Labat to say goodbye to Mémé.

If Sarah seems hard on her biological mother, it does appear that this mother, no doubt out of extreme anxiety and the stress of trying to survive with six children in Nazi-occupied Paris, often resorted to beatings, threats, and other behaviors we might now, and in the United States especially, see as abusive. Thus, the Hitchcockian split mothers, recalling strongly Melanie Klein's theories of the good and the bad breast in the infant's imaginary, spoke directly to Kofman's fantasies of her two "mothers." How could the little girl understand that her need for the "mirroring" (which D. W. Winnicott argues is essential for the child's developing a secure identity) was only possible to obtain from Mémé? How could she understand the subterranean sexual appeal of Mémé, which only comes close to surfacing in the recollection of a night they once spent together in a hotel?

It seems that the guilt about preferring Mémé to her mother was never satisfactorily resolved. The mothers continued to be at war over Sarah—to be rivals and enemies, even as Sarah grows up and goes to college—and so how could Kofman find a way through her ambivalence in regard to both women, and, most centrally, in regard to her own subjectivity? Given the vast differences between the two women, and Sarah's alternating identifications with each of them, it seems that her identity was always in crisis. She might settle into one identity, only to long for the other, or to miss what the other offered. A constant, traumatic oscillation, then, between opposed mother-imagos. And along with this, the constant fear of losing either mother, exacerbating her inherent need to feel safe and secure as a result of the terrors of being a Jew in Nazi-occupied Paris.

Kofman resorted to illness and reading as escape mechanisms when everything got to be too much. Her many references to vomiting made me think of her need to vomit up the horrible world she was living in, to expel her anxiety in this way. She eagerly sought from her various female teachers the mirroring she needed, falling in love with one after another. The memoir ends with mention of Mémé's "recent" death, preceded by her sad physical decline. Unable to attend her funeral, Kofman significantly notes: "But I know that at her grave the priest recalled how she had saved a little Jewish girl during the war" (85).

But what about the father whom Kofman evoked so powerfully in the opening pages of her text, and whom she saw at the start as the prime mover, as it were, for her writing? He disappears from the text as he had from her life. Kelly Oliver has argued that this is because Kofman displaced the paternal law into her birth-mother, who indeed, in an anecdote others have commented on, seemed often (paradoxically) to represent the very rigid Judaic and paternal law that, with its prohibitions, excluded the mother. In turning from the law of the father, then, Kofman turns from the mother (Oliver 186–187). But it is also possible that the father remains powerfully present in the unconscious rage at her mother for coming between Sarah and her father. In turning to the philosophical fathers to escape the claustrophobic relationship with her birth-mother and claim her father, did Kofman fail to reconnect with her birth-father with whom she identified strongly, and who impels her to write? Is it the traumatic (and intolerable) memory of the split mothers that leads Kofman to her death shortly after writing the memoir? Could it be that the real trauma was not so much the split mother identifications, but her father's suddenly being deported, suddenly taken away? Is it that recalling her lost father—and his tragic end that overwhelmed the little girl's consciousness—evokes a traumatic gap that never healed?[28] Perhaps the combination of these traumas, brought to consciousness as testimony, proved unendurable.[29] Kofman's suicide raises many questions about whether in fact writing or recalling trauma can be a way of "working through," or whether at least in some cases it provokes a new crisis, a new acting out (in Dominick LaCapra's terms).[30]

Gender and Aesthetics in Trauma Memoirs

These three memoirs, then, precisely because of their differences, establish the contexts for discussions in chapters that follow. First, the gendering of the trauma is significant, although there are some obvious similarities across gender difference. Both Freud and Kofman suffered the trauma of Nazi annihilation of so many Jews, despite the fact that neither ended up in a camp. Freud endured exile, Kofman the terrors of fragile daily survival, with the ever present fear of discovery and deportation. But the family traumas that accompanied this larger political terror were remarkably different. Freud's interest in, and identification with Moses, I've argued, had to do with his fears of losing his power and authority as the leader of his psychoanalytic followers, partly through illness and aging, partly through eager younger analysts discovering their own, if related, theories. He fears the loss of a particularly male position of power. And his text represses the feminine in Freud's preoccupation with the primal father.

Kofman, meanwhile, suffers from her need for dependency—a situation produced, perhaps, though insufficient mirroring and nurturing on the part of her anxiety-ridden, terrified, and often helpless mother in Nazi-occupied Paris. The mother-daughter conflicts that emerge as the major theme of Kofman's memoir are commonly suffered by women, and will figure in other texts studied in this book. However, the particular intensity of the conflicts and the split subjectivity Kofman endures have to do with her particular situation. We will see how other situations produce analogous, though different, crises of identity. If Freud's text represses the feminine, Kofman's seems to repress the masculine. The much-loved father—in a way the reason for the writing itself—disappears from the text, or is present only in the very process of Kofman's writing.

Meanwhile, Duras, read in the context of both Freud and Kofman, stands apart from their obviously psychoanalytically inflected texts. Her text is perhaps best linked with phenomenology—a phenomenology often remarked as characteristic of the traumatic attack. Duras's unconscious seems overwhelmed, so that she lives in the present, writes in the present tense, and leaves no room for infantile desires and wishes to surface. If I read back from the text into possible unconscious reasons for Duras's writing, seeking what the texts brings to life, I have very little concrete evidence with which to work.

The differences between the texts' aesthetic forms are striking. Trauma marks Freud's and Duras's texts in the moments showing paralysis, in the endless repetition, the unheeded circularity—all aspects of the nonrepresentability of trauma and yet of the search to figure its pain (via narration of a sort). This first kind of trauma aesthetic shows trauma as narration without narrativity—that is, without the ordered sequence leading to a determined end we associate with narratives. Yet both texts do have a sort of "ending," a kind of "closure," belying attempts to radically oppose traumatic narration and narrative. Thoughts irrupt into both Freud's and Duras's textual space, unheralded in the telling as in an individual's consciousness. Fragments, hallucinations, and flashbacks are modes trauma often adopts.

But it does not always do that, as Kofman's text shows; Kofman's text would seem to belie most of the characteristics outlined in relation to *Moses*. Kofman writes in a calm, clear prose, detailing remembered events vividly. However, let me briefly comment on two aspects of the text that indicate trauma beneath this smooth surface: First, the memories are not always in chronological order: they are fragments, pieces, that weave back and forth between different phases of Kofman's childhood, and they have surely been worked on by unconscious fantasies in intervening years. There is less linearity than might at first appear. Second, the more one reads the text, the more sharply emotional intensity emerges. While many memories are recalled without explicit reference to emotion, the events that were especially traumatic and that are accompanied by emotional signifiers stand out all the more. One such event is the memory of Kofman and her siblings wailing as their father was taken away—a memory that seized her when, as an adult, she read a lament in Greek tragedy (*Rue Ordener* 7). The other is the image of Miss Froy in Hitchcock's film being replaced by the cruel, harsh look-alike—the image standing in for Kofman's terror regarding her own splitting, mirrored in the two mothers. As suggested earlier, however, perhaps the difference in aesthetic form has to do with Kofman being at a point where she is almost standing outside of her trauma, writing "close to the bone" with the clarity that may come as one anticipates death.

Despite their differences, however, all the texts, whether implicitly (in the case of Freud) or explicitly (in the case of others), address the impact of trauma on an individual in the context of, and closely allied with, the overarching social, political, and cultural conditions of the Holocaust and World War II. The focus in this chapter has been on how trauma performs in the individual in the context of particular sociopolitical conditions. In what follows, I look at how the sociopolitical arena "manages" cultural trauma and thus shapes how individuals react to it.

Chapter 3

Melodrama and Trauma

Displacement in Hitchcock's *Spellbound*

This chapter investigates cultural trauma, and argues that politics intervenes in how such trauma is "managed." How is collective trauma translated across different groups with differing relationships to a traumatic event? May cinema, in its classical and dominant Hollywood form, "translate" an event for a culture, unconsciously colluding with dominant political forces? These are some of the questions addressed in what follows.

The question of collective or cultural trauma is a difficult one. While individual trauma is always linked to the social sphere, given that social conditions shape trauma's impact (e.g., 9/11 and the memoirs studied in chapter 2), traumatic events may affect the discourse of an entire nation's public narratives. It would be reductive to apply to the collective or nation trauma phenomena common in individuals, such as post-traumatic stress syndrome with the "splitting" or dissociation it may involve. Yet history seems to provide examples of national "forgetting" or displacement that require explanation, such as the long delay in wide public and international discussion of World War II suffering, especially the Holocaust, or the delay in confronting slavery or the decimation of Native Americans in the United States.

But even here there are problems. Does an entire nation forget? Or only the perpetrators? Do dominant and powerful groups engineer a "forgetting" through controlling discourses? Groups that have been victimized in a nation don't "forget"—at least not in the same way as do the perpetrators. We need to heed Dominick LaCapra's warning that "historical trauma is specific, and not everyone is subject to it or entitled to a subject position associated with it" (*Writing History* 78). Yet, people in a nation who have been through a catastrophe such as war may need to "forget" those experiences because they are too painful to deal with in the immediate aftermath of suffering. Kai Erikson "has argued that the social tissue of a community can be damaged in ways similar to the tissues of mind and body" (Robben and Suárez-Orozco 24). Robben and Suárez-Orozco go on to explain, "Massive trauma ruptures social bonds, undermines community, destroys previous sources of support and may even traumatize those members of a community, society or social group who were absent when the catastrophe or persecution took place" (24).

The question of when and how a national discourse can allow recognition of its past sufferings, or can permit knowledge about violent crimes directed at marginalized groups to surface in the public sphere, is extremely interesting. Yet, the question may be difficult to answer since evidence of the mechanisms by which knowledge is shelved is hard to obtain. How could one discover the strategies by which dominant power groups in the United States developed mechanisms to engineer a "forgetting" of traumas that they originally inflicted on victims (such as slavery or the decimation of Native Americans)? How could one investigate the displacement of traumas that a nation shared (such as the experience of wars)? South Africa was the first nation to investigate and bring to light specific crimes by individuals perpetrated on victims in the name of the state. The Truth and Reconciliation Trials provide a unique and brave, if ultimately only partially successful, attempt by a nation to confront crimes that were hidden from the public and that were enacted within a massive discourse of pernicious racism. As LaCapra notes regarding South Africa's experiment, "This complicated past was now to be disclosed truthfully in order for a process of working through to be historically informed and to have some chance of being effective ritually and politically in creating both a livable society and national collectivity" (*Writing History* 44).

One has to turn to theory. First, it is necessary to distinguish between discussing public or official discourse—that is, talking about what gets attention and when by the media, by public intellectuals, by scholars doing research in academia—and discussing the collective memory of a particular group within a nation who may have been victimized. Such groups, like a nation as a whole, may need to "forget" traumatic events perpetrated on them, but even when these groups are ready to bring forth historical catastrophes, the nation as a whole (those in power especially) may not be ready to hear from the victimized. This is why the South African reconciliation "experiment" is so important, especially since it is being repeated in other nations and situations.

New work in an anthology, *Cultures under Siege: Collective Violence and Trauma,* coedited by Antonious C.G.M. Robben and Marcel M. Suárez-Orozco, brings together essays by anthropologists and psychiatrists in an effort to understand the impact of massive cultural trauma. While not quite addressing the problem of whether or not one can talk of an entire nation being traumatized and suffering the kind of "forgetting" that trauma involves, the essays do discuss ways in which social violence pursues its victims long after the slaughter ends and the peace treaties are signed (Robben and Suárez-Orozco 5). The destruction of the symbolic order within which people live and can make sense of their lives can have devastating results. Trust in "the social institutions and cultural practices that structure experience and give meaning to human lives," must be reconstructed for healing to take place. Anthropologists in the volume discuss the dynamic relation between society and trauma, showing how "the social context influences the self-perception and recovery of the traumatized, and . . . the victims themselves, as a social group, have an influence on the society at large" (21).

Authors discuss ways in which "violence continues to shape the inner, interpersonal, and socio-cultural worlds of victims and their children," and they note how social violence has multiple sequelae (5). Transgenerational trauma is one such result. Many scholars studying trauma today are doing so because of the effects of transgenerational trauma. As Nicholas Rand pointed out when introducing the crucial research by Nicolas Abraham and Maria Torok in this area, "The idea of the phantom has implications beyond the study of individual psychology or even familial psychology" (Rand 169).[1] He goes on to note that the concept has the potential "to illuminate the genesis of social institutions and may provide a new perspective" on cultural patterns and cultural ideology. Rand concludes that the phantom may show how silence is the breeding ground for the return of shameful secrets "on the level of individuals, families, the community and possibly even entire nations" (169).

Similar arguments were made in many papers delivered at a conference organized in Germany, in summer 2002, by the Trauma Research Networking group. Sibylle Rothkegel, discussing "Ethnocultural Aspects in International Work on Trauma," observed, "Without regard for political-historical and social contexts, we can neither hope to gain insights into the circumstances in which trauma occurs, nor to develop effective treatments. Cultural context should not be excluded from trauma research, for it determines how symptoms are experienced and expressed and provides a framework for understanding traumatic events, opportunities for healing and therapeutic possibilities."[2]

In arguing here, then, that cultures too may be traumatized, and that they too may "forget" horrendous actions performed in the past and simply split off from the daily consciousness in the culture, I concur with the Freud of *Moses and Monotheism* that the "latency" phenomenon he discovered in the individual may also apply to cultures.[3] Although cultural traumas are not "remembered" in the usual sense because of the specificity of trauma, I will show that the impact of past crimes in a nation-state may evidence itself in the form of cultural "symptoms" analogous to those in individuals explored in previous chapters.[4] However, unlike Freud, I argue that the phenomena of "forgetting" are not always innocent, for political interests generally enter into processes of national memory or non-memory, as the case may be.

Trauma and modernity are inherently intertwined. But how did the "shocks" to Euro-American cultures produced through modernization evidence themselves culturally? What symptoms can be found through which such shocks were registered, and perhaps negotiated and controlled? How did cultures manage not to "know" the history they had participated in? How could memory be tricked into not remembering? While there are many possible answers to these questions, I have chosen here to investigate the degree to which a pervasive popular genre, the melodrama, might have served the function of registering *while negotiating* the cultural traumas of modernity, including those of war, race, and gender, through the mirror of what I am calling "quiet" or "common" trauma.

While theatrical melodramas preceded film, film melodrama could reach large numbers of people and respond quickly to cultural and political events. I am especially interested in the match between the visuality common to traumatic symptoms (flashbacks, hallucinations, dreams) and the ways in which visual media like cinema become the mechanisms through which a culture can unconsciously address its traumatic hauntings. The phantom-like quality of cinema discussed by Tom Gunning—a quality that some viewers in cinema's early days found in itself to be traumatic—now serves to allow spectators to register what they (and the culture at large) do not want to consciously "know" (Gunning, "An Aesthetic of Astonishment").

But since this is the first chapter in which I discuss cinema and trauma, it is appropriate to briefly address debates ongoing in cinema studies about the new interest in trauma. These debates bear some relation to the general concerns about trauma studies discussed in chapter 1, only now they emerge specifically in regard to the impact on cinema studies of interest in trauma.

At one pole is the worry that "trauma theories already dominant within literary studies and history subjugate Screen Studies too" (Radstone, "Introduction" 189).[5] At the other (a more realistic worry) is that trauma theory will become, in Thomas Elsaesser's words, "too handy a catch-all for resolving the aporias or lacunas of previous theoretical configurations in the field of film and television studies" (Elsaesser 201). This was an issue raised years ago by Michael Roth in terms of theory more generally and then it had a certain validity. But now, given that there is a "crux" of trauma theories currently being debated, and given the strong criticisms of trauma theory, any such temptations are too obvious to be viable.

In between are other concerns that require attention, such as that the attention to memory and history encouraged by trauma theory "prompt[s] a retreat from film theory's imbrication with questions of fantasy and spectatorship" (Radstone, "Screening Trauma" 191). Radstone remarks that "trauma theory runs the risk of returning Screen Studies to [a] model of passive spectatorship, and the retention of fantasy may be our best insurance against such an outcome" (191).[6]

In considering these worries, let me highlight a certain confusion between tendencies that European scholars see in United States culture and how this culture is understood in work on going by mainstream American film scholars interested in trauma. The concerns about the purported "victim culture" of the

United States or the ways in which "psychical mediation has been sidelined in the interests of litigatory clarity" (Radstone, "Introduction to Trauma Studies" 190), observed from London or Amsterdam through whatever media reports do not necessarily reflect as great a validity as reports received in Europe might indicate. Scholars follow controversial critics like Allan Young, and popularizing writers like Elaine Showalter, rather than going to less polemical work by authors such as Dominick LaCapra or Robert Jay Lifton.

Secondly, I am reminded of the ways in which American feminist film scholars were accused of essentialism by European scholars because they focused too much on the figure of woman as an embodied entity (in lived experience) in exploring film images, instead of studying images as specific signs within a culturally produced signified. There's a parallel attribution now to United States scholars of a literalism regarding the traumatic event and its latency or belatedness, of "history" being written on the body, instead of scholars meditating "on the illusory but shocking indexical 'otherness' of the moving visual image" (Radstone, "Introduction to Trauma Studies" 190). I'm not sure how many film scholars in the United States working with trauma are in fact abandoning the depth model of the mind, ignoring fantasy, failing to attend to cinematic indexicality, or reverting to the notion of a passive spectator. But in this book I aim to distinguish kinds of filmic address in films dealing with trauma so that passive or voyeuristic spectatorship is only predominant in some genres, and quite absent in others. Indeed, a main purpose is to foreground the spectator as active, as having agency and as receiving multiple positions with which to identify.

Elsaesser usefully points out that trauma theory in film studies is important in prompting a reconsideration of referentiality. Trauma theory is more about recovered referentiality, he says, than about recovered memory. Trauma invokes a historicity that is needed while "acknowledging (deconstruction's) deferral and (psychoanalysis's) double time of *Nachträglichkeit*" (201). But because of the nature of trauma, referentiality can only be recovered through interpretation.

This is relevant to uncovering cultural trauma, the project of this chapter. "Interpreting" classical film may enable one to uncover historical events displaced into a narrative about something closely related but not the event itself. In the example of such displacement that follows, I link trauma studies to film studies by building on prior research. In the case offered here, I link melodrama and trauma, building out from earlier film theories about melodrama. In this way, trauma studies does not undo earlier theories; rather, trauma studies' perspectives bring to light what was already implicit in early theorizing about melodrama but not yet "seen" as such. The political context was not right for 1970s and 1980s film theorists to "see" trauma in what they were discovering about the cultural formation and functioning of melodrama. The appropriate political context appears to be in place in the millennium, so that the relevance of trauma studies to melodrama emerges.

Literary and film scholars in the 1970s and 1980s did not necessarily agree on definitions of melodrama or on the causes or dates for its emergence any more than now we agree about trauma theory. Debates hinged on whether to ascribe melodrama's emergence mainly to loss of medieval and even Renaissance constructions of a sacred world (as Peter Brooks argued in *The Melodramatic Imagination*), or to the political upheaval of the industrial revolution in which the bourgeoisie, emerging out of feudalism and then out of the working and entrepreneurial classes, replaces the old aristocracy whose decadence inflicted traumas on the aspiring class (as Geoffrey Nowell-Smith and Thomas Elsaesser argued).

For instance, for Brooks, melodrama's origins are in the French Revolution—a moment "that symbolically and really, marks the final liquidation of the traditional Sacred and its representative institutions (Church and Monarch)" (15). Melodrama "becomes the principle mode for uncovering, demonstrating, and making operative the essential moral universe in a post-sacred era." Brooks notes that resacrilization can only be conceived in personal terms—the sphere of melodrama. Thus melodrama is a "mode of conception and expression . . . a certain fictional system for making sense of experience . . . a semantic field of force" (xiii), which he sees coming into existence in the form vital to the modern imagination "near the start of the 19th century" (xi).

Meanwhile, in his "Minnelli and Melodrama," Geoffrey Nowell-Smith claims that melodrama, as genre, arises from "a set of social determinations, which have to do with the rise of the bourgeoisie, and a set of psychic determinations which take shape around the family" (Nowell-Smith in Gledhill 1987 70). For Nowell-Smith, what's new is the assumption of a "world of equals, a democracy within the bourgeois strata) . . . [and] a world without social power" (71). Thomas Elsaesser meanwhile, in his "Tales of Sound and Fury: Observations on the Family Melodrama," sees the continuation of the French romantic dramas Brooks discusses in the plots of British eighteenth-century novels (themselves leading to Italian operas) such as Richardson's *Pamela*. This novel images "the quasi-totalitarian violence perpetrated by (agents of) the 'system'" (such as Lovelace, who, as an aristocrat, tries through violent means to force the lower-class Pamela to marry him, ending up with rape) (Elsaesser in Gledhill 45). The ideological "message" of novels like *Clarissa* is recording "the struggle of a morally and emotionally emancipated bourgeois consciousness against the remnants of feudalism" (45). In the era of a "bourgeoisie in its militant phase, protagonists come to grief in a maze of economic necessities, *Realpolitik,* family loyalties, and through the abuse of aristocratic privilege from a still divinely ordained, and therefore doubly depraved absolutist authority" (45–46).

According to these critics, then, melodrama, evolving in eighteenth-century

Europe proliferates and develops into a genre in modernist nineteenth-century Europe and America, as the newly formed bourgeois family seeks to represent itself to itself. This need for images is part of the effort by the bourgeoisie to shape an identity other than that of either the aristocratic classes it is displacing, or the working and lower classes it emerged from.

The focus of these early critics on class and religion is complemented by the work of feminist critics on melodrama and gender, who argued that melodrama exposed female suffering if it was unable to oppose it.. Debates and differences continued, not surprisingly, since, as Elsaesser remarked, there was indeed "a radical ambiguity attached to the melodrama," whether in the French pre-revolutionary and Restoration forms, or the nineteenth-century British melodramas or the later Hollywood film. As he put it, "melodrama would appear to function either subversively or as escapism—categories which are always relative to the given historical and social context" (Elsaesser, "Tales of Sound and Fury" 47).

Feminists have made strong arguments for melodrama as a genre that not only "corrects" the misogynist bias of male-dominated culture, but one that also images forth the sufferings of women suppressed in most male-centered Hollywood genres (Mulvey, "Notes on Sirk"). It has also been seen as a genre that permits women's multiple identifications with different figures on screen, providing a certain sense of being in control (see Williams). Feminists focused less on class than on the specificity of women's roles and women's unconscious processes as melodrama might permit a certain subversive image within an overall reinscription of normative female models.

The loss of constructions of the sacred provided the conditions for industrialism and other changes of modernity more generally. The shocks of modernity lead in turn to trauma in individuals and in the culture (as I showed in chapter 1). I see melodrama as an aesthetic form (on the stage and in popular fiction) as produced from the traumas of class struggle and in the context of a search for identity, social order, and clear moral rules by which to live in modernity. Stories and images, giving shape to fictional lives, were needed as a disruptive modernism got underway to bolster other modes creating a new stable society. Personal and social traumas were displaced into fictional melodrama forms where they could be more safely approached. By the twentieth century, as Miriam Hansen has argued, the cinema also "attracted and made visible to itself and society an emerging, heterogeneous mass public," and "engaged the contradiction of modernity at the level of the senses, the level at which the impact of modern technology on human experience was most palpable and irreversible" (Hansen, "Introduction" in Kracauer xi).

The links between melodrama and psychoanalysis are evident in Freud's own understanding of the functions fiction fulfills. In his essay "Thoughts for the Times on War and Death," Freud notes: "In the realm of fiction we discover that plurality of lives for which we crave. We die in the person of the hero, yet we survive him, and are ready to die again for the next hero just as safely" (307). Hollywood melodramas from the 1920s to at least the 1960s endlessly repeat family and war traumas and recoveries, bringing audiences back time and again by ensuring closure and cure at the film's end. As Lauren Berlant argues in a project somewhat related to mine, "The politics of rage and pain and powerlessness that motors so much of the sentimental complaint and protest industry [in America] has been accompanied by a desire for amelioration at any cost."[7]

The notion of melodrama repeating in fictional form a suppressed cultural trauma to do with the overthrow of prior authority parallels Freud's theory developed toward the end of his life in *Moses and Monotheism*. Freud theorizes that the trauma of the Jews in the killing of Moses repeated an earlier crime of the primal horde's murder of the powerful father-leader. Traces of the crime continue throughout history. Extending Freud's theory, it is reasonable to argue that at certain historical moments aesthetic forms emerge (sometimes in a useful way) to accommodate fears and fantasies related to suppressed historical events. In repeating the trauma of class struggle, melodrama, in its very generic formation, may evidence a traumatic cultural symptom.

But, importantly, Kaja Silverman made an argument for trauma as a cultural symptom some years before Felman and Caruth introduced trauma studies as such. In her *Male Subjectivity at the Margins,* Silverman studies films made in the context of World War II. She develops the concept of historical trauma and in so doing makes a bridge between Fredric Jameson's theory of the political unconscious and prior theories of melodrama summarized above. In his groundbreaking *The Political Unconscious,* Jameson was the first to theorize a cultural "unconscious" that paralleled Freud's well-known individual unconscious. Silverman's concept is important in relation to the question of memory, since, like Freud, she introduces the idea of a cultural trauma as against only being concerned with individual crises: By "historical trauma," Silverman means "an historical ramification extending far beyond the individual psyche" (*Male Subjectivity* 55). Such historical trauma depends for its impact on what Silverman (following Jacques Rancière, quoted in Burgoyne 15) calls the "dominant fiction," namely "the mechanism by which society tries to institute itself as such on the basis of closure, of the fixation of meaning, of the non-recognition of the infinite play of differences" (Silverman 54). Following upon Jameson's idea that "history is what hurts," Silverman states that historical trauma is what "interrupt[s] or even deconstitute(s) what a society assumes to be its master narratives and immanent Necessity" (55).

Stipulating trauma as a split-off cultural process relates to Silverman's formulation: traumatic memory is not "unconscious" in the manner of ordinary neurotic repressed memory. It is, rather, memory shifted to another part of consciousness mainly accessible in the familiar traumatic phenomena of flashbacks, phobias, and dreams.[8] In light of this, Hollywood's melodramas are arguably impelled to repeat the rent in the dominant fiction occasioned by historical trauma while at the same time seeking unconsciously to repair and reveal that rent.

Revisiting melodrama from the perspective of trauma theory suggests looking for what the texts cannot know because that knowledge has been "displaced." This is not because the events are literally unable to be recalled, but because, for political or social reasons (or a mixture of the two, including guilt or criminal activity), it is too dangerous for the culture (or powerful political figures) to acknowledge or recall, just as the "forgotten" contents in individual consciousness are too dangerous to remember. Individuals and cultures, then, perform forgetting as a way of protecting themselves from the horrors of what one (or the culture) has done or what has been done to oneself or others in one's society.

Significantly, Hollywood producers were attracted to this very theme of forgetting in the period right after World War II, very much as producers in 2003 and 2004 are in the wake of terrorism and the Iraq War.[9] However, melodramas only portray a traumatic amnesia in individuals and rarely deal directly with the politics of cultural "forgetting."[10] It is one such melodrama about amnesia that I will discuss as an example of the cultural processes that concern me here, namely first, a process of displacing cultural traumas into fictional form; and second, Hollywood's uncannily selecting the very theme (traumatic amnesia) that the culture is itself manifesting. It is as if the knowledge of United States culture's choosing to "forget" war suffering is so close to the surface that a whole series of displacements have to be instituted in order to keep that split-off part in its place. The films try not to remember what ultimately has to be remembered. But in that process, they usefully expose catastrophe.

I have chosen Alfred Hitchcock's *Spellbound* (1946) as my example partly because it was made right after World War II and is thus marked however unconsciously by that war, but also because of its odd reference to modernity—and modernity's special visuality—through the collaboration with Salvador Dali, perhaps *the* icon for avant-garde art in the prewar period. The film also highlights links between cinema and psychoanalysis by situating the film within a psychiatric institution, and including a character loosely modeled on Freud himself. If the film arguably "manages" the trauma of World War II, it also "manages" psychoanalysis, as we will see.

The text, then, is multilayered: There is first World War II as social, political, and ideological event, including the well-known traumatic experiences of returning war veterans; there is Selznick's (the producer's) own psychological problems (like many immigrant Jews, he sought psychoanalytic help for symptoms no doubt linked to the Holocaust); there is the fact that Hollywood as a commercial institution reliant on profit needed to take into account pervasive public opinion, and prevailing social codes, mores, and ideas about sexuality, psychoanalysis, and the like. In addition, there are the needs of Selznick's director Alfred Hitchcock, and suggestions of his designers, his stars, and so on. A text like this then becomes in its very formation a confused mixture of the demands of art and of life, including the life of society and that of the individuals involved.

If acknowledging the war traumas soldiers suffered in World War II was slow to gather public momentum, this was understandable. While a war is ongoing—especially a war against Fascism that had to be fought—the public needs to give it their full support. Too much information about the traumas their loved ones were suffering might be counterproductive. The flurry of debates about war trauma during World War I (debates that contributed to Freud's developing his "properly" psychoanalytic theories of trauma) reemerged, if with more understanding, during World War II. The idea that physical symptoms of returning soldiers could be the result of psychic stress still made people uncomfortable. But it was precisely this situation that moved David Selznick to make a film dealing with psychoanalysis if not yet directly with war trauma. The film is interesting precisely because there is a producer who "knows" and at the same time does not "know" exactly what his film is about, and because it put psychoanalysis (if in a reductive manner) squarely into the public sphere at a time when this practice was viewed with suspicion, and rarely encountered by the general public.

Since there had been so much concern with war illnesses both during the war and increasingly after it with the returning veterans, Selznick's interest in the project is understandable; he wanted a film that would educate Americans about psychoanalysis, but not directly about their most urgent problem, namely postwar trauma illnesses in veterans. How self-conscious he was of his own "amnesia" about his project is a question that cannot be answered. Nevertheless, the unlikely working collaboration of a sophisticated European like Hitchcock with a smart Americanized Jew, David Selznick, is intriguing. Hitchcock's (also unlikely) interest in a tale about psychoanalysis (Hitchcock never warmed to Freud, it seems) happened to coincide with Selznick's preoccupation with psychoanalysis on both an individual and a social level, bringing the two men together to make *Spellbound*.

According to Leonard Leff (116), in the early 1940s many producers felt psychoanalysis was too removed from the experience of audiences to interest them, and it also made studios vulnerable to censorship.[11] But with the return of the GI's and their need for psychiatric counseling, the U.S. public changed. Many people had experienced war traumas themselves or seen their loved ones suffer. Leff writes, "The American popular press became a vigorous advocate of psychological counseling, especially for returning GI's" (116). In addition, as a

European Jew struggling to assimilate, Selznick himself had periodically undergone psychoanalysis with May Romm, one of the top Los Angeles psychoanalysts, for depression and mood swings. In 1943, he produced *Since You Went Away*—which touched on war trauma. He was profoundly influenced by the film, which includes brief reference to a shell-shocked soldier benefitting from psychoanalysis, to respect what this practice could achieve for people.[12] Evidently, working on the film lifted him out of his own depression.

Now that psychoanalysis had purchase, Selznick decided that a movie directed by Hitchcock might help his flagging studio. Hitchcock's rights to Francis Breeding's *House of Dr. Edwardes* about a madman who takes over an insane asylum seemed a perfect choice. Hitchcock, for his part, not only told François Truffaut that he "wanted to do something more sensible, to turn out the first picture on psychoanalysis" (Truffaut, *Hitchcock* 163), but noted his luck in working with Ben Hecht, whom he says "was very keen on psychoanalysis" and "in constant touch with prominent psychoanalysts" (163).

The many trials and tribulations—especially those concerning Salvador Dali—in the course of making this film have been adequately documented and do not as such concern me here. Most problems arose from Selznick's (usual) interventions, lack of funds for Dali's vision of the famous surrealist dream sequence, and Hitchcock's unwillingness to be interfered with. Hitchcock developed the first screenplay in London with the advice of prominent British psychiatrists only to find that Selznick's advisers thought there was too much psychiatry in the film, and also that psychoanalysis was becoming too much of a trademark in Selznick films. The screenplay was accordingly adjusted.[13]

In their melodrama, Selznick and Hitchcock managed to represent something of the visuality of what I will term the "affect aesthetic" of trauma phenomena. However, this affect aesthetic does not emerge in the elaborate dream analysis, which Dr. Brulov, standing in for Freud, performs for the troubled imposter, John Ballantine, who is pretending to be Dr. Edwardes (I retain this name for the character since his impersonation is only uncovered at the very end). The visuality of this belabored dream analysis is quite different from the visual phenomena of Edwardes's panic attacks, and usefully highlights the difference between dream per se, and trauma's phenomena.[14]

The dream analysis takes place when the imposter and Dr. Petersen (played by Ingrid Bergman as a rare female psychoanalyst) stay in Brulov's house. Dr. Brulov, speaking not only to his patient (who does not believe in dreams—"That's Freud's stuff, a lot of hooey," he says), but to the American audience as well, paraphrases a passage in Freud's *The Interpretation of Dreams*. Dreams, he says, "tell you what you are trying to hide. But they tell it to you all mixed up, like pieces of a puzzle that don't fit. The problem of the analyst is to examine this puzzle and put the pieces together in the right place, and find out what the devil you are trying to say to yourself." That Selznick and Hitchcock had Freud's text in mind is clear, not only in this speech but in the following dream analysis in which Dr. Brulov indeed assigns to each separate dream image a particular meaning. But he does this in a pedantic, reductive way that does not do justice to Freud.[15] Edwardes's affect-relation to the dream is hardly touched upon, and (as actor) Gregory Peck's blank, dazed state in reporting the dream only encourages the rational focus.

The visuality of trauma attacks and their emotional suffering emerge in the representation of Edwardes's classic trauma symptoms of flashbacks and hallucinations rather than in the reductive pseudo-Freudian dream analysis of Dr. Brulov (standing in for Freud). Hitchcock seems more at ease in cinematic rendering of these episodes than in the dream images. The hallucinations occur periodically throughout the film, starting with the first time Edwardes has lunch in the asylum, when fork marks on the white tablecloth set off a panic reaction that he can barely control (fig. 18). The cinematic techniques attempt to render how trauma symptoms feel to the victim, subjectively. Cinema becomes trauma, and as it does so, it draws the spectator in. A second attack happens when Edwardes notices Dr. Petersen's white bathrobe with lines on it. This intrusive trauma effect comes unexpectedly and awkwardly when he and Petersen are engaged in their first embrace. The sequence reveals the contrasting psychic states of the

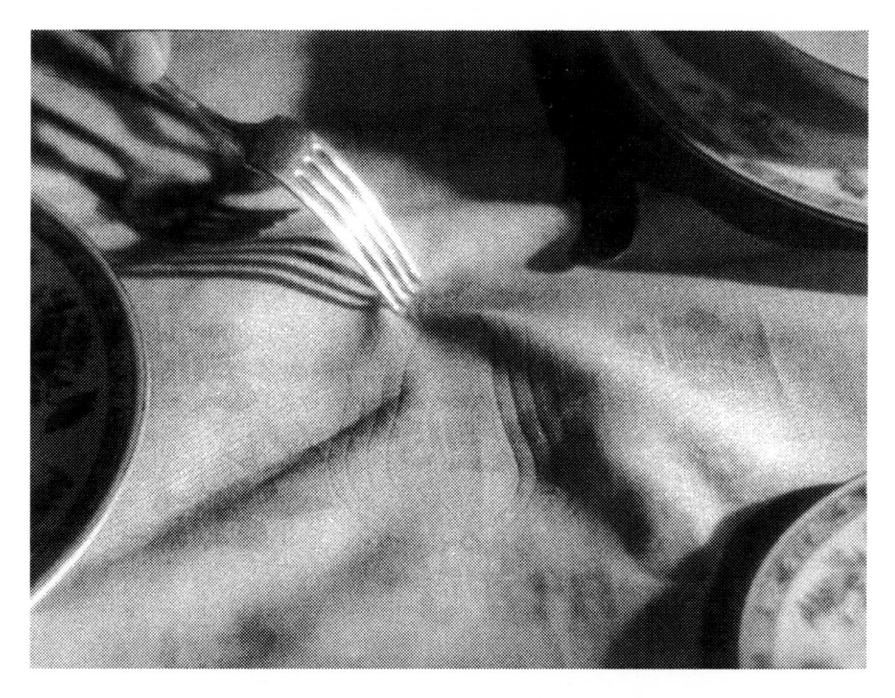

18. First panic attack: Lines on a white tablecloth. *Spellbound* (Photofest)

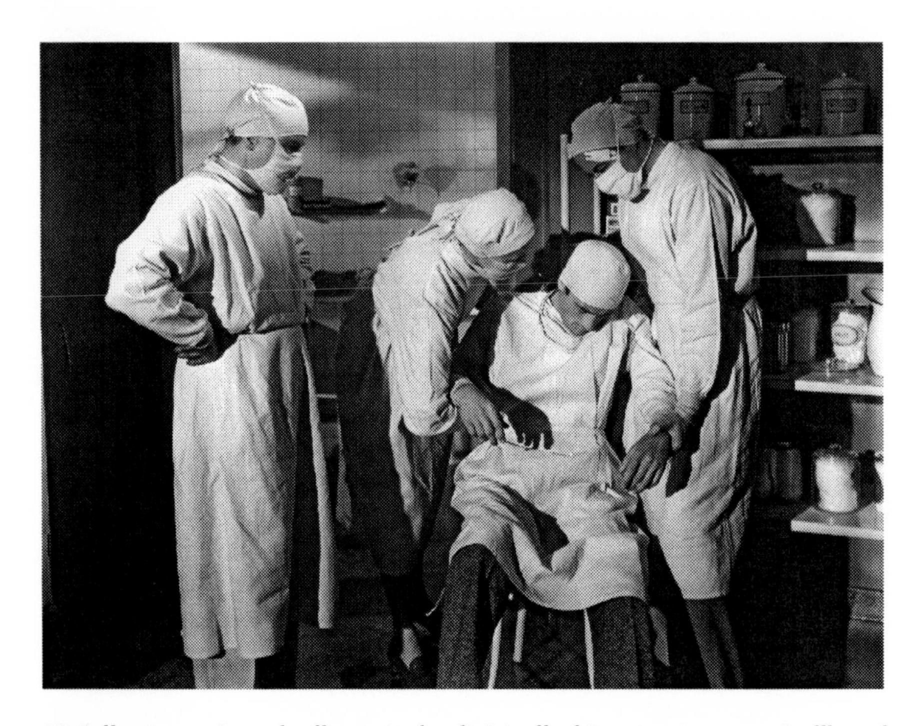

19. Ballantine panics and collapses in the clinic's all-white operating room. *Spellbound* (Photofest)

protagonists: it begins with the kiss and Hitchcock's (somewhat clumsy) visual metaphor of opening doors (reminiscent of René Magritte's paintings) to indicate Petersen's first sexual arousal; and then rapidly changes to represent Edwardes's traumatic response to lines on whiteness. The narrative is suspended as the viewer is asked to experience the flashback to some incomprehensible past event that at this point has no meaning for us or for the hero.[16]

Edwardes's/Ballantine's attacks get progressively worse until, called upon in the night to help with urgent surgery, he collapses and loses consciousness (fig. 19). It is then that Petersen realizes Edwardes is unwell. When she finds that Edwardes has fled (not wanting to involve Petersen anymore), she plans to follow him and to bring him to her old psychiatrist mentor, Dr. Brulov. But significantly while briefly in the Empire Hotel in New York, Edwardes has an attack. Petersen grabs his hand, and in the course of this sees that it has been badly burned. She begs him to remember, saying, "You have third degree burns. Your hand is burned. Where?" Edwardes mutters only "It hurts." Petersen encourages him to remember: "Open your mind," she says, "and the pain will leave." But Edwardes again collapses. When he asks what happened, Petersen says: "You relived an accident you were in. Your memory only touched the part of your brain that feels. But it's a beginning. . . ." Here World War II is

20. Railway lines trigger memory flashback to Ballantine's World War II trauma. *Spellbound* (Photofest)

introduced, but sideways, as it were. Petersen does not at this or at any other point choose to focus on Edwardes's obvious war trauma.

The police having caught up with them, Petersen rushes Edwardes to the train station. She urges Edwardes to recall where he had been going by train before the amnesia, and he mutters "Rome." Petersen then gets tickets for Rochester, where Dr. Brulov lives. On the train, Petersen remarks that they have made progress: they have some facts. They know that he was a doctor, that his hand and arms were burned, and that he was in Rome, perhaps Rome, Italy. "When did you go to Rome? What did you do in Rome?" she asks. As Edwardes tries to remember, his eyes catch sight of railway tracks outside the train window, and these trigger another attack (fig. 20). We hear gunshots and the roar of planes on the sound track, while Edwardes in a trance says, "Fighter planes spotted us." Petersen interjects, "You were flying?" He responds: "Transport, Medical Corps; flying over Rome they hit us. Bailed out." When he can't recall more, Petersen queries, "You left the army?" He replies, "Probably deserted: I hated it. I hated the killing. I remember that much."

Given this interchange, the lines now are clearly related to the displaced cultural memory of World War II underlying the film's narrative; they have previously been related to the skiing accident only—which in turn, as we'll see, will be linked to a family trauma. Edwardes was presumably horribly hurt and burnt, and no doubt traumatized. But Petersen does not ask him to discuss his war trauma, which she might well have seen as directly involved in his amnesia and strange panic attacks. Why not? Clearly, Selznick did not want to create disease in his audience by coming in any closer to the real topic of the film, namely a World War II veteran's traumatic memories. Yet he inserted this brief sequence precisely referencing war trauma.

Another attack happens in Brulov's house, again awkwardly, when Petersen and Edwardes first enter the bedroom. The white bedspread has furrows, and Edwardes panics. Petersen tries to engage Edwardes briefly but unsuccessfully in a discussion about his past. The attacks escalate rapidly as Edwardes reacts to the white foam when he is shaving a bit later on, and to the shining shaving-razor that inspires murderous thoughts.

At this point, melodrama merges with film noir, as Edwardes approaches Petersen as she sleeps—his shaving knife seen dangerously close to her neck. The lighting is now as in film noir, with Edwardes's shadows looming large on the white walls of the room. Somehow, he pulls himself away and goes downstairs, where Dr. Brulov, suspecting Edwardes was possibly dangerous, has stayed up pretending to work. Hitchcock keeps Edwardes's knife in sharp close-up (in accordance with noir conventions) in the front of the image, as in the rear Brulov prepares milk with something to make Edwardes sleep. When he awakens, Edwardes describes his dream to Brulov, with Petersen taking detailed notes. Dali's surrealist images splash across the screen as he talks, with barely concealed references to Dali's painting and to the film he made with Luis Buñuel, *Un Chien Andalou*. Film noir, melodrama, and the avant-garde all fuse in an interesting way at this moment in the film.

As noted earlier, Brulov decodes the dream in a manner deliberately referencing Freud's *The Interpretation of Dreams*. For Selznick, this is another opportunity to educate his audience about psychoanalysis, while, in the reductive rendering of Edwardes's psyche, also "managing" psychoanalytic practice, domesticating it, making it rational and logical. The dream sequence serves the narrative in providing Petersen with the clues that will lead her to Dr. Murchison, the mad director of the Psychoanalytic Clinic who was to be replaced by Dr. Edwardes (she actually brings the notes she has taken to her confrontation of Murchison, using Edwardes's dream as evidence of Murchison's guilt).

After describing his dream to Dr. Brulov, Edwardes panics yet again at seeing the sledge marks in the white snow outside the house (fig. 21). In the case of each panic attack, very similar cinematic techniques are used. This duplicates the repetition that trauma victims in fact experience, namely the return time and again, each time as if for the first time, of the same physical responses, the same beating heart, and automatic aversive bodily reaction to leave the triggering event. (I should note that Edwardes's complete collapses are not usually associ-

21. Lines in the snow trigger a panic attack in Dr. Brulov's office. *Spellbound* (Photofest)

ated with traumatic attacks, although feeling faint is common. But I later discuss the gender implications of these scene of Edwardes collapsing.)

The attacks make clear that Edwardes is possessed by a terror of whiteness and tracks in this whiteness, but that he cannot recall anything about what caused the terror in the first place. Evidently overwhelmed by some past event that could not be cognitively registered, its impact remains, full of affect but not meaning. It is this panic, together with what the dream revealed, that makes Dr. Petersen believe something must have happened at a ski resort and leads to her unraveling the mystery surrounding her patient's amnesia. In the end, the dream analysis does not cure him; rather, the cure comes from Petersen's daring to bring Edwardes back to the site of the onset of his amnesia at a ski resort. In a sense, Selznick and Hitchcock extend to a literal level Freud's early theory about psychoanalysis and trauma, namely that through hypnosis the patient must be led back along the paths that were blocked by the overwhelming event so that a full discharge of affect can take place.

The return to the ski resort evokes yet again severe panic in Edwardes, but finally also memory of a childhood accident that took place years ago. Being back in the ski resort in the place where Edwardes thought he had murdered the doctor recalls his split-off traumatic memory of the way his brother died in a

22. Dr. Petersen asking Ballantine about his attacks. *Spellbound* (Ohlinger)

horrible accident as the two children played on balustrades outside their house. In the flashback, the young Edwardes watches as his brother is impaled on the fence. He evidently believed the accident was his fault and simply repressed any knowledge of it. However, the skiing accident is analyzed by Petersen as repeating his unconscious trauma about how his brother died, and precipitating onset of a new and much more complicated amnesia. Perhaps the brother's sudden death evoked guilt because of sibling rivalry: if this were the case, the apparent repetitition of a similar structure at the ski resort would be especially traumatic. The skiing accident Ballantine witnesses (with Murchison pushing the real Edwardes over the ravine) evoked memories of the prior traumatic situation, worked on by fantasies and unconscious desire. But Petersen does not include in her delight at discovering this split-off childhood trauma the other traumas Edwardes suffered in the war—traumas that no doubt would have been exacerbated by the earlier childhood incident, and that made doubly traumatic this new skiing accident. In fact, the prior war and family traumas account for why Ballantine believes he has killed Edwardes.

Like the scene in which the railway lines trigger the memory of war trauma, thus fusing the family and war events, so now the two are fused: Ballantine's brother's accidental impaling on an iron fence mimics horrible war deaths when soldiers are impaled on barbed wire. In this context, the skiing terrain emerges like a battlefield, with the figures racing for their lives. The other brief references to the war, as discussed, are when Petersen notices Edwardes's burn scars on his hand, triggering Edwardes's memory of being caught in cross fire over embattled Rome. An additional war reference appears when Petersen (after the skiing revelations) is rehearsing with Ballantine (he now knows who he is) how we came to be with Edwardes in the 21 Club and later at the ski resort. Ballantine casually mentions that he wanted to talk to Dr. Edwardes about his war-produced shell shock.

Melodrama's demands force an exaggerated unraveling of the mystery of Ballantine's traumatic amnesia. Melodrama departs from the realities of trauma in the neat "cure" that results. Yet my interpretation has shown that behind the narrative lie two traumatic events, one personal and familial, the other war trauma. Most likely, the displacement of the war trauma into the familial one is for the sake of spectators at the time, whom producers did not want to leave distressed.

I have argued that *Spellbound,* made in 1945 and in the context of the traumatic impact of World War II on soldiers (and, I should add, on civilians), displaces war trauma into Edwardes's accidental observing of his brother's terrible death. But war and its traumatic impact on men and the masculine symbolic order is also evident in the representation of gender relations in the film. As Kaja Silverman argued in her discussion of *The Best Years of Our Lives* and the mutilated soldiers returning from the war to civilian life, war trauma exposed the failure of the paternal function. It laid bare the illusion of male mastery (*Male Subjectivity* 65). Veterans were in addition shocked to find that women had taken their places in the factories while they were away; they had moved out of their roles in the home as wives and mothers and managed relatively happily without men. *Spellbound* unconsciously images the changed nature of gender relations, while unable to fully work against them. Petersen is imaged at the start as a career woman, a doctor, but also as a classic "bluestocking" intellectual—frigid with glasses and hair tied back. But while, in typical Hollywood style, Petersen softens and becomes properly feminine upon falling in love with Edwardes, she does not give up her intellectual role. Motivated by love to figure out the mystery of Edwardes's amnesia, she becomes stronger as Edwardes becomes weaker. The two reverse roles: Petersen's femininity is masculinized by her needing to be active and in control while his masculinity is muted by his physical and psychological weakness. Playing the role of detective (as in film noir) she brilliantly figures out that Murchison is the murderer and is brave in facing down his threat to kill her. Yet the film is anxious about the shift in gender relations and the collapse of masculinity literalized in Edwardes's many fainting spells. Sometimes Petersen is the trigger for the spells, suggesting perhaps that women, not war, cause male trauma (see Philip Wylie). At least twice, Edwardes berates Petersen in gendered terms. For example in the train sequence as she tries to explain his guilt fantasies for being a soldier, he retorts: "If there's one thing I hate, it's a smug woman." Hitchcock and Selznick knew they had to leave the audience with everyone back in their proper places, and the trauma "cured." Hence, the very last image is of Petersen and Edwardes going off on a honeymoon, kissing as their tickets are taken by the collector.

Yet this ending can only seem tacked on. The real ending is of the viewer being shot at, vicariously traumatized as it were. This shot (very near the film's end) suggests that the war and its traumas were present in the film's unconscious. In this shot, Murchison is confronted about his crimes by Petersen; he grabs a gun and turns it on Petersen, whose point of view spectators are first asked to share. But there is a quick cut to that of Murchison aiming the gun at Petersen: she calls his bluff, remarks that to kill her would put him away for life because it would be a cold-blooded murder, and bravely turns her back to leave the room. The camera then rotates the gun toward Murchison, whose point of view spectators still share, as he prepares to commit suicide. The gun now looks directly at the spectator. It makes the viewer the target; we are about to be shot. While Hitchcock no doubt had in mind the famous shot of the gun in close-up pointed at the viewer from *The Great Train Robbery* (1904), surely he also had war in mind. In addition, the scene may reference the "shocks" of early cinema that Tom Gunning has talked about (see Gunning, "The Cinema of Attraction").

Spellbound is an example, then, of a text pulled in numerous directions, trying to serve divergent ends and of course failing to do so. For my purposes, the most telling conflict is between on the one hand, wanting and not wanting at the same time to address war trauma, and on the other, Selznick's self-conscious desire to educate the American public about psychoanalysis, partly so as to be able at some point to address the realities of shell shock—something that Selznick on some level wanted to do—while not wanting to deal with the complexities and uncertainties of psychoanalaysis regarding any "cure"—thus "managing" it in the sense of making it unthreatening.

My evidence for reading the film as dealing with a cultural trauma the nation is not ready to address, or, in different words, as manifesting a politics of terror and loss—an attempt to manage such loss—is the presence in the film of two different accidents, and the fact that the film seems not to know that it has these two quite different accidents as alternate suggested "causes" for the hero's amnesia. The war trauma (in which Ballantine was shot down, was badly burned, and suffered shell shock) is just inserted and not followed up, "left hanging" as it were, while the other—the second, "family" trauma—becomes the sole explanation for the hero's amnesia and troubled mental state. Yet the film cannot unconsciously help showing how the two accidents worked together (viz. the scenes of the railway lines and the skiing accident) to produce Ballantine's amnesia after the murder of Edwardes: the childhood trauma no doubt triggered traumatic symptoms when Ballantine was involved in World War II killings, and perhaps contributed to the shell shock he mentions as the reason he was seeing Dr. Edwardes. But Selznick's desire to "educate" the American public about basic Freudian concepts (such as repressed memory of traumatic childhood events and their impact on adult life) together with his desire not to confront shell shock directly, led to the displacement of war trauma into "family" trauma.

American films continue to repeat war themes, with increasing awareness by the 1990s of repressed guilt for the damage done to others. While not directly about war trauma, *Spellbound* does provide a hero with trauma-produced panic attacks such as many returning war veterans were experiencing at the time. Salvador Dali's involvement with the film creates links to modernity and French surrealism, but the aspects fit somewhat uneasily with postwar United States' still somewhat puritanical orientation and dis-ease with psychic disturbance. French surrealism (heavily in debt to Freudian ideas) assiduously sought to make visible unconscious processes, so that traumatic images frequently occur in surrealist art, especially in Dali's paintings. André Breton's much quoted "Manifesto of Surrealism" (originally written in 1924), describes surrealism as "psychic automatism in its pure state, by which one proposes to express—verbally, by means of the written word, or in any other manner—the actual functioning of thought" (Breton, *Manifestoes* 26). Obviously French surrealism dealt with the unconscious and with terror in the wake of World War I in painting and visual culture as well. I have shown that *Spellbound* registers the special visuality of trauma in its depiction of the freezing of the image in representing the traumatic attack.[17]

Because this is a Hollywood melodrama, the narrative in *Spellbound* has to end with the real murderer exposed, and the heterosexual couple united. Bergman's female analyst has all along been in a rather feminine position of mother/lover even though she's the "detective" as well. In terms of how melodrama is able to deal with trauma—that is, at once revealing but needing to seal it over—the trauma in the film is explained, cured and "framed." It is relegated to an unhappy past, now safely over. Psychoanalysis is seen as having a comforting closure. This is how United States culture also wanted to think about World War II—as an unhappy event, now safely over, rather than as an event whose impact and proliferating results are only beginning to be understood in the millennium.

Most films in the wake of World War II continued to tell stories of heroism, bravery, and triumph and repressed direct address to the war's horrors (*The Best Years of Our Lives* was a rare exception). Once World War II veterans were no longer so obvious, dominant discourses in the United States and Europe took other directions. The 1950s saw the United States "forget" the war as bourgeois ideology and consumer culture reached a new high. In the 1960s and 1970s different rebellions and wars eclipsed World War II. If the Holocaust is the most obvious catastrophe that was split off from dominant discourse in the 1950s, other aspects of the suffering and struggles of World War II were also "forgotten." This "belatedness" in relation to the war (it was not until May 2004 that a National Memorial to Veterans of World War II was built in Washington) is not unusual. It seems that fifty years or so must lapse before a culture or an individual finds the right time to return to trauma. The Vietnam War did revive memories of the war and directed new attention to soldiers' disorders including a new war syndrome, PTSD, discussed earlier.

CHAPTER 4

Vicarious Trauma and "Empty" Empathy

MEDIA IMAGES OF RWANDA AND THE IRAQ WAR

WHILE PRIOR CHAPTERS have focused on different techniques film directors or authors used in representing a particular mode of trauma, here I contribute to film studies first by using data from interviews with trauma therapists to illuminate what happens to spectators of traumatic events in popular media; and secondly, by developing the concept of "empty empathy" to understand the effect of other kinds of media reporting about catastrophes.

VICARIOUS TRAUMA AND THE MEDIA

Psychologists have been studying how the narratives therapists hear in the course of treating trauma survivors may evoke such strong reaction that the therapist is "vicariously" traumatized, but film scholars have rarely addressed the issue of vicarious trauma in people's response to popular media. Studying vicarious trauma is especially important in an era when global media project images of catastrophes all over the world as they are happening. Most of us generally encounter trauma vicariously through the media rather than directly. Since such exposure may result in symptoms of secondary trauma, we need to know as much as possible about the process. After discussing vicarious trauma in therapists, I show that secondary trauma may also apply to media response. The question I then ask is, how might vicarious trauma in spectators facilitate or interfere with pro-social individual and cultural change? Arguably, being vicariously traumatized invites members of a society to confront, rather than conceal, catastrophes, and in that way might be useful.[1] On the other hand, it might arouse anxiety and trigger defense against further exposure.

Let me start, then, with clinicians who do not often ask questions about the broader social relevance of their clinical findings, or their applicability to other cultures. What does it mean that clinicians suffer vicarious trauma effects? Can one extrapolate from clinical findings something for cultural meanings and purposes broadly defined? How relevant are findings such as those discussed here to other cultures? Both Pearlman and Saakvitne and Martin Hoffman do briefly address the question of culture (if not multiculturalism) in ways useful for my project. The former end their volume *Trauma and the Therapist* with a hopeful note about the enrichment of doing work with trauma victims, despite the vicissitudes described above. In their chapter "The Rewards of Doing Trauma Therapy" (400–406), Pearlman and Saakvitne claim first that "trauma therapy works," and second that despite the experiences of vicarious trauma they have detailed, "the act of listening is part of the process of healing. It is personally transformative, inspiring and rewarding to witness and be part of people's healing." They continue to assert that the work "has deeply transformed us, as therapists, as women, as people, and as members of society" (Pearlman and Saakvitne 400). They express gratitude to their patients, colleagues, and teachers for those transformations, and include comments from clients showing changes in their relationships albeit it often small. Finally, they cite the emotional nourishment and intellectual rewards of the work, and what they have learned from their clients (402–403).

Hoffman also argues for a pro-social result of vicarious trauma, again despite the wealth of data detailing the pain and suffering endured by clinicians working with victims. Toward the end of his paper, Hoffman usefully notes that "VT is a misnomer in that clinicians do not feel the patient's trauma. They feel the pain evoked by empathy arousing mechanisms interacting with their own previous traumatic experience" (17). Hoffman goes on to show that empathy for the suffering of victims does increase nurses' and clinicians' motivation to help. Is there anything in the comments by clinicians that can contribute to understanding the impact, on viewers living in many different national contexts, of films or journalism that deal with global crises? Given the clinical observations, can one theorize that viewing such films, perhaps enduring vicarious trauma in the process, could generate beneficial empathy for the sufferings of peoples far removed from one's own communities? Before considering some of these questions, it is necessary to recall earlier discussions about brain circuitry and trauma.

I suggest three possible kinds of brain function in people experiencing a traumatic situation. First, there is the response of dissociation, when the event only registers on the amygdala, and does not reach the cortex;[2] second, there is a process in which temporary repression is followed by registration of the event in the cortex, involving cognition and therefore possible recall of the event; finally, there is the process that is not mentioned by neuroscientists and that goes back to the later Freud after he abandoned his "seduction theory," where the victim is partly implicated in the traumatic situation. In this case, the situation triggers earlier memories and unconscious fantasies, which then become mixed in with memories of the new event.[3]

The question is, do any of these three possibilities apply to the situation of vicarious rather than direct trauma? And can we find links between references to visuality in clinicians' accounts of work with trauma victims, and the cinematic situation? In regard to the latter question, some of the responses given by clinicians to Hoffman and Friedman's questions would suggest that visuality links cinema, victims' accounts, and therapists' responses to those accounts. In reporting their work with trauma patients, for example, therapists use language that sounds as if they were creating a film in their minds of the events people narrate. One respondent in Hoffman's study actually alludes to this when she says: "I created an image in my own mind, like a movie, of what she was describing [being thrown from a Disneyland ride]" and of another case, "As I write this, I see the picture of the man who hurt her in my mind's eye (the picture I created in my imagination as she spoke)." Another therapist recounts that she "had images of her in the situations she described. She was usually very articulate so her narrative created flashes of visual images of her traumas, along with the feelings that went with those images" (Hoffman, unpublished manuscript 8–9). Others seem haunted by images, as when a clinician reported "horror and images of faces, body parts, smells of blood and flesh." One therapist notes that she "was hypervigilant for three days, worried over what she might do, about suicide. . . . " Another respondent said, "Sometimes after hearing incidents like this, I cannot be exposed to anything else that hints of violence against people as I cannot get enough distance from the event. I think about what if such had happened to me or to my children. As it is, I watch very little TV and I refuse to watch violent movies, as it feels too real to me." Here, the border between television or movie images and the "reality" of her patient's experiences is blurred for the therapist. The comment also confirms the power of visual media to trigger symptoms of vicarious trauma, at least when the viewer is primed by treating trauma victims or by having been a victim himself or herself.

In discussing therapists' reports Hoffman argues that there is an important neural difference between trauma and vicarious trauma: "Whereas," he says, "direct trauma circuits may or may not involve the cortex . . . VT circuits probably always do. This is because decoding patients' verbal trauma descriptions requires high level cognitive processing by the clinician: that is, semantic integration and (usually) perspective-taking" (15). Hoffman concludes, "Clinicians are therefore far more likely than patients to know the origin of their distress: They know their distress is empathic and due to exposure to the patient's trauma." Pearlman and Saakvitne, like Hoffman, also imply that therapists may have fantasies about their victims' experiences and that sometimes the therapist's unconscious can be triggered by what she hears. Therapists with a prior personal history of trauma are especially vulnerable to this reaction and to symptoms of vicarious trauma. Several in Hoffman and Friedman's study note they suffered similar traumas to a patient and the triggering effect of patient's accounts (11–16). This would mean that they partly identified with the patient and her narration, partly entered the scene, and that the patient's words evoked past memories and possibly fantasies linked to their own experiences.

Reading the therapists' responses, it occurred to me that differing levels of vicarious trauma in the clinicians, aside from what the therapist brings to the encounter, may reflect the differing ways in which victims narrate their experiences. That is, the more vividly a patient recounts an event, the more graphic details included, the greater the likelihood of the clinician suffering vicarious trauma.[4] Unfortunately, the reports do not include the victims' actual words, but much can be learned nevertheless from clinicians' reports of accounts. One clinician in the study states: "I was amazed at the clarity of her thought processing and ability to verbalize her feelings, which enabled me to visually imagine the scenes she described."[5] Hoffman also mentions different degrees of vicarious trauma depending on the therapist's style, such as how visual she is to begin with, or the degree of suggestibility of the material related.[6]

This discussion of vicarious trauma and clinicians may be relevant to the situation of watching a film, since as a spectator one remains conscious. One's cognitive functions are needed to follow the story and to decode images, and one knows that one is watching a film. Only in rare cases may a spectator be so overwhelmed by images of extreme suffering or of violence that his or her cortex is bypassed and cognition is prevented. Usually, in that case, the person simply leaves the theater, thus avoiding an increase of secondary trauma. For most moviegoers, the cortex remains active, even if powerful emotions are being registered on the amygdala. However, as with therapists, if the story deals with traumatic situations that the viewer may have experienced either directly or indirectly, his or her response to the images may be more powerful than that of another viewer lacking such past associations. One spectator may suffer secondary trauma effects while another does not.

To summarize: In a certain sense, all media response should be seen as at most vicarious trauma, not as experiencing trauma itself. Even then, in some cases, vicarious trauma (as Hoffman noted for clinicians) may be a misnomer, since (to adapt Hoffman), spectators do not feel the protagonist's trauma. They feel the pain evoked by empathy—arousing mechanisms interacting with their own traumatic experiences. Such mechanisms are especially powerful when a viewer has had firsthand traumas that are similar to those being portrayed. Nevertheless, it is possible to distinguish among spectator responses, as with therapists' reactions, in terms of degree of arousal.

Vicarious trauma is but one of several kinds of response to media dealing with catastrophe. Whether or not a film or piece of journalism elicits this response depends very much on the filmic or literary techniques used by the director or in reports, as I have explained elsewhere (Kaplan, "Melodrama, Cinema, and Trauma").[7] The little research that has been done by psychologists using film to study stress supports the idea that films can produce vicarious trauma in the sense of "belatedness" of response, of overwhelming the spectator, and of spectators avoiding screen images. Richard Lazarus et al., for example, studying stress in the 1960s, turned to using film in laboratory experiments because film avoided both deception and "losing the realism of the naturalistic state," of the usual experimental laboratory conditions in psychology research (2). His, and later studies by Mardi Jan Horowitz extending Lazarus's use of an Australian film about circumcision rites, cited symptoms now commonly known as vicarious trauma, including the delayed reaction: "This delay in obtaining a disturbed response was surprising" (Lazarus et al. 8); Horowitz says, "The period after the traumatic film lead to more reports of film references, and more instances of forgetting" (556). It should be noted that these psychology researchers were not interested in the pro-social impact of trauma films, in their moral or political import, or in the aesthetic strategies that produce traumatic effect in the viewers.[8]

As one of the few film scholars to discuss vicarious trauma in any depth, Joshua Hirsch notes that despite the mediation involved in seeing images, "the relaying of trauma to the public through photographic imagery" can be most graphically demonstrated in Susan Sontag's description of her initial reaction to photographs of concentration camps.[9] Sontag describes her life as divided into two parts, "before I saw those photographs (I was twelve) and after, though it was several years before I understood fully what they were about" (Sontag, *On Photography* 19–20). She goes on to describe how "when I looked at those photographs, something broke. Some limit had been reached, and not only that of horror; I felt irrevocably grieved, wounded, but a part of my feelings started to tighten; something went dead; something is still crying."[10]

As Hirsch notes, Sontag's account provides a clear example of vicarious image-induced trauma, such as "the sense of shock, of numbing, of being forever changed," along with references to the "belatedness" characteristic of traumatic reactions (Hirsch in Kaplan and Wang 6).[11] But I wonder if the impact has to be so clear to qualify for a vicarious trauma response? Would it be useful to open the term to refer to related but lesser discomfort—and a discomfort of shorter duration? And in any case, what may be the socially useful effects of either symptoms or discomfort?

Such questions are perhaps impossible to answer without an intensive interview study of viewer-response to different kinds of trauma cinema (i.e., something analogous to the data collected from clinicians by Pearlman/Saakvitne and Hoffman/Friedman). But it may be useful, as a start, to offer the following series of distinctions that need to be born in mind in thinking about visuality and vicarious trauma. For example, let's consider the following relationships to perception of trauma: 1) direct experience of trauma (trauma victim); 2) direct observation of another's trauma (bystander, one step removed); 3) visually mediated trauma (i.e., moviegoer, viewing trauma on film or other media, two steps removed); 4) reading a trauma narrative and constructing visual images of semantic data (news reader, three steps removed); 5) hearing a patient's trauma narrative (perhaps the most complex of all the positions, since it not only involves both visual and semantic channels, but includes the face-to-face encounter with the survivor of the bystander while involving the intimacy of the counseling session).

What follows focuses on the third relationship to trauma, that is, visually mediated trauma. Most discussion about the impact of cinema dealing with traumatic situations has arisen in regard to films about the Holocaust.[12] But that work rarely addresses the specificity of spectator response that I have been inspired to think about through Hoffman and Friedman's study of therapists and vicarious trauma. Let me give an example of my being overwhelmed by a media depiction of trauma that will at the same time demonstrate the difficulty of generalizing about spectator as about clinicians' responses to trauma.

My example comes from teaching a course titled "The Politics and Aesthetics of Crisis" at Green College, University of British Columbia, Vancouver, in spring 2001. A journalism student presented her research on a documentary about Rwanda in which women were interviewed about the violence, including rape, of the tragic interethnic war, showing long clips of the film. My response was complex: I found the film very difficult to watch, even though I thought the French journalist making the film went about it in an extraordinarily sensitive manner. Simply seeing the women she was interviewing in their desperate plight, seriously hurt physically, psychologically damaged, living in miserable quarters without proper food or water, with maimed, numb children, some of whom also had been raped, was nearly more than I could bear. I was alternately furious with the perpetrators of the deeds, and pained by the women's suffering. I wondered how I could have borne such treatment. I hurt for the women. While I had read about such events, seeing the women on film, hearing them talk so sadly and in so much pain, and watching their deprived surroundings, brought everything much closer to me. The larger context for their suffering—that is, the violent interethnic hatred—was abundantly clear and made the women's suffering seem senseless.

However, several students in the class had quite a different response. They did not have anything like my (or the journalism student's) emotional response, but rather argued that the director had exploited the Rwandan women and produced a voyeuristic and sensationalized view of events. They objected to the women being asked questions about what had happened to them, seeing the journalist as interfering in their lives. There seemed no way to resolve these differing responses. I pointed to the very quiet camera that I thought treated the women tactfully, keeping a respectful distance; they referred to the voice-over commentary that they thought was too sensational. I was reminded of debates about Holocaust films and how difficult it is to get agreement about certain kinds of images.[13] Ultimately, this documentary sits at the border between evoking an informed empathic response and producing vicarious trauma effects. I was in the situation of some of the clinicians in the Hoffman/Friedman data—shocked, identifying with the victims, feeling their pain, and unable to put the images out of my mind (even now after the lapse of time, they return with surprising intensity and vividness). I might have left the room and simply chosen not to look at more images if this hadn't been a class. I responded by being overwhelmed by the images.

My students had touched upon some important problems with such documentaries, and they showed their knowledge of work in film studies on documentary cinematic methods. But the theoretical framework that they brought to the film provided a screen between them and the images being shown. The framework perhaps blocked an empathic response. I believe they confused sensationalism with this particular documentary filmmaker's ability to inform viewers about a terrible tragedy. But they might say (were they familiar with psychological research) that I allowed empathic overarousal to determine my response. This example shows the complexity of theorizing about vicarious trauma and viewer response to certain films.

"Empty" Empathy and Images of the Iraq War

Earlier, I mentioned several scholars' objection to a culture of "wounded attachments" and sentimentality. What follows suggests how a certain kind of media reporting encourages sentimentality by presenting viewers or newspaper readers with a daily barrage of images that are merely fragments of a large, complex situation in a foreign culture about which audiences may know very little and that reporters usually omit. What I call "empty" empathy is empathy elicited by images of suffering provided without any context or background knowledge. While empathy, as Hoffman (*Empathy and Moral Development*) has amply shown, may have pro-social aspects, it is hard for pro-social motives to be aroused through mere isolated images of violence, aggression, deprivation, and death. While my earlier example of Susan Sontag's reaction to images of concentration camp victims would seem to offer a counterargument, in fact it does not: for these images were inherently situated in the specific context of a familiar Jewishness and of a war (i.e., World War II) that had surely taken up the psychic space of Sontag's family and the United States as a whole. Although specific knowledge of the camps had not reached her consciousness, the workings of transgenerational trauma meant that on some level the catastrophe had touched her.

In raising the issue of "empty empathy," my point has something in common with John Berger's short piece on "Photographs of Agony." In that essay, Berger is discussing photographs in connection with the Vietnam War (a war often mentioned alongside the Iraq War), asking what the effect of shocking photographs really is (42). Berger argues that the photographs are "arresting," and that viewers are either filled with despair or indignation. The first reaction, he says, takes on the other's suffering to no avail, while the second suggests action. Yet what action is commensurate with the agony witnessed? Berger concludes that what we need to do in this case is realize our lack of political freedom—our inability to have any influence on wars engaged in, in our name.

Clearly, much of what he says rings true for the Iraq War. However, unlike photographs of Vietnam, until recently shocking images of American casualties were not widely circulated. It took the unplanned release of digital photos of abuse in Abu Ghraib prison to bring attention to this withholding of photos of American suffering mainstream American newspapers (one could always find more explicit images in the foreign press). It is because the images we were allowed to see were not that shocking that the concept of "empty empathy" applies. As we will see, most of the photos offer viewers a chance to empathize with the difficult situation of our marines and ground forces, and mainly with Iraqis whom our forces are helping. It is for this reason that the response can be called "empty empathy."

My case study here is the March 2003 coverage of the war on Iraq. I'll argue that the media coverage aroused only "empty" empathy, closely allied to sentimentality, through its practice of providing fragmented images of individual pain. CNN predictably had the most continuous television coverage, but I will mainly focus on the also continuous *New York Times* coverage because of easy access to the images.[14] What was new in CNN and BBC coverage of this war was the ongoing presence of journalists broadcasting from their posts alongside the troops. New wireless and cell phone technology allowed the journalists to relay images as things were happening. Viewers were thus more or less placed right on the battlefield—so much so that people worried families might actually witness their sons or daughters being killed in battle. I could hardly believe that I was seeing an actual war taking place and not watching yet another war movie. There were the huge tanks rolling by with the soldiers so young they looked like children sitting there with all their elaborate gear weighing them down as they spoke into mouthpieces to those directing their movements. The night scenes were momentarily scary—in a sort of sensationalized way—in that the reporter was speaking to viewers in the forefront of the television image, while in the not-so-far distance one would see great flashes of fire as explosions went on reaching far up into the sky.

The empathy I felt for people in these scenes was "empty" partly because what I was seeing hardly seemed *real*. Where the film about the Rwandan women had seemed only too real to me, and thus overwhelming, coverage of the Iraq war seemed unreal even though it was clear that the reporters talking to viewers were actually there in Baghdad, or elsewhere in Iraq.

What added to the sentimental response (and its "empty" empathy) was the focus on individuals rather than on the larger issues to do with the reason for war on Iraq, its global impact, its effect on America's political alliances worldwide, and especially its devastating impact on Iraqi women, children, and innocent civilians. A typical kind of coverage involved a reporter locating an individual soldier or commander and interviewing him or her on camera about his or her experiences. The supposedly heroic recapture of Jessica Lynch (later debated as having been less heroic than at first appeared) is an example of this individualized, sentimental focus.[15] The Lynch story occupied hours of television time with details of Jessica's life, interviews with her family, and retelling of her original capture by the Iraqis, her wounding, and her recapture by American forces. Lynch's photograph made the front cover of *Newsweek* (April 14, 2003), with an inside story showing images of Jessica's childhood and of her family. Subsequently, a television movie was made about the episode. In this kind of media reporting, spectators are asked to peek in on an individual's life in war rather than to think about the ethics of the war, human rights, and other important topics. We are encouraged to identify with specific people—to enter their personal lives.

Newspaper coverage of the war followed similar lines, as is clear in daily images in the *New York Times*' "A Nation at War" coverage. On Sunday, March 30, 2003, the focus was "the faces and stories of the first American casualties" (A1, B7). Portraits of the twenty-seven dead soldiers (whether deliberately intended by the *Times* or not) remind one of the portraits of those killed in 9/11. And there are similar stories to those told about 9/11 victims in the accompanying article. A characteristic series of fragments of the war in images can be seen: a street in Nasiriya in the background, with marines in the foreground keeping guard; an image of a marine doctor sitting on the sand near the front line at Rifa, holding a little Iraqi girl (whose mother had been killed in cross fire) cuddled in his capacious arms (fig. 23); and an image of marines killed in a taxi suicide blast. One's empathy moves from the soldiers seeming vulnerable, to the little girl's loss (reflected in the sadness on the doctor's face) and onto the dead marines. But one soon forgets these images because of their fragmented nature.

The March 31 "A Nation at War" has contrasting images of marines in huge tanks coming into Nasiriya to reinforce the men already there, and of a child's crying and frightened face as her family flees Basra (fig. 24). The cameraman capturing the cover image for the April 2 "A Nation at War" must have been traveling with the troops entering Umm Qasr, since the picture was taken just ahead of the men, and shows them communicating through their mouthpieces as they run toward the camera, loaded with gear and guns. Other images show explosions from bombs dropped by coalition aircraft. On April 3, "A Nation at War" covers the battle for Baghdad. The cover image for the section shows faces of very young men sitting in huge tanks. One has a sense of being in the midst of the ongoing battle, and yet distant. Again, we are peeking in on the action, fascinated by the technology and postmodern weaponry, but we have no context through which to organize empathic feelings for the soldiers.

23. A marine doctor holds an Iraqi girl whose mother was killed in cross-fire. (Daniel Sagolj/Reuters)

24. A little Iraqi girl is held as families continue to leave Basra on March 30, 2003. (Pool/Reuters)

Inside pages of this report include gruesome pictures of seriously injured children and young people undergoing surgery inside a hospital in Hilla that has just come under attack. The image of a dead Iraqi man in a bombed-out car, with civilians walking along the street with a white flag, is especially shocking and suggests that American forces were attacking in a civilian neighborhood (fig. 25). I withdrew from these pictures, since they sickened me, very much as some images in the Rwanda film had.[16] But unlike the case of Rwanda, where I fully understood what had gone on, here everything was murky. Why were the children injured? Why are the people carrying a white flag? What are our soldiers really doing in Iraq? One of the rare photos of Iraqi women shows them crowding into the hospital looking for relatives. A huge photo just beneath the images filmed inside the hospital takes the viewer into the heart of battle. The image is black with the smoke of explosions. Two huge fighting vehicles can be seen on the move in the foreground as a soldier runs between them.

By April 5 the coverage is already discussing who will rebuild Iraq and also the search for Iraqi weapons sites. The image for "A Nation at War" shows grim-faced marines, guns alert, hastily evacuating an injured buddy. Inside pages show images of an army captain greeting Iraqi citizens and showing family pictures. The children seem fascinated. The wariness of soldiers entering Iraq about what their reception will be is highlighted in a photo of a British lance captain, who is quoted: "I think they are getting a wee bit more faith in us" (*New York*

25. Iraqi men and women pass a car with dead Iraqi fighters in the town of Kifl. (Peter Andrews/Reuters)

Times, April 5: B3). The front image shows a soldier inspecting a wrecked Iraq army headquarters. An image inside the section captures medics giving emergency treatment to a wounded soldier. One is yelling urgently for help, it seems; the other looking very anxious holds the IV bottle over the soldier. Again, the viewer feels pulled into the details of battle while being at a safe distance.

The section ends with portraits of the dead, as before. This time the headline explicitly references 9/11: "Many Took Arms in Iraq with Images of Sept. 11 Etched in Their Memories" (April 6: B7). Interviews with relatives (as before) detail aspects of the soldiers' lives and how 9/11 influenced their wish to serve.

The Tuesday, April 8, front-page image is of soldiers on the roof of an Iraqi Republican palace, while below the camera catches a gas station on fire with marines patrolling near to it. The headlines deal with efforts to kill Hussein and debates about the role of the United Nations after the war. Inside coverage continues the theme of American casualties and how the American public is tolerating them. The large cover image of "A Nation at War" section is of a small child standing before his stepfather's coffin at a funeral service in Georgia. Inside photos show the impact of the war on Iraqis, something muted in coverage so far. The emphasis has been solidly on what the troops were doing, on their battles and injuries, with only a rare glimpse of Iraqi suffering. A huge photo on April 8 finally shows an Iraqi man walking through the rubble of his neighborhood. Below, an image of two completely distraught Iraqi men sitting next to their ruined home conveys the suffering of Iraqis. The center section includes an astounding series of images taken as American troops fought fiercely to capture a bridge in Baghdad. The cameraman must have been storming the bridge with the marines in order to provide images showing the men yelling (we can't know for what reasons) as their buddies fight their way across the bridge. Other photos show the soldiers entering and resting in Hussein's palaces, or moving through the streets in tanks, guns raised, while citizens cower in doorways. One image shows looters with a truck full of goods waving at the camera; another shows a young boy walking past a marine guarding a street; yet another has an Iraqi man sitting beneath a huge smiling image of Saddam Hussein. The series provides across the two pages glimpses of the complicated and contradictory events unraveling as the troops move into Baghdad.

The April 9 *New York Times* is the last issue to be discussed here since my focus was coverage during the war, not the equally interesting (and continuing) postwar urban guerilla war that began once Hussein's official troops were defeated. This issue's large image shows Iraqi men being taken to a marine position in Baghdad with arms raised. Inside, images show the troops searching houses in a neighborhood for weapons. One shot shows amused children, another anxious adults, and then, once an Iraqi male with guns claimed to be a deserter, there's an image of the soldiers taking tea in his house. Other images show onlookers going into one of Hussein's feared prisons after it was bombed, reading secret files that were blown out with the blasts. The text deals with Iraqi reaction to the American invasion, with who will control the oil, and with plans for policing postwar Iraq.

As in all this coverage there is no analysis of a sort that would allow questions about the war. I have shown how viewers of the images are offered the position of peeking into large slices of war activity and small fragments of Iraqi life, response to the war, and occasionally, suffering. The main focus, whether when dealing with troops or Iraqis, was always on individuals. One is encouraged to identify with specific people, to enter into their experiences rather than to think about what we are looking at, or to engage on any larger intellectual or analytical level.

Significantly, the April 9 paper appeared just after three journalists were accidentally killed by American strikes on Baghdad buildings: The damage included the famous Palestine Hotel from where so many reporters spoke on CNN. This confirmed what many of us already knew, namely the danger that the journalists faced to cover the war. In a rare moment of self-reflexivity, a reporter, Sarah Boxer, made connections between a celebration of the well-known media analyst, Marshall McLuhan, and the Iraqi War ("Arts" section of the April 3 *New York Times*). Boxer attended a celebration of Marshall McLuhan held at the Graduate Center of the City University of New York as the war was ongoing. In looking at connections between some of McLuhan's ideas about the "global village" and the war in Iraq, Boxer notes that McLuhan's image of people now living in "a highly sensitized global village," in which "the world 'is like a buzzing forest, stirring all around you,'" strikes Boxer as a fitting image "to take home as the war in Iraq began on television" (*New York Times,* April 3: E6). Boxer notes (agreeing with my own sense) that "with the war rolling ahead on television, you the viewer are made a part of the invading army. . . . Meanwhile, just as the audience feels part of the army, the army becomes part of the audience. American troops on an aircraft carrier watch CNN to see how the war is playing and progressing. Soldiers are watching other soldiers on television" (E6). Boxer concludes that there is "general confusion as to who is acting and who is watching. And at the crux of the confusion are the traditional eyewitnesses to war, the journalists, 'embedded' with the troops" (E6). She perceptively asks: "Are the television cameras witnesses to war, or are they part of the weaponry? Or both?" (E6). For McLuhan, "all technology can plausibly be regarded as weapons," says Boxer. McLuhan understood the cold war "as an electric battle of information and of images." Certainly such was (and remains) the case in the coverage of the Iraq War.

These examples reveal a good deal about how commercial visual media function in relation to the "real"—that is, we can see that visual media shape how we perceive and construct our lived worlds, how they "hail" us as particular kinds of American subjects, how they construct the impact of war trauma on United States citizens, and how difficult viewing such images is for many. As Martha A. Sandweiss observes, "Photographs are powerful, and Americans have long found it difficult to face those that capture the horror of war."[17] Yet, as Susan Sontag reminds us, film and television images change how we see the world. The fact that we are "not totally transformed" by images of atrocity, says Sontag, "does not impugn the ethical value of an assault by image" (*Regarding* 116). "Images," she says, "have been reproached for being a way of watching suffering at a distance, as if there were some other way of watching" (117). "There is nothing wrong," she continues, "with standing back and thinking" (118). As John Leonard puts it, Sontag insists that "such images cannot be more than an invitation to pay attention, to reflect, to learn, to examine the rationalization for mass suffering offered by established powers" (10)—a point not unlike Berger's with which I began. Yet Berger also notes that the moments of agony that the war correspondent captures "are in reality utterly discontinuous with normal time (43). He claims that "it is not possible for anyone to look pensively at such a moment and emerge stronger" (43). This is because of the violence involved in the moment itself and in the camera's capturing of it. Without context and a continuity that would bring events into our own lives, such images can only elicit empathy that in the end is "empty."

Thus, we have to invent other strategies for communicating and understanding trauma. Therapists and their patients, with which this chapter began, may bring experiences from visual media into their discourses, and may use their imagination to reinvent lived relations, to "re-memory" trauma experiences as part of working them through. Therapists, like viewers of certain kinds of noncommercial film or literature, may come to occupy the position of the "witness." In chapter 6, I will examine what spectator positions, different from both the Rwanda documentary and from the *New York Times* war coverage, are possible when one is offered the situation I define as "witnessing." But before that, I turn to another this time *post*–World War II case study, looking at how trauma is translated in the postmodern, postcolonial contexts of Australia, Canada, and the United States.

Chapter 5

"Translating" Trauma in Postcolonial Contexts

Indigeneity on Film

In focusing on *translation* in this chapter as yet another modality for sharing trauma, I build upon ways in which trauma has been discussed hitherto. I move from studying the pattern of violence and its ensuing effects, to exploring translators who mediate across difference. My effort may be seen as itself an act of translation in which I explore texts representing other such acts already underway or imagined.

I will focus on cross-cultural conflict in Australia, Canada, and the United States, looking at select contact-zones between Western and indigenous peoples in order to investigate processes of translation. Since the 1980s and 1990s, postcolonial theory has critiqued colonialism from diverse disciplinary perspectives. But more attention should be given to indigeneity and to the differences between nations that were colonized (such as India or African states) but later won independence; and "settler" societies such as Australia, Canada, and the United States, where the colonialists came and stayed. This chapter draws on both postcolonial studies and indigenous studies but aims to make a contribution by using the concept of "translation," and by rethinking the ambiguous but possibly useful notion of "embodied translators."[1] Since I am working with images in film rather than as an ethnographer, let me say something about studying cultural interaction through research on representation. I will then situate myself in this work.

Representation and Ethnographic Film

I have elsewhere discussed the importance of work on representation in general, arguing that studying images should be central in transnational research, complementing historical, sociological, and anthropological study (Kaplan, *Looking for the Other*). I would suggest that fiction or documentary films by or about indigenous peoples offer concrete and "bounded" spaces representing varied contact-zones. Since they are "bounded," "out there," as it were, they are unencumbered by the difficulties, complications, and "embeddedness" of face-to-face interaction (as in interviews) or participant-observer status (as in anthropology). While what we see on film is heavily mediated by photographic or cinematic processes of selection, editing, framing, inclusion/exclusion, or the choice of topic, nevertheless there are bodies and voices to watch and listen to from a distance. This distance allows thought, emotion, close observation, and reaction by the spectator. Some have argued that such images represent a kind of history in process, as against the "dead" fixed history of records and documents.

Films about other cultures, traditionally known as ethnographic cinema, are a familiar genre. As Bill Nichols writes, "Ethnographic film has represented a valuable, concerted effort by those who share anthropology's principles and objectives regarding the representation of other cultures to members of our own" (*Blurred Boundaries* 63), but he also says that "ethnographic film is in trouble" because of the new voices of those traditionally only objects of the ethnographer's camera, namely "women/natives/others."[2] While ethnography and anthropology may contribute greatly to understanding other cultures, studying films and photographs by peoples from diverse communities reveals how communities choose to represent themselves, including what issues they select to make films about. Such work is producing new genres. As Nichols points out, "Ethnographic film no longer occupies a singular niche. Other voices call to us in forms and modes that blur the boundaries and genres that represent distinctions between fiction and documentary, politics and culture, here and there" (*Blurred Boundaries* 64).

Meanwhile, critical study of ethnographic images of non-Western peoples by Western artists (whether in fiction or documentary film) illuminates the Western imaginary of the "Other"—an imaginary that needs to be changed (see Kaplan, *Looking*). Indeed, the more indigenous and ethnic peoples make their own images, the more the Western imaginary is slowly being destabilized. In the following discussion of works by both "insiders" and "outsiders," I tease out the implicit ideology or self-positioning in each film.

POSITIONING THE SPECTATOR/CRITIC

But let me briefly situate myself in this work. Whereas in discussing World War II my position could be seen as that of victim of German aggression, here, I belong to the descendants of imperial British aggressors.[3] While I lived through World War II, I have not personally experienced racial discrimination. What impact may this have on my work on films by and about Australian Aborigines, First Nations, and Native Americans? If my position, far from being one of mastery, is that of wanting to listen and learn, as a critic I still have to render interpretations. By what right can I do this?

It seems that my interest in the traumatic situation of indigenous peoples arises in part from a sense of responsibility for what happened to them.[4] That is, I trace my interest in indigenous and other ethnic groups to my unconscious guilt about the violent legacies of English imperialism. There is also guilt at being born into a world in which the Holocaust was taking place just across the English Channel, with a certain well-known English complicity. Nicolas Abraham and Maria Torok have shown that such guilt may be unconsciously absorbed through a "phantom" process by children of parents suffering or perpetrating aggression (174). Nicholas T. Rand, discussing theories of Abraham and Torok, points out that "the concept of the phantom moves the focus of psychoanalytic inquiry beyond the individual being analyzed because it postulated that some people unwittingly inherit the secret psychic substance of their parents' lives" (Rand 166). In the case of perpetrators, he says, the work of these analysts enables us to understand how "the falsification, ignorance, or disregard of the past . . . is the breeding ground of the phantomatic return of shameful secrets on the level of individuals, families, the community and possibly even entire nations" (169). I return to these important issues below.

Pursuing my interest in cultures very different from the ones I knew, I once made an argument in a now "classic" essay on "Problematizing Cross-Cultural Analysis: The Case of Women in the Recent Chinese Cinema" (40–50), that if there was to be cross-cultural research and interaction, and if one came from the West, one had to dare to read a Chinese film through Western frameworks; since there was no way, given the language barrier and the complexities and length of Chinese culture and history, that I could make myself an expert, it was either this or ignoring such films. My claim was that there would be value in putting forward my readings since that gesture invites dialogue with the "Other," and through that process knowledge can move forward. My readings could be negated, corrected, or rejected by Chinese scholars.[5] Through dialogue of this kind much can be learned.

Some years later, I offered a different model, namely that of an "interracial gaze," developed in *Looking for the Other* (see especially 292–303). Drawing an analogy between theories of a mutual mother/child gaze suggested by psychologists—a gaze that obliterated the parent/child hierarchy—I proposed a mutual gaze between peoples from different cultures, a gaze in which power hierarchies were hopefully avoided.[6]

But are we ready yet for such a mutual gaze? My earlier model—that of cross-cultural dialogue about film images and about "readings" of films—seems rather to be the best that we can expect at this juncture.[7] A truly interracial, nonhierarchical mutual "gazing" that does not objectify, stereotype, or in other ways come in between interchange is a good way off. I thus hope to engage in dialogue as critics respond to my readings and interpretations, and to the ways in which I choose to enter texts by and about indigenous peoples. At the same time, I am seeking here to develop a third model—that of translation.

Sherry Simon's 1996 book on *Gender and Translation* suggested to me that her ideas about gender might be relevant to cross-cultural work. Simon shows how women translators have revalued a historically devalued position. Translation not only creates new subject positions, but is an activism, a process for change. Instead of an essentialized concept in which two known fixed entities exchange ideas or languages, translation for Simon is a third space—it changes and renews in its processes, even if it fails. In Simon's words, "Instead of serving as a bridge between already given cultural entities, translation becomes an activity of cultural creation. The bridge . . . brings into being the realities which it links" (152).

One way, then, to bring about a transfer from traumatic violence to something else may be through a concept of self-conscious "acts of translation." I use the word "translation" both in its literal sense of translating one language into another, and in the larger sense of explaining any particular culture to people from another culture. My "act of translation" is to examine the field and identify works that move across cultural and ethnic differences with the aim of engaging in cross-cultural dialogue and exchange. A concept of "embodied translators," who do not "transfer" one culture to another but (following Simon's lead) are part of a process of meaning creation, may be useful. Together on both sides of any cultural divide the embodied translators create new meaning, enter that "third space" that others have named, and forge new subjectivities in the process of their movement across borders. For my purposes as a film scholar, I turn to works in which that movement has been captured on film, and thus becomes part of a living history—history in process.

"Translation" then implies working to convey the experiences of one culture to people in another culture, but not in the old ethnographic sense. And it can move in many directions, from indigenous peoples educating their own communities about their histories, to ethnic artists educating Western peoples; to diverse indigenous peoples interested in learning about other indigenous or ethnic cultures, including an interest in learning more about Western peoples. The model here is that of a network of interchange, not simply a set of binary relations. Translation also implies that interpretation (such as that by Western critics about films from elsewhere) is an attempt at understanding on the critic's part—a sort of feeling out toward the other culture (something which is very different from the condescending stance of traditional ethnographic cinema). In a sense, film itself becomes a crossroad or a border between cultures that the critic uses to further his or her own and his or her readers' learning.

But in order to set the stage for theorizing "embodied translators," I first look at representations of the traumatic contact-zones that precede any possibilities of translation. It is only since the 1970s protests on the part of indigenous peoples everywhere about their continuing oppressions that Western cultures have begun to face their crimes and consider reparation. It could be that the need to deal with traumatic aspects of contact-zones is felt more strongly by Western scholars because of their ancestry and their renewed awareness of violence perpetrated on the innocent.[8] Applying psychoanalysis to the psychoanalytically oriented trauma research in postcolonial studies suggests that Western scholars may write from the perhaps unconscious, guilt-ridden perspective of descendants of colonial perpetrators of crimes. Meanwhile, if many previously victimized indigenous peoples are moving beyond mourning and forward to a new future, others are still concerned with pain and loss, as we know from films by indigenous directors such as Alanis Obomsawin. In other words, a whole variety of positions can be found in transcultural research on the part of indigenous and ethnic artists and scholars, as well as among white critics and artists. Given the proliferation and diffusion of daily traumas in visual media discussed in the last chapter, I am interested in what positions indigenous productions provide for spectators. Which techniques produce empathic understanding across cultures? Which produce misinformation about or alienation from groups still viewed as "the Other"?

Contact-Zones, Phantoms, and Traumatic Memory

Coined by Mary Louise Pratt in a groundbreaking volume, the term "contact-zone" refers to cross-cultural relations that can take many forms.[9] For Pratt, in her words, the concept of "'contact-zone' is an attempt to invoke the spatial and temporal consequence of subjects previously separated by geographic and historical disjunctures and whose trajectories now intersect." Her aim is "to foreground the interactive, improvisational dimensions of colonial encounters so easily ignored or suppressed by diffusionist accounts of conquest and domination" (Pratt 7).

My interest, however, is specifically in what prevents harmonious relations in colonial encounters. For relations need not necessarily be traumatic; indeed, accounts of early interactions between Native Americans and Europeans reveals a good deal of collaboration and working together for mutual interest or mutual exploitation.[10] Contact becomes traumatic when, for example, the invading groups determine simply to expropriate the land and resources that originally belonged to indigenous peoples; or when such groups determine that all indigenous peoples should adopt Western religions, values, and ways of being, and snatch children away so as to eradicate original languages and cultures.

Trauma studies usefully illuminates processes following from contact between indigenous groups and Western invaders that was catastrophic. Understanding trauma's overwhelming impact helps us comprehend the mental state of peoples who were victims of catastrophic inter- (as well as intra-) cultural contact, and who nevertheless find strength to resist and fight for rights. But most interesting is the way that the trauma of one generation is passed down to later generations through their indirect recall. Exactly how this happens is still being debated, although the phenomena of transgenerational trauma continue to be observed.[11]

Nicolas Abraham and Maria Torok were among the first to theorize transgenerational trauma, building on, and moving beyond, Freud's metapsychology. As Nicholas T. Rand, translator and editor of Abraham and Torok's *The Shell and the Kernel,* notes, the psychoanalysts draw on folklore in their use of the terms "phantoms," "ghosts," and "revenants." However, in their extension of such lore "the dead do not return, but their lives' unfinished business is unconsciously handed down to their descendants" (167). In his essay "Notes on the Phantom: A Complement to Freud's Metapsychology" (1975/1994), Abraham writes, "The presence of the phantom indicates the effects on the descendants, of something that had inflicted a narcissistic injury or even catastrophe on the parents" (174). The phantom, that is, works like a stranger incorporated into the subject, like "a foreign body lodged within the subject." It speaks, Abraham says, to the gap in speech—that is, to what could not be said by the parent but was nevertheless unconsciously communicated. As in folklore (and in drama and fiction from the ancient Greeks to Shakespeare and beyond), the dead return to haunt the living, so for Abraham "the phantom which returns to haunt bears witness to the existence of the dead buried within the other." It is in this way that the phantom "is the formation of the unconscious that has never been conscious," because "it passes . . . from the parent's unconscious to the child's" (173).

This makes a great deal of sense in the context of ancestors of indigenous peoples who suffered violence and catastrophe through Western invaders of their land. Much Native American fiction (such as that by Louise Erdrich) includes images of powerful haunting, and readers will see the relevance to the phantom in Toni Morrison's *Beloved.*[12]

In these cases, subjects are haunted by the trauma of their parents even as their lives may take on less catastrophic forms. Those to whom the catastrophe happened may only recall the past indirectly or dimly because of the blockage to cognition; they may suffer a delayed response in the form of repeated, intrusive hallucinations, dreams, thoughts, or behaviors. But in transgenerational trauma subjects are haunted by tragedies affecting their parents, grandparents, or ancestors from far back without conscious knowledge. In a sense, transgenerational trauma is a kind of unconscious vicarious trauma. It is partly in order to bring such tragedies to consciousness that filmmakers like Alanis Obomsawin undertake their work.

In what follows, I look briefly at two examples of late twentieth-century feature films (with an ethnographic slant) made by white Western male directors about indigenous peoples, and then contrast images and cinematic techniques with films by indigenous artists. Reasons for producing each film vary, and in each case (as appropriate) I will show that different issues in regard to translation, transgenerational haunting, and acts of translation are involved.

WESTERN IMAGINARY OF WESTERN/INDIGENOUS RELATIONS AND CONTACT-ZONES

Werner Herzog's *Where the Green Ants Dream* (Germany/Australia, 1984), and Kevin Costner's *Dances with Wolves* (USA, 1990) represent a huge move away from the blatant stereotyping of indigenous peoples as brutal savages, closer to animals than humans, that were evident in earlier commercial films, and from the condescending images of ethnographers. But both films in their different ways circle back more or less to the eighteenth-century concept of the "noble savage." Both suggest that "translation" is ultimately impossible, that indigenous peoples live in an inexorably Other mental and physical universe, and that either the peoples are left to carry on their traditional ways or their traditions and languages are lost, annihilated by Western invaders. According to these films, the only way that Westerners can engage with indigenous peoples in a relatively "positive" way is by abandoning Western ways and joining an indigenous community. It's a black and white, binary vision that, I'll argue, possibly comes from the unconscious transgenerational haunting of violence toward indigenous peoples passed down to the current generations of Western artists.

Both films represent the "outsider" artist vision, as against the works discussed below as emerging from an "insider" perspective. Werner Herzog, a German filmmaker, went to Australia in 1984 to make *Where the Green Ants Dream,* a film partly inspired by the groundbreaking 1992 Eddie Mabo land rights case,[13] and modeled after an actual case brought against a mining company wanting to drill on an Aboriginal sacred site. *Where the Green Ants Dream* is firmly on the side of the Aborigines who stage a peaceful sit-in on the sacred site the company has started to mine. The film's identification with the Aborigines is mediated through the liberal-minded, decent Australian mining engineer, Lance Hackett, who gradually comes not only to respect the Aborigines' position, but, like the white anthropologist in the film, "goes native."

This "going native" (or indigenization) is a very complex kind of cultural "mingling," a special sort of "contact-zone." It requires a complete reversal of identity for the white person, yet does not overcome the cultural and historical gap that exists between the cultures. "Going native" may be one of the ways in which people belonging to the historical colonizing group try to deal with their unconscious guilt arising from their forefathers having appropriated someone else's land. In "going native," such people simply give up their white identity and their past life, and settle down among indigenous peoples, adopting their ways of being and learning their languages.

The flip side of indigenization is believing there is utter incommensurability between Western peoples and indigenous groups, which is the position that Herzog appears to adopt in this film. Herzog is not a philosopher, but (as Bill Readings once argued) the film can be read in relation to Jean-François Lyotard's

26. Aboriginal leaders confront the company tractor. *Where the Green Ants Dream* (Photofest)

notion of *le différend*. Herzog's film does suggest that the Aborigines must remain "over there" in their uniqueness and exotic beauty.[14]

Lance Hackett, the white Australian engineer, and the anthropologist called in to testify on behalf of the Aborigines, are so overwhelmed with guilt at what mining companies and others have done to the Aborigines that they cannot return to their prior existences within white society. They become nomads, displaced persons. If Herzog implies that the West should retreat, he does not expect it to. Indeed, the film is filled with a terrible sadness from its apparent position that any utopian solution is impossible. These beautiful people will eventually be extinct, their purity eradicated by the white settlers, their languages and land taken away.

Meanwhile, the Aborigines in the film bring to the present contact over the desecration of their spiritual site a culturally transmitted transgenerational knowledge of traumatic historical contact.[15] They do not want to communicate with whites presumably because the traumatic historical wound is still open, the destruction too severe. But they are not passive exotic objects in the way that the film tries to suggest, despite evidence to the contrary; they actively resist the company's mining on their site, they hold sit-ins, they refuse to move, and ultimately, they bring about a remarkable court hearing of their rights to the land (fig. 26). The judge seems to regret having to rule against them. Mystically, the Aboriginal leaders manage to fly a defunct plane (that they associate with the Green Ants whose sacred ground the mining disturbs) (fig. 27). It is a scene in

27. Aboriginal leaders prepare to take off in the "Green Ant" airplane. *Where the Green Ants Dream* (Ohlingers)

which one senses the phantom-like presence of the people's ancestors bringing about a different order of reality. Word comes of the pilots having returned the ants to sacred ground, but the actual fate of the people is left unclear. Hackett, meanwhile, leaves Western life and takes up residence in an abandoned old hut in the desert near the sacred site being mined.

What might explain Herzog's vision? Born in Germany toward the end of World War II, Herzog belongs to a generation educated under the American occupation of Germany. In his case, it seems, he is infused with sadness, and perhaps unconscious transgenerational guilt, at the desecration of six million Jews and destruction of non-Aryan groups (like the Roma), homosexuals, and Communists. Herzog became fascinated with the madness of omnipotent leaders like the Spanish conquistador, Gonzalo Pizarro, who lead men into the Peruvian mountains in search of gold (see Herzog's *Aguirre: The Wrath of God,* 1972), and who clearly resembles Hitler. He was also concerned about the decimation of indigenous groups, like the Australian Aborigines, whose fate seems analogous to that of the Jews. Perhaps the unutterable sadness in the film arises partly from the hopelessness that young Germans must have felt (and perhaps still feel) in the wake of the Holocaust perpetrated on their land by "their" leaders—their fathers.[16] It is interesting to compare the situation of Herzog in Germany with what Anne Anlin Cheng calls "The Melancholy of Race" in the United States. "While all nations have their repressed histories and traumatic atrocities," Cheng notes, "American melancholia is particularly acute because

America is *founded* [*sic*] on the very ideals of freedom and liberty whose betrayals have been repeatedly covered over" (Cheng 10). In being educated in the post–World War II imposed democratic ideas, Herzog's melancholy might also be termed a "melancholy of race." However that may be, Herzog's identification with the Aborigines is so strong and their integrity and beauty so well depicted that some personal connection may have been at the heart of the film.[17]

The case of Kevin Costner's film is somewhat different if within a similar general category of films that exoticize and stereotype indigenous peoples. It is more hopeful and idealistic about Native American/white American relations than was Herzog's film about white Australian/Aboriginal contact, and in this way serves as a convenient bridge between the mourning and melancholy of Herzog, and the self-representations of Australian Aboriginal, First Nations, and Native American groups. Nevertheless, the "melancholy of race" that Cheng describes may be seen in the comments touched on below by Costner and Michael Blake, who wrote the film script.

Unlike Herzog's independent film, which got relatively little play (no one seems to know the film, although the subtitled VHS video is in circulation), Costner's was an expensive Hollywood product, highly successful at the box office, and winner of many Academy Awards. Video copies are readily available and DVDs include the "backstory" to the film. The set for the film is available for tourists to walk around at Fort Hays, four miles south of Rapid City, South Dakota. The film is important in bringing to audiences new, more realistic views of Native Americans in a commercial film that reached huge numbers of people.[18]

Costner's film offers viewers far greater insight into nineteenth-century Sioux life and culture than Herzog's did for contemporary Australian Aborigines. As with Herzog, Costner had a personal investment in making the film. As part Cherokee and part German, he had always been fascinated with the frontier and with the American past on the frontier. He says of the film that it's "a romantic look at a terrible time in our history," and that it will "always complete the picture I have had of myself since I was a little boy. It will forever be my love letter to the past" (Costner, Blake, and Wilson viii). Like Costner, the author of the novel and screenplay, Michael Blake, is also preoccupied with Native American history, "often a sad study of genocide, of cultural annihilation perpetrated by our forefathers in the name of growth and of the 'future generations' that we now comprise" (*Dances with Wolves* 14). Blake seems very much to share Herzog's mourning for all that has been lost through the decimation of indigenous life and culture.

The sadness evident in Blake's novel underlies Costner's film, but Costner is also invested in showing the vitality and sophistication of Sioux culture. There are extended sections in which Sioux dialogue ensues with English translation.[19] For once, the English-speaking audience has to experience the alienation of not knowing what is being said, and is put in the unusual position in a Hollywood film of having to read the (approximate and always inadequate) translation in subtitles.

Symbolically, Costner is attempting to convey the history of Sioux culture to the modern viewer. But within the narrative the protagonist, Dunbar, is unable to translate Sioux life and culture to the invading American military forces. These do not want to know anything about the Sioux: They want to kill them and their buffalo.

Dances with Wolves is still a Hollywood film, fulfilling deep desires for romance, visual pleasure, heroism, and "closure." Unfortunately, the Pawnee, a hostile tribe the Sioux fight in one section of the film, fall back into earlier Hollywood stereotypes of vicious brutes. The scene of the decimation of the white frontier family might have been lifted from John Ford's one-sided view of frontier/Native American relations in *The Searchers* (and is perhaps intended to reference that film). Yet, interestingly, in his review of *Dances with Wolves,* Roger Ebert focuses on the way the film "abandons the contrivances of ordinary plotting to look, in detail, *at the way strangers get to know one another*" (my italics) (*Chicago Sun-Times* 2003). Dunbar, the American cavalry officer isolated on a lone Western army outpost, keeps a diary documenting the way he gets to know the Sioux, who discover him there. Dunbar becomes the kind of "embodied translator" that I define below, in the sense that he teaches the Native Americans about white culture and its negative aims. He is extremely curious about Sioux culture and ways of being—and in a sense, like Hackett, "goes native" (fig. 28). Only in this case, he actually joins the community, falls in love with a woman (who seems to be Sioux but who significantly is actually a white and was captured as a child), and eats and fights with the group (fig. 29).[20] However, this knowledge does not get "translated" because the Americans do not want to live with the Native Americans; they want to annihilate them.[21] The film unfortunately remains within the consciousness of Dunbar, the white hero, so that we mainly see the Native Americans through his eyes and experiences. He is still the central focus for spectators, and it is his change and growth that are at stake.

The concluding scene in which we see the American soldiers, led by Pawnee scouts, tracking the path of the retreating Sioux, forebodes only too clearly the devastation that is to come but that Costner tactfully (and correctly) leaves to our imagination. Not seeing what we know is to transpire is much more powerful than the violence we have already seen in microcosm when the soldiers find Dunbar dressed as an Indian. The camera at the end tracks not the fleeing Native Americans but the white couple going their own way.

Herzog's (and to a lesser extent Costner's) vision leads to a melancholy if not despairing notion like that of Clifford Geertz, that mutual understanding is impossible.[22] The films also run the danger that Ernest Van Alphen has pointed to, namely of contaminating a critical discourse through inserting a repetition of oppression. As Van Alphen puts it, "Sometimes the critical scholar or artist ends

28. Costner "going native." *Dances with Wolves* (Photofest)

29. Costner joins the Sioux warriors looking for buffalo. *Dances with Wolves* (Photofest)

up reveling in the material s/he objects to, especially when this material combines racism with sexism" (273). Van Alphen's larger point is that "images can do damage." They may produce historical trauma for the black audience, and repetition of colonialism for the white audience (273).

Others have addressed the serious dangers in the ways in which Western cultures are seeking redress and reconciliation. Talking about *Dances with Wolves* (Costner, 1990), and the hero Dunbar's "going native," Sara Ahmed states that "through becoming [like] them [the Indians] he is able to undo the history of violence which fixes Indians into the bodily life of strangerhood" (124). Ahmed notes that the narrative of becoming always "reimagines violence as the opening out of the possibility of friendship and love" for the Western subject. This narrative confirms the white man's agency, "his ability to be transformed by the proximity of strangers, *and to render his transformation a gift to those strangers through which he alone can become*" (125; italics in original).[23] Similarly, Elizabeth Povinelli observes in the case of Australia how "mourning a shared shameful past would not more, and no less, than propel the nation into a new cleansed national form" (26). This new cleansed national form is also fueled economically as "the public consumed indigenous traditions in the form of art, music, and cultural tourism" (30). Ecofeminism, ecotourism, and New Agism, Povinelli says, "plowed into the national consciousness a commonsense feeling that this ancient order made Australia a special country" (31). However, as she later details, all of this puts enormous pressure on the Aborigines to recall a traditional law that, for many, was simply no longer available, making it hard for Aboriginal men and women "not to see the failure of cultural identity as their own personal failure rather than a structure of failure with which they are urged to identify" (35). This seems to me a case of grave "mistranslation" on the part of dominant white Australia vis-à-vis its indigenous peoples. It is also possibly an effort to overcome a prior moment when the shameful secrets of earlier generations returned phantomatically to haunt white Australians. By publicly assuming this shame, instead of being haunted by it, white Australians hope to cleanse themselves, while not seeing that this does not address the situation or grievances of the Aborigines.

But as postcolonial critics have shown, it is also true that cultures are adaptive and malleable; both the colonizing culture and that of the colonized are mutually impacted and change. Mingling inevitably takes place, and racial/ethnic purity is a myth. Thus it's not clear that understanding between vastly different groups is impossible. We should bear in mind Robert J. C. Young's warning that theories "must always be reshaped, resituated and redirected according to the specific, contingent location of the moment."[24] Theory as activism presupposes that it intervenes in a particular context against the politics of its adversary; once that context has passed, Young says, "the political impact of a strategic intervention is lost" (11). Theories too have a history and need to be freshly thought out in relation to specific conditions at a particular moment.

If understanding seemed impossible to Herzog, born in Germany in the post-Nazi, post-Holocaust era, perhaps recent events, including renewed investigation of the Holocaust's senselessness but also of people's resilience in the face of it, now require different interpretations. Costner's vision, meanwhile, is part of, but has also contributed to, a changing consciousness on the part of the general United States public about grave injustices done to Native Americans. Books, films, and journalism about such injustices are being circulated at an increasing rate, bringing to light knowledge hitherto suppressed and in the process dramatically changing perceptions about Native Americans *and* white Americans—that is, reversing stories of white heroism and Native American brutality.[25]

It's healthy that Western artists are mourning great injustices done to innocent peoples, but this may have little benefit for indigenous peoples and could seem an indulgence, as both Ahmed and Povinelli suggested. In any case, we see that indigenous people are moving on to new worlds in modern life—something that makes more sense than blindly holding onto traditions. This is not for me to say, of course. Comments in the online Free Encyclopedia note that people fighting for self-determination of indigenous peoples "are simply replacing the stereotype of the barbaric savage with another—that of the noble savage possessing mystic truths and at peace with nature [a danger in Costner's film as well], and that this second stereotype ignores some of the real issues of indigenous peoples such as economic development." Yet even this has been objected to as well, by those asking why "economic development" should suddenly be an issue when it never was before and that such arguments are made by industrialists hoping to further exploit indigenous peoples.[26]

Indigenous Filmmakers Represent and Translate Their Struggles

The two indigenous films by women discussed below, one by an Australian, the other by a First Nations director, counter the feature films made by Western males.[27] The first by Essie Coffey counters the exoticized images in Herzog's film by showing a contemporary Aboriginal woman's struggle not only to survive but to communicate something of the ancient Aboriginal traditions to her young family. The second counters Costner's film in that Alanis Obomsawin, a First Nations director, addresses the continuing suffering of First Nations groups in regard to their sacred sites and other long-held rights that belong to their communities.

Essie Coffey's My Survival as an Aboriginal *(1978)*

Coffey's film needs to be set within recent turns of events in Australia. As in the case of Canada and the United States, many books and Web sites detail specifics of the various Native Title Acts instituted in different historical periods, from when Australia was a British colony until it became independent (though like Canada still with a relationship to the British Crown).[28] The concept of "Terra Nullius" (that is, of the land being vacant when the Europeans arrived) for some reason prevailed in Australia for a long time. It was assumed that Aboriginal title to land had not survived British settlement of the continent, until cases began to be put forward in the 1950s gathering steam and increasing from the 1970s on.

While traumatic contact and residues of past colonial encounters still dominate some Australian communities, other psychic and social processes are also starting to be experienced.[29] The groundbreaking Australian government report, *Bringing Them Home,* began the important process of reparation and mourning by detailing stories of suffering that Aboriginal children had undergone through policies of forced separation. Peter Read and Correll Edwards's account of their work with the organization Link Up, helping reunite Aboriginal adults with their birth-parents, has done much to change the climate in regard to white Australian policies.[30] Material from their extended interviews with Aboriginal children who were snatched from their parents is detailed in Peter Read's volume, *A Rape of the Soul So Profound.* Much detailed information in fiction, film, and journalism about what Aboriginal people experienced is being published. Most recently, and perhaps familiar to readers, is Doris Pilkington's compelling account of her mother and aunt's incredibly brave and daring escape from the Moore River Native Settlement established for Aboriginal children with white fathers—known as "half castes," and often despised as much by their own communities as by white society. (Pilkington's book was made into a riveting film, *Rabbit-Proof Fence,* by Philip Noyce in 2002: the violent emotions on the part of the Aboriginal families, the intelligence and bravery of the children, and the arrogance, racism, and cruelty of British officers is beautifully conveyed in the film narrated from the perspective of the Aboriginal characters.)

Coffey's short film is unusual in being a collaboration between a white Australian filmmaker, Martha Ansara, and Essie herself. Essie is the central figure, and the collaborating director is invisible. The film was Essie Coffey's idea in that she wanted to address her own community about their joint struggles to survive while also opening up an opportunity for other Australians to learn about the situation of many indigenous Australians—the sort of knowledge that white Australians do not necessarily want to learn about, given their needs described by Povinelli for the Aborigines to embody some ancient traditions that reflect what was there before, a "purity" that would redeem the violence of the Western invaders. A sequel to the film, *My Life as I Live It* (1993) made just before Essie died, refers back to the earlier film's images and shows that some progress has been made, while some things remain the same.

The film moves at a leisurely pace, as appropriate to Coffey's ways of being. Coffey is seen not only teaching her children how to hunt groundhogs and how to skin and cook them outside, but also attending to people in her community who, out of work, depressed, and living in what amounts to a shanty town on the edge of an Australian city, have nothing much to live for. Coffey encourages them to find meaning, tries to prevent them from overdrinking, and in general provides social services for her people. Her courage and endurance are admirable. The film allows the viewer to enter Coffey's world and to empathize with her struggles, the more so because Coffey does not complain or bemoan her lot. She is rather interested in doing something to improve her and others' lives, and in attempting to pass on lost knowledge to her many children.

Coffey has managed to make a heartwarming film out of what could have been a merely depressing vision. While the film was made more than twenty years ago, and things may have improved slightly for Australian Aborigines in the meantime, the sorts of struggles Coffey shows still prevail in many parts of Australia.

Alanis Obomsawin's My Name Is Kahentiiosta *(1995)*

Alanis Obomsawin's film references the centuries-long struggles by aboriginal peoples to hold onto their lands, cultures, and languages in spite of waves of various European invading groups seeking access to the resources of Indian lands. Treaties and negotiations go back in North America to 1763, and indeed, the various Indian tribes (now Bands), located in the United States and Canada at that time came under similar royal proclamations, since all these areas were under the British Crown. After the Revolutionary War and the establishment of the United States, followed in 1867 by the Canadian Constitution Act, Indians in the different nations had to negotiate their own treaties. The history and complete documents detailing legislation vis-à-vis Indians in the different nations and provinces, along with copies of the many treaties involving Indians in all areas, can be found on valuable Internet Web sites. There one can also find legislation and establishment of institutions by Indians and First Nations.[31] In regard to the notorious Indian Act, one Web site noted that "the attitude that others were the better judges of Indian interests turned the statute into a grab-bag of social engineering over the years. . . . Indian children were removed from their homes, under the Minister's authority to educate them, and send to residential schools." Further, in regard to the definition of "person" in the statute until 1951, "Indians could only become persons by voluntarily enfranchising—renouncing Indian status—and in many circumstances were involuntarily enfranchised by the Act" (from Web site cited in previous note, pp. 1–2). A post–World War II Hawthorne Report amendment to the act attempted to abolish Indian status in the effort to force total assimilation of all Indians into Canadian identity. However, due to pressure from Indian and other groups, the

Hawthorne Report was withdrawn and in 1973, the government began to deal seriously if intermittently with land claims. Again, details of all these land claims, disputes, and crises (over such issues as desecration of lands, fishing rights, radioactive waste, and Canada's "colonialism") can be found on Web sites noted. Particularly useful are the various news reports and journalistic commentary from 1995 to 1998 reprinted on the site.

One crisis that had a profound impact on First Nations people in Quebec is documented by Alanis Obomsawin. In 2002, Obomsawin completed her fourth (and longest) film about the so-called Oka Crisis, *Rocks at Whiskey Trench* (2000). Obviously, this event was traumatic for Obomsawin and First Nations peoples as a whole, so that the need to return again and again to different aspects of the crisis led her to make this quartet of powerful documentaries. (The fact that at least two other First Nations or Métis filmmakers have made documentaries about or including the same crisis attests to the profound and lasting impact it had on the people abused by Canadian authorities.) Obomsawin has been making films for thirty-five years, and in a personal communication about her 2002 film, *Is the Crown at War with Us?* (which deals with yet more protests about rights and land), she made clear to me that her aim from the first was educational in the sense of wanting First Nations peoples to hear their own voices, learn about their histories and traditions, and sit in classrooms where they could recognize themselves, feel good about themselves (fig. 30). Obomsawin noted how many of her films have helped make changes in social issues, in law. What is important for Obomsawin is to counter pervasive media images that distort the reality of the people. Those who want to know more, she says, can find out more. Obomsawin stresses that her works are intended also for the generations to come to learn from.

In her *My Name Is Kahentiiosta,* Obomsawin represents the part of the Oka Crisis that involved an ongoing sit-in by Oka peoples demonstrating against the attempt by Canadian authorities to further desecrate their land by building a golf course and a housing development on a sacred site. She chose to represent this aspect of the crisis through a first-person narration by the protagonist after whom the film is named. What can we learn from how Obomsawin chooses to image her protagonist? How does she represent the struggle to prevent the tearing down of pine trees so as to build houses and make a golf course that would further disrupt indigenous life in the area? What can we learn from differences between these images and those used by Herzog and Costner in their full-length feature films?

What is immediately clear from listening to Obomsawin's central figure talk to the camera about her lived experiences of the Oka Crisis is how "constructed" Herzog's and Costner's images seem by contrast. We are dealing with completely different kinds of representation. Given the "bounded" nature of these works, spectators can reflect on the very different meanings produced in each

30. Supporters of the Esgenoopetitj First Nation gather. *Is the Crown at War with Us?* (Photo Pamela Mitchell, © National Film Board of Canada)

case by the positioning of the narrator, by the kind of address performed, and by the camera techniques. Obomsawin brilliantly uses visual means to disrupt the normalized view of demonstrations against governments taking away land that belongs to indigenous peoples, or violently disturbing their ways of life.

To begin with, her subject's in-person confrontation of the camera, as she speaks directly into it, challenges normalized documentary cinematic codes that usually distance the subjects and master the storytelling via an omniscient commentary. While both Herzog and Costner move beyond usual Hollywood techniques by offering the perspective of the indigenous peoples, there is still a white male central figure in each film whose narration is privileged, albeit he has sympathy with and empathy for the peoples. But here Obomsawin keeps to the subjective voice and position of her protagonist who describes the demonstration her Mohawk peoples joined to support the Oka warriors' closing of the bridge that would bring construction vehicles to the area—The Pines—the sacred site that is to be destroyed.

While a main feature of the film is the fight for the land and the determined resistance to the Canadian police and military organized by the group, another main point slowly emerges. The demonstration is traumatic; a policeman is killed, and the Mohawks thought *they* would be killed. But in a certain sense, awful as they are, such demonstrations and resistances seem almost a natural part of people's lives. However, the refusal of Kahentiiosta to provide a Canadian name to the authorities so that she can be "processed" through their institutions when she is arrested makes a further point. Her insistence on her indigenous name—on, that is, her identity—conveys as vividly as anything how authorities attempt to snatch identity from people as they have snatched the land.

The filmic strategy invites the spectator into the subject's world. It's not quite clear whom Kahentiiosta is addressing; she could be telling what happened to people in her community who were not there or had not heard about it. The narration is very informal and conveys powerfully if in tactfully restrained manner the pain of the violence threatened to land that contains memories of ancestors and represents links to the earth vital to the community. The protagonist, indeed, offers an example of the transgenerational trauma referred to earlier as passed down from parents to children, without children necessarily knowing consciously of the violence done or realizing the trauma they are dealing with. Inured as she is to injustice and violence against her people, Kahentiiosta struggles to keep tears back as she describes the events. At times, she seems so inured to her land and her identity being stolen, that this is just another day when she has to put up yet again with the nonsense of the Canadian authorities. But at other times, the suffering breaks through.

Obomsawin's strategy works to radically destabilize the non–First Nation viewer, who is invited to share a radically other perspective on such events. Without the overarching commentary, there is no way that this can or should be a "balanced" view. But such purportedly "balanced" narrations are what viewers have been educated to expect from television and other standard documentaries. Obomsawin's film then deconstructs cultural authority through her visual images that belie normalized patterns, normalized ways of narrating, which themselves hide their one-sided pro-government views. The melodramatic aura that clings to Costner's film and even also to Herzog's is here stripped away. Our eyes have to see differently.

In this sense, Obomsawin's hero is one kind of "embodied translator." She communicates her world and the fight for identity by speaking directly to the spectator. A person in her community would be informed about something she missed or only heard about from a distance; a person outside her community is invited to share her experiences, and to learn from the very undramatic, flat narration about what seem like incredible hardships and struggles, and about how much injustice people have had to endure over so much time.

This chapter has argued for documentary and fictional texts as central to understanding cultural difference. I have, secondly, argued that the concept of traumatic contact-zones is useful for understanding how traces of a violent past impact both victims and perpetrators, although not similarly. While since the 1980s, the commercial feature films by white male (or Métis, in the case of Costner) directors within the context of national cinema production offer far more empathic images of indigenous peoples, they nevertheless are narrated from the position of the white male seeking to understand the Aboriginal people, rather than showing the voices of the people themselves speaking about issues that concern them. Thus, we cannot say that the process of translation was at work in these films.

The last two films made by or close to aboriginal people allow those voices and perspectives to be heard and the people's points of view take center stage. Unlike the feature films that, by comparison, could be seen as somewhat narcissistic (the white male mourns the loss of something he sees as closer to the truth, a higher kind of life than the Western industrial one), the documentary films speak at once to each group's community, but also hope to educate Western viewers about the history and culture of that community—to correct misleading images in the dominant media.

Different methods of resistance are undertaken in the different contexts surveyed here. In some cases, as in the Oka Crisis, resistance (which can become violent) seems essential or the only way. In others, as in the case of Herzog's film, Aborigines use what legal recourse they have to make their claim to ancestral land. All the indigenous films leave the viewer with a sense of the strength and resilience of peoples who have kept fighting for their rights, and who now seem on the brink of attaining some justice through the bravery of those willing to take a stand, to translate a community's values, beliefs, and rights to the larger public through their films.

These two films may perhaps usefully be categorized within the genre of the testimony. As Rosanne Kennedy and Tikka Jan Wilson have pointed out, such testimonies may serve several different functions. Referring to the Australian government report *Bringing Them Home,* they note that the testimonies collected there provide historical and quasi-legal evidence for the policy of forced removal; they provide evidence that such removal caused harm, including symptoms of post-traumatic stress disorder; as autobiographical narratives, they enable the witness to make sense of what happened, and to form his/her identity as a member of the "stolen generations"; and finally, the testimonies appeal to the wider Australian community to take responsibility for past actions ("Constructing Shared Histories" in Kennedy and Bennett 120–121). It is this last feature that interests me here and in the following chapter, in that the process of "witnessing" is vital to reparation. While this term, like many in trauma studies, is under debate and has been used in many different contexts, I use it to refer to assuming a responsibility toward historical injustice, and to argue for a moving beyond only empathy and identification with suffering.

Mainstream culture has tended to start with recognizing white crimes by situating the "Other" as a victim, as if this makes up for prior vilification and degradation. Rejecting white culture because of its violence against the innocent, and "going native" does not solve anything for indigenous or colonized peoples; it can also seem condescending. But the documentaries by Essie Coffey and Obomsawin enact the concept of witnessing because the protagonists in the films do not ask for empathy or situate themselves as victims. Rather, these strong women are seen actively resisting suppression, actively trying to make a difference by helping their people. This invites the nonindigenous viewer to reflect on her role in events. As Ruth Leys notes (drawing on Judith Herman's *Trauma and Recovery*), "It is because personal testimony concerning the past is inherently political and collective that the narration of the remembered trauma is so important" (Leys, A Genealogy 109).

In chapter 6, I explore a somewhat different subject-position produced by certain (usually but not necessarily noncommercial fiction films) that I also define as "witnessing," if in a different sense than that involved in testimony. While testimonies are badly needed, so are films that figure forth catastrophe in indirect, less explicit ways. It is to two such films that I turn next.

CHAPTER 6

The Ethics of Witnessing

MAYA DEREN AND TRACEY MOFFATT

BUILDING ON DISCUSSION of documentary films representing "testimonies" of indigenous women in chapter 5, this chapter explores to what degree an ethics of witnessing involves different psychic mechanisms and aesthetic strategies than those studied earlier. How should one differentiate between empathic reactions, including vicarious traumatization, in a reader, listener, or viewer, and witnessing? Arguably the difference involves distance; empathic sharing entails closeness but may lead to the overidentification of vicarious trauma. Witnessing has to do with an art work producing a deliberate ethical consciousness, such as we saw earlier in testimonies but with even greater distance.

Martin Hoffman implies that, through its very symptoms of discomfort, vicarious trauma may have a socially useful effect (Hoffman, "Empathy and Vicarious Traumatization" 15). Could it be that vicarious trauma can be prosocial in the case of clinicians, because as Hoffman shows "empathy can intensely distress clinicians and increase their motivation to help"? Hoffman concludes, "The clinician-patient relationship may therefore count as an empathy-based pro-social moral encounter." He states that what makes this moral encounter significant is its "role-demand."

While witnessing also involves a "role-demand," it is of a different if related order than that of the therapist. For in bearing witness, in the sense I intend here, one not only provides a witness where no one was there to witness before, but more than that, one feels responsible for injustice in general. Witnessing involves wanting to change the kind of world where injustice, of whatever kind, is common.

VICARIOUS TRAUMA AND WITNESSING

Vicarious trauma in the clinical situation takes place in the context of one individual helping another, while witnessing implies a larger ethical framework that has to do with public recognition of atrocities. While individual efforts, as in therapy, are immensely important, there is also a need to mobilize the consciousness of large communities, such as the nation-state, in which people elect their leaders and vote for or against policies that affect people's daily lives. "Witnessing" is the term I use for prompting an ethical response that will perhaps transform the way someone views the world, or thinks about justice. Vicarious traumatization may be a component of witnessing, but instead of only intensifying the desire to help an individual in front of one, witnessing leads to a broader understanding of the meaning of what has been done to victims, of the politics of trauma being possible.

Dori Laub has offered one powerful set of insights about witnessing that illuminates witnessing as against the more usual empathy or vicarious trauma. In his essay "Truth and Testimony: The Process and the Struggle," Laub points to the urgency of finding a witness where there was none before. For Laub, what makes the Holocaust so horrifying is that "during its historical occurrence, *the event produced no witnesses*" (65). The terrifying aspect for survivors is having been forced to participate in the evil, and becoming bearers of a secret never to be divulged. Referring to Martin Buber's work, Laub says, "There was no longer an other to whom one could say 'Thou' in the hope of being heard, of being recognized as a subject, of being answered" (66). Just because of this, Laub emphasizes how important it is for the narrative that could not be articulated to be told, transmitted, and heard (69). Even more important is that the interviewer-listener "takes on the responsibility for bearing witness that previously the narrator felt he bore alone, and therefore could not carry out." Most importantly for my purposes, "it is the encounter and the coming together between the survivor and the listener which makes possible something like a repossession of the act of witnessing. This joint responsibility is the source of the emerging truth" (69).

Kelly Oliver, a philosopher, builds in interesting ways on Dori Laub's notion of responsibility. In developing a theory of subjectivity based on witnessing (Oliver, *Witnessing* 85), Oliver usefully distinguishes between historically determined subject positions and subjectivity, which she defines as "an infinite responsibility" (87), as "testifying to both something you have seen with your own eyes and something that you cannot see" (86). To be a subject, for Oliver, is to be responsible in this larger sense; "That which precludes a response destroys subjectivity," Kelly notes (90). Agency is only possible if one takes up subjectivity in this way.

Like Laub and Oliver, I too am concerned with the issue of responsibility, that is, with finding ways to enable us to be responsible. To do this, one has to learn to take the Other's subjectivity as a starting point, not as something to be ignored or denied. It is only in this way that we can gain a public or national ethics. Certain films may be pertinent in constructing a position for the viewer that enables him or her to take responsibility. Oliver is correct that "to recognize others requires acknowledging that their experiences are real even though they may be incomprehensible to us" (106). This idea of experiences being possibly incomprehensible to us is also mentioned by Laub when he distinguishes three distinct levels of witnessing that he has learned from his interviews with Holocaust survivors. The first is the position of "being a witness to oneself," which, in his case, comes from his being himself a Holocaust survivor. The second level is his participation "not in the events, but in the account given of them, in [his] role as the interviewer of survivors who give testimony" (62). This level involves his becoming part of the struggle "to go beyond the event and not be submerged and lost in it" (62). The third level is one "in which the process of witnessing is itself being witnessed." Here, Laub says, he and the narrator are both struggling to reach a truth that is elusive. In Laub's words, "The traumatic experience has normally long been submerged and has become distorted in its submersion. The horror of the historical experience is maintained in the testimony only as an elusive memory that feels as if it no longer resembles any reality. The horror is, indeed, compelling not only in its reality but even more so, in its flagrant distortion and subversion of reality" (62).

It is interesting that Laub does not refer to empathy or to being overwhelmed, thus suggesting that witnessing in his sense has little to do with vicarious traumatization. Laub's first level, that of being a witness to oneself, might involve empathy and identification with the subject, even though Laub does not say so. Vicarious trauma, in the sense Hoffman defined it in relation to the client-therapist relationship, might indeed also take place. Laub's second level—the struggle to attend to the event without being submerged by it—certainly relates to Hoffman's scheme. Where Laub departs from psychological research is in his third level—that of being witness to witnessing itself and understanding the elusiveness of the event, including the distortions of traumatic memory, and the haunting by an event that no longer seems real, or that does not accord with one's new, postwar "reality." (In this formulation, Laub's position resonates with Abraham and Torok's concept of a phantomatic return of what subjects consider shameful and secret events, even when they were not responsible for what happened, or even when they were victims.)

It is this element of trauma's elusiveness and subversion of reality that is echoed in the films I discuss in this chapter. These works position the viewer as a "witness" to trauma in an elusive, disturbing, perhaps haunting way that nevertheless provokes in the viewer a need to take responsibility. Each film explores the structure of injustice and its accompanying rage; in only alluding to a specific "quiet" or "family" trauma, each film enables the spectator to generalize to many specific cases.

One of the main characteristics of the witnessing position as formulated by Laub is the deliberate refusal of an identification with the specificity of the individuals involved—a deliberate distancing from the subject to enable the interviewer to take in and respond to the traumatic *situation* (see David Becker, "Dealing"). When a film constructs this sort of position for the spectator, it enables attention to the situation, as against attention merely to the subject's individual suffering, and this positioning thus opens the text out to larger social and political meanings.

MAYA DEREN, *MESHES OF AN AFTERNOON* (1947)

For reasons of chronology but also so as to retrace from a different vantage point themes taken up in prior chapters, I begin with Maya Deren's 1947 independent American film, *Meshes of an Afternoon,* and move onto a very different postcolonial (also independent) Australian film, *Night Cries,* made in 1989. While definitely not commercial cinema, each film situates itself in relation to Hollywood between them thus drawing connections between usually distinct types of film. We saw the public benefit in Hitchcock's *Spellbound* of addressing a cultural problem even if only indirectly. These films rely on spectators' knowledge of Hollywood films and genres to flesh out what the directors want to show. While both are technically independent films, both deliberately make links to classical Hollywood cinema. Where *Meshes* pays homage to and uses strategies of film noir, *Night Cries* references the Hollywood melodrama.

Deren, a pioneering experimental film maker (also known as Eleanora),[1] made *Meshes* in the wake of the Pearl Harbor attacks, and soon after Hiroshima. In 1947, the United States was on the verge of a new post–World War II order that included critical discussions about the atom bomb. Whereas a Hollywood melodrama such as *Spellbound* retains a clear separation between the realist illusion of a "normal" world in the film and the protagonist's traumatic attacks that are triggered by a visual phenomenon, Deren produces a visual correlative to the subjective, emotional, and visual experience of trauma, leaving the situation uncertain or to be deduced by the viewer. That is, the entire world of her film is "inside" the traumatic experience, with its visual distortions, its hallucinatory repetitions of actions, its terrifying dissociations and splittings, its uncanny intertwining of inside and outside, and its crossing of borders normally held firm in ordinary life.

I suggest that the world of the film is basically that of a traumatic hallucination related to the destabilization created by Hiroshima and the knowledge of the atom bomb but perhaps specifically alluding to the gender struggles following World War II. The women who had learned to take responsibility for themselves and their children while the men were away, and who had done jobs normally reserved for men, were suddenly forced back into being wives and mothers within what came to be seen as a stifling home. While Deren's film is not specific about the cause of the traumatic landscape we enter, its strategies place us as "witnesses" to the heroine's extreme distress and mental destabilization, with suggestions that a violent patriarchal order is responsible.

Some critics have viewed the film as Deren problematizing waking and dream states. But I would argue that even these images of possibly differing psychic states are themselves within a hallucination—that there is no "outside" to the visual experience within the film. It is this enclosure within the self that expresses or relays the experience of trauma. But Deren's techniques prevent us from fully identifying with the heroine, leaving space for us to witness her mental landscape and respond to it in terms of an elusive truth being conveyed. Or perhaps, following Abraham and Torok (1987), we witness a certain kind of haunting by a shameful secret.

This may not be such a radical reading as may appear. A good deal of research has been done on Deren's interest in anthropology and especially her intimate knowledge of Haitian voodoo rituals (Nichols, *Introduction to Documentary*). Many critics discuss the ways in which Deren's work seeks to address another world—one reached through voodoo rituals, including not only dance and music as triggers, but the trance states themselves as well. People have discussed Deren's interesting "choreocinema" as a way of explaining her focus on the body and its movements, its changeability. It seems to me that in certain ways trauma also produces an "other" world; in trauma as in trance, one is outside one's body. Indeed, one of the ways of working oneself through a traumatic attack is to self-consciously focus on getting back into one's body—such as through deep-breathing exercises. People engaging in trance, on the other hand, aim to get outside the body. Nevertheless, the visual and bodily phenomena in the two states may not be that dissimilar, despite the different causes for each state.

Meshes of an Afternoon is a multilayered film, with different meanings for each layer, but I will focus on the ways in which the film presents traumatic visuality—a vision of a hallucination. At the same time, one can posit a historical and personal context for the state expressed in the film as at once potentially about Deren's spiritual preoccupation with voodoo and Haitian ritual and as expressing her World War II context (that is, general anxiety about the war and especially the atomic bomb, including certain feminist perspectives stimulated by wartime realities).

Trauma, as discussed, is characterized by two main phenomena: visuality (including sound) and absence or delay of symbolization. Indeed, visuality is central to trauma precisely because of the absence or delay of symbolization. Hitchcock's *Spellbound,* as in many Hollywood representations of trauma, offers images of extreme dissociation and traumatic amnesia such as is rarely found in real life, but which nevertheless convey something of traumatic phenomena. But while *Spellbound* deals with male trauma having to do with killing and/or murder, *Meshes* embodies female coded traumatic imagery, female psychic and unconscious preoccupations.

Having been active in Socialist and artistic circles in and around New York City in the 1930s, by 1939, according to Clark, Hodson, and Neiman, "In a climate of world war and death, Eleanora reasserts her will to be creative," and joins choreographer Katherine Dunham, who "swept her off to California." There, we are told, "Eleanora was introduced to artists whose radical experiments in the arts enticed her precipitously, it would seem, into film-making" (Clark, Hodson, and Neiman 396). It was particularly the meeting with filmmaker Alexander Hammid that inspired Deren to make *Meshes*. This unusual, disturbing, and powerful film resulted from the combination of Hammid's expertise in editing, lighting, and photography, and Deren's strong visual and poetic sense. Crucial also was her fascination with dance, the body, music, together with her growing interest, once in California, with "primitive peoples" and their rituals, including voodoo (as described in a "Letter to a Friend" in Clark, Hodsen, and Neiman 470–473).

While Deren apparently had little directly to do with the French surrealists, she wrote a thesis on French symbolist poetry at Smith College and she was multilingual. It is hard to imagine that she did not know of Salvador Dali's paintings (Hitchcock, as we saw, invited Dali, then resident in the United States, to make sets for the traumatic dream in *Spellbound,* so his presence must have been known to artists), André Breton's manifestoes, or Antonin Artaud's theater of cruelty, to say nothing of surrealist cinematic experiments—especially since Hammid had made surrealist films before. Yet her Russian-Jewish background and American socialist agendas would make French surrealism—developed before World War II—perhaps seem too intellectual. Parallels with Dali/Buñuel's *Un Chien Andalou*—if only on the visual level—inevitably come to mind.

Deren and Alexander Hammid (then her husband) first made the film without sound, so that only the visuality of trauma prevailed. Once Deren was working with her third husband, Teiji Ito, a composer, they added the music track that, to my mind, increases the sense of terror and danger that the film expresses. Deren works at a self-conscious and high emotional pitch. While her work methods involved very precise planning for specific filmic effects, her stated aim was to deal with emotions. Her complaint about much avant-garde cinema, and especially the surrealism she is so often associated with, was that it was too "intellectual," too "rational." Ito's sound track is able to convey (more than the images alone) the sudden shocks and abrupt confrontations that the protagonist endures. The music punctuates and registers the heroine's emotional states.

But first, something should be said about the possible genesis of the film. That *Meshes* may embody a female-coded trauma is born out by the letter to a friend included in papers collected in *The Legend of Maya Deren*. The letter (written in 1941) perhaps contains germs of the traumatic feminine world in the film for in this letter Deren alludes to her Haitian and Trinidadian friends, and to her profound involvement with Haitian music and dance. She notes her interest in "the profound truth and reality . . . in the ritual of the most primitive peoples. I feel as if I perform ritual as they do . . . primitive rituals are the instruments for the invocation of deities" (Clark, Hodsen, and Neiman 470). In a scene that anticipates *Meshes,* Deren describes a kind of "séance" (but what is also a sort of daydream) that she performs in her apartment. She notes her sense of comfort in her space, her home, and her pleasure in putting records on and dancing to them. But then a sudden terrifying moment happens, when she senses being on the verge of "possession." "It frightened me," she says." I ran to the phonograph and lifted the needle and grabbed my head with both hands to stop it. I felt terribly exhausted and sank into a chair . . . I was alone and it is hard to stop and the idea of relinquishing my mind without anyone responsible to take care of me was frightening" (472). In this same letter, Deren distinguishes herself from a Catholic priest (perhaps a prior friend?) who is "treacherous, very clever and heartless. Thinking of him, I arrive at the distinction between myself and an intellectual." She goes on to describe herself as using her mind "as the instrument for the successful satisfaction of values which emerge and develop organically from, basically, my emotions" (472), rather than as being an intellectual.

Elements in this letter are possibly reworked to produce the powerful hallucinatory mental landscape of *Meshes*. One of the first things the film's hero does is to enter the house and lift the needle from the phonograph. Traces of the Catholic priest in the letter appear in the androgynous figure on the garden walk at the start of the film whose image is repeated throughout, and who seems like a phantom haunting the protagonist. The figure appears to have male shoes and to be wearing trousers, and yet the garb is that of a nun rather than a priest. The face, however, is a mirror, reflecting only its surroundings, not producing its own ideas—a fake kind of intellectual, perhaps. The house changes quickly from a place of comfort and ease to a terrifying space, as in 1940s film noir or melodramas (like *Gaslight*) in which women become prisoners of criminal males.[2] As Lauren Rabinovitz (1991) points out, visual images focus on doors and windows, and on ordinary domestic elements becoming uncanny and claustrophobic. Going up to take a rest, the hero (played dramatically by Deren) finds herself swayed from side to side. The very walls of the house seem to be caving in upon her; as in film noir, the camera offers strange angles, and, in this case, the hero's body is upside down in an action that is dizzying and terrifying. Once upstairs, the woman finds a knife in her bed, suggesting fear of male sexuality and the phallus as knifelike, wounding, dangerous. Traumatized beyond belief, the heroine splits into three subjectivities, three different identities—a mild white woman, a woman in blackface, and a murderous white woman. Woman's unconscious desire for revenge against male dominance is indicated. While the man who enters the house at first seems mild and kindly, he turns cold and is associated with the terrifying nun phantom.

Compared with *Spellbound, Meshes* exemplifies the "affect aesthetic" of trauma. The film embodies Deren's statement that her mind is at the service of her emotions, compared with the Catholic priest, who was all intelligence at the expense of heart. Deren works to find visual correlatives for the powerful emotions that nightmares produce. She does this by clever combination of Teiji Ito's musical track—often consisting of screeching, piercing sounds, or repeated unharmonious notes—and carefully chosen camera angles in the images.

Typical of the literalness of trauma, there are images and happenings in the film, but no causal sequence. There are strong emotions—fear, disgust, and rage—but no specific meanings. Set within the home for the most part and dealing with the heroine's perspective, this traumatic world projects the female-coded trauma affect aesthetic noted above. While technically "framed"—since this is a film—Deren far more than Hitchcock pushes at the borders of her frame, resisting the intellectualizing of Hitchcock's Dr. Brulov, and resisting the heterosexual closure of *Spellbound* with the assigning of trauma to the past. On the contrary, *Meshes* ends with a traumatic hallucination, as the heroine sees herself lying in her chair, apparently dead, with weeds around her neck.

31. Maya Deren in *Meshes of an Afternoon* (Photofest)

Yet the scenes in which we see the heroine outside the house apparently chasing the male nun figure along the path, or shots where huge feet take gigantic steps on a beach, suggest that the world of the film also represents the larger public space in which impoverished leaders without ideas (represented in the mirror-faced phantom) bring about national catastrophe. The emotions the film inspires suggest legacies of unconscious cultural violence producing death, symbolized by violence within the domestic space.

TRACY MOFFATT, *NIGHT CRIES—A RURAL TRAGEDY* (1989)

A different approach to the representation of trauma, to the ethics of witnessing, and indeed to the tension between deep personal and linked social traumatic impact may be found in another independent film, this time by the Aboriginal Tracey Moffatt. Moffatt's film, *Night Cries—A Rural Tragedy,* was made in 1989, just as Australia's Aboriginal peoples were asserting more forcefully than before their rights to their land and were demanding reparation for past crimes committed by white Australians. While only indirectly about any of this, *Night Cries* evidences the cultural trauma haunting Australia at the time through the story (at once real and metaphorical) of conflicted relations between white mothers and Aboriginal daughters. The film offers an explicit example of individual trauma as a combined result of unconscious internal and brutal external assault. Themes of aging, cultural loss, and abandonment are central in the film in relation to women from different racial backgrounds.[3] As in Deren's film, the trauma takes place literally in the domestic sphere—traditionally, and in many places still, a female world. Yet implicitly, as in *Meshes,* the domestic trauma is inseparable from the public sphere, in this case the world of Australia's white, postcolonialist national agenda. Finally, *Night Cries* provides a useful example of a work that produces the modalities of trauma through its cinematic techniques, but that also (like *Meshes*) offers spectators an example of the possible social utility of the "witnessing" experience.[4]

The film follows the structure and performative modality of trauma, very much as did Freud's *Moses and Monotheism* and Duras's *The War* (*La Douleur*), while self-consciously pitting that trauma against the illusory comforts of melodrama in the form of Aboriginal entertainer Jimmy Little. While Freud, as we saw, displaced his traumatic situation into obsessive inquiry into Moses' national identity—making melodrama, in a sense—Moffatt deliberately evokes melodrama not only in the figure of Jimmy Little but also in the opening quotation from a well-known Hollywood melodrama, *Picnic,* while avoiding melodrama. But despite Moffatt's highly stylized control of her story, the intense hatred between her protagonists remains unexplained, as if, like Freud's *Moses,* reflecting a psychic trauma the text does not itself fully know. Once again, the struggle Laub referred to, namely, to reach a truth that is elusive, is enacted. As in Deren's film, we enter a world, in Laub's words, "that feels as if it no longer resembles any reality."

As in Freud's *Moses,* the spectator has to manage a kind of double trauma; there it was the trauma of Freud's exile together with his fears of aging, implying loss of authority and loss of his analytic powers. In *Night Cries,* the text first performs the middle-aged daughter's childhood trauma involving an episode by the sea, perhaps linked to her forced adoption as an Aborigine by a white mother.[5] But, second, the spectator experiences the infirmity of the very aged, helpless mother, dependent on her obviously angry, frustrated, and unhappy daughter. Both are evidently trapped in some Outback location—clearly Australian while at the same time mythic. While the reader of *Moses* is invited directly into Freud's struggles through his first-person address, Moffatt keeps the viewer somewhat distant—part of producing the spectator as a "witness" to the events in the narrative.

The film mimics the structure of trauma in the way the daughter's images intrude increasingly into the narrative without being given meaning. Although it would be wrong to tie the daughter's traumatic attacks too rigidly to a single event—the film refuses us that sort of closure in accordance with the elusiveness that characterizes traumatic memory—in the wake of Corell Edwards's and Peter Read's research on the "lost children" (and Read's own 2000 volume, *A Rape of the Soul So Profound*), it is hard not to associate some of the images and themes in the interviews transcribed with the Aboriginal daughter's traumatic episodes.[6] Some of the people Edwards and Read talked with show traumatic symptoms. When asked what she recalls about being taken away, Jean Carter says, "Can't remember, sort of all blank" (Edwards and Read 51).[7] Much has yet to be written about the traumas of these "stolen generations," and the topic lies beyond my task here.[8] But, as Marcia Langton (who, an anthropologist, plays the daughter in Moffatt's film) notes, Moffatt inverts colonial history "to play out the worst fantasies of those who took Aboriginal children from their natural parents to assimilate and 'civilise' them" (Langton 47). As a spectator of flashback images in which a sullen Aboriginal child, in pretty party dress, is washed and her dress smoothed by a white woman with resigned face, we might ask if the little Aboriginal girl hated being made over in the image of a pretty, middle-class white child. It's impossible to tell. The image is purely visual and emotional, as in traumatic attacks. No explanation or meaning is assigned to these images and emotions for the viewer, and I consider this one of the film's strengths. Traumatic symptoms often float free of a specific event, becoming mixed with fantasies, and Moffatt evidently understands this process well.

The third and longest flashback dramatizes a painful trauma. It is stimulated, as were earlier traumatic intrusions, by an activity involving water—this time the daughter is washing her mother's feet in the only intimate and loving scene before the closing shots. The two hum "Onward, Christian Soldiers," highlighting the white Christian culture imposed on the daughter and many other Aborigines, and reminding viewers of the opening credits, when Jimmy Little sang a Christian gospel song about finding safety through a direct telephone line to God. The daughter pauses a moment and her hallucination of the childhood seaside scene starts. Like other flashbacks, this one too is in black and white, as against the stylized, exaggerated Technicolor of the scenes in the present (Moffatt was mimicking 1950s Hollywood color schemes, perhaps). The little Aboriginal girl is left in the care of two young Aboriginal boys, while the mother gazes out to sea, lost in her own thoughts. The play turns ugly as the boys "strangle" the girl with seaweed. Repeated shots of the child's terrified face with weed around her neck recall, perhaps, the umbilical cord wrapped around the neck of a fetus. The loud noise of waves crashing on the rocks together with claps of thunder prevent the mother from hearing her child's cries of terror.

Typically, as Freud noted, the event that stimulates a traumatic response is in itself often not that traumatic. But, significantly, the traumatic scene collapses the Aboriginal and the white mothers in that the loss of the former is perhaps reactivated by the white mother's apparent abandonment of the child in her need. Moffatt leaves the issue open for the viewer's interpretation, but in the midst of shots of the child's panic, Moffatt inserts images of Jimmy Little, now singing an Elvis love song, but *soundlessly* at this point. His message of love cannot help the little girl, as she experiences profound abandonment and the terror of being hurt, lost, and drowned.[9] Indeed, Little's message, and its apparently easy, tuneful mode accompanied by his hopeful face, only throws into relief the child's pain. This amounts, possibly, to a parody of Little that works to enhance the spectator's sense of trauma, much in the mode of Shakespeare's tragedies when the presence of the Fool only sharpens the tragic sense.[10] The contrast between the figure of Little and the scratched sounds of failed transmission that intervene in place of music or silence emphasizes the child's original trauma and its reworking in the present of the sea scene. The triggering by the seaside event of the original trauma cannot be repaired, despite a later shot of the mother comforting and warming the little girl after her crisis.

At the same time, as spectators witnessing this trauma, we also witness the trauma of the mother's aging that the protagonist daughter seems oblivious to—in fact, as oblivious as her mother was of *her* childhood traumas. The first sounds of the old lady are those of her prosthetic hand, banging on her plate as she tries to eat her food. As the camera pans across a table full of varied objects, to where the sound is coming from, we focus on the mother's ungainly apparatus and on the food barely making it into the woman's mouth. Later on, we experience the mother's total dependence for bodily care on her daughter, who must push her wheelchair to the outside toilet. There the daughter waits impatiently, while noise of metal scraping on metal fills the scene (fig. 32). While the mother is

32. Frustrated daughter in *Night Cries* (Courtesy of Tracey Moffatt)

inside the toilet, helpless we might say, the daughter's first flashbacks to the past begin. Finally, we see images of the mother's toothless mouth as she breathes at night with difficulty, flailing about in her bed, shrieking out having nightmares. Her aging trauma is that of a Victorian woman, presumably never active in the public sphere, never holding power other than over Aboriginal peoples, now left helplessly dependent on her angry mixed-race daughter.

The daughter's vivid rage, which brings its own harsh sounds as she angrily bangs on a bucket creating the sound of the train she yearns for to take her far away, or gleefully wielding a whip while her mother dozes, contrasts with this trauma of aging. Through a creative use of sound and silence, the film conveys the characters' contrasting situations and emotions, all without dialogue. Some argue that silence—choosing not to speak—befits trauma. The only words spoken in the film are those in Jimmy Little's songs. At the end of the film, as if to mark the pain rather than ease it, Moffatt brings back to the viewer the image and sound of Jimmy Little airing his illusions of safety with a direct line to God—illusions that the film has shown are empty fantasies.

Moffatt's art is syncretic; she draws on a broad range of styles from melodrama to surrealism, from trash television to classical art, from playwrights as diverse as Samuel Beckett, Garcia Lorca, Eugene O'Neill, and Tennessee Williams—playwrights well known for their dysfunctional families. At the same time, Moffatt's art includes reference to Australian landscape painting by white artists (like Drysdale or Arthur Boyd) as much as by Aboriginal ones (such as especially

Albert Namatjira). But Moffatt's film, while technically more related to independent or "new wave" European cinema and drama than to classical cinema, also positions itself vis-à-vis American film melodrama.[11]

The quotation from *Picnic* placed in the opening title sequence for *Night Cries* honors American melodrama and symbolically the forces of good and evil that melodramas rely upon. "Look at that sunset, Howard: It's like the daytime didn't want to end; the day is putting up a big scrap to keep the nighttime from creeping on." This is spoken by Rosalind Russell in the 1950s melodrama *Picnic,* playing the role of an aging schoolteacher, a spinster, desperate to be married and to have fun. She too is "putting up a scrap" to prevent her descent into loveless age with death "creeping on." This is a "descent" that haunts Moffatt's film, filled as it is with ambivalent, elusive memories of the heroine's past. Moffatt transfers the evils of a deadly, small, puritanical American town in Kansas to the bleakness of the Australian outback, where her Aboriginal protagonist too is aging and bitterly confined taking care of her aged, ill white mother.

Yet the film, like *Meshes,* may also be seen as a metaphor for the larger Australian tragedy of the near annihilation of its indigenous peoples, now returning to haunt the culture. The deadly weight of a dying white colonial culture is possibly symbolized in the aged white mother, whose weakness and vulnerability contrast with the virility and rage of the Aboriginal daughter, much as William Holden's character's rage and virility contrast with the vapid nouveau-riche family in *Picnic.*

In making this link back to American melodrama, Moffatt seems to support the concept of a genre that repeats unutterable historical struggles below the level of cultural awareness, much as Freud had argued in *Moses.*[12] White colonialism's ravages on Aboriginal life and culture similarly have remained below conscious awareness in Australia in the past. What Ken Gelder and Jane Jacobs name "uncanny" Australia has partly to do with the estrangement of white Australians learning that the land they thought was theirs really belongs to others.[13] As always with national crimes too horrible to fully know, the blocked knowledge returns in cultural symptoms that betray the crimes, such as following attempted annihilation of Aborigines by rendering them (until recently) absent from the Australian national imaginary.[14] But Moffatt's film refuses to close off the crimes; rather, in taking us into her heroine's elusive traumatic memory, she asks us to witness those crimes.

The ethical movement in *Night Cries* is produced partly via the daughter's emotional release at the end. The mother's death frees the daughter into mourning for her loss. Movingly, the film shows the daughter curled up in a fetal position beside her mother's corpse. Viewers first see the couple at eye level, but on the sound track we hear now only a baby's soulful cry. The angle then moves to an overview shot so that the daughter appears in a fetal position—as if returned to the position within the womb. Can we say that the daughter has moved through her trauma to find her unexpressed love for her pathetically aged mother—a love that seemed impossible before? The pain of her trauma remains with the viewer, as do images of the aging mother, with her failing body, difficulty eating and caring for herself, her terrifying dependency on others, and her utterly empty life. The triadic structure of *Night Cries,* with the viewer contributing to the film's meanings as against the usual passive position the viewer occupies in classical melodrama, arguably enabled a performative "working through" to take place for viewers as well as for the protagonist of the film. This "working through" does not mean, as it did in *Spellbound,* that there is a "cure" or healing; rather, in Moffatt's film, working through means accepting ongoing mourning, keeping the wound open.

Through this example, I conclude that art that takes trauma for its topic but does not allow the spectator so easily to "survive" the protagonist's death or wound, refuses the safe closure that melodrama perhaps vainly seeks. Art that leaves the wound open pulls the spectator into its sphere in ways other kinds of art may not. Both *Meshes* and *Night Cries* leave the viewer with an uneasy, disturbed feeling, but with the sense of having been moved empathically and ethically. The distance that both films achieve allows the viewer at once to participate in the experience of each hero's trauma through the aesthetic devices used, and to have a perspective on injustice broader than that of the main protagonist herself. While the films may require contextualizing for the broader view to be appreciated, this in no way mitigates their power to move the audience ethically, to expose the structure of injustice and to invite viewers to take responsibility for related specific injustice.

Both films arguably support Dominick LaCapra's concept of "working through" as mourning—an idea related to that of witnessing.[15] LaCapra's point is that we must find ways in public education and practice to move emotion and value toward victims "who are indeed deserving objects of mourning" (214), and in so doing facilitate processes of mourning and of discovering viable rituals. While LaCapra mainly has victims of anti-Semitism in mind, the same holds true for victims of family trauma who are largely women. Meanwhile, communities everywhere need to establish structures within which there can be "witnesses" for the testimony of women, who are still subject to patriarchal violence even as new subjectivities are being drastically revised in postmodernism, postcolonialism, and multiculturalism. People require structures within which often silently endured traumatic experiences can be "spoken" or imaged, as in Moffatt's and Deren's powerful short films, and in the documentaries by Essie Coffey and Alanis Obomsawin. In such processes, people can begin the task of working through via mourning.

Epilogue

"Wounded New York"

Rebuilding and Memorials to 9/11

This books ends, as it began, with 9/11 and its aftermath. The great yawning crematorium at the end of Manhattan continues to fester like a sore without bandages or healing salve. The great pit can be watched from inside the spacious Winter Garden, increasingly the site to which relatives of victims return to peer into the crematorium as if into their loved one's grave. I have returned many times to gaze as well, still in disbelief at what I am seeing—namely the footprints of those great towers now no more, surrounded by the "disturbing remains" of so many.

But while something has to be done with the crematorium, the "disturbing remains" continue to haunt any discussion of what to do with it. The city seems caught between two processes focused on in this book, namely providing an adequate form of "witnessing" in the aftermath of the catastrophe, and also finding ways to "translate" it so that the city can resume its life, and can move on from the trauma. It is hard for the city and its people to move on from related processes of "acting out," that is, remaining within the traumatic event and repeating it endlessly (something similar to Freud's melancholy), to "working through," the stage of accepting what has happened, mourning the many kinds of loss, and providing—not closure or healing (the wound to New York will remain forever)—but a fitting witness, a fitting way to memorialize the catastrophe. It is as if traumatic phenomena of splitting and unconscious guilt, mixed with fantasies of revenge on the perpetrators ("we'll show that we cannot be beaten, that life and commerce in the United States will go forward") could not be avoided. As Thomas Laqueur has noted, "Nations, like individuals, sustain trauma, mourn and recover. And like individuals, they survive by making sense of what has befallen them, by constructing a narrative of loss and redemption" (25). But he also says that "defeat is the greatest trauma in the life of nations."[1]

Traumatic residues of "acting out" may be seen in the tensions, conflicts, and intense debates about the site that moved to the fore as the city began to think about rebuilding. The different interest groups involved in planning what to do with the site cannot agree about what is most fitting. The traumatic event has impacted in such diverse ways with each interest group, and the needs and concerns of these groups are so different, that conflict was inevitable.

In what follows, I explore some of the debates about what to do with the site with a view to illuminating how hard it is for a community to stay united under the stress of competing interests and of groups occupying diverse personal, political, and cultural positions vis-à-vis the catastrophe. The problems New York, qua city, faces in rebuilding offer in microcosm the problems humans have in many situations worldwide where consensus is being sought about memorials. Splitting, denial, guilt, unconscious motives for revenge, fame, financial reward, all make such decisions enormously complicated.

Partly because of the experience of having one's entire world shaken at its very foundations, New Yorkers struggled to find ways to make meaning of what had happened, to work it through on many levels (personal, political, intellectual), so as to continue with life in the city and as citizens of the world in the wake of the attacks. Part of the problem is that people have been caught between efforts to make meaning of what happened—to provide the fitting witness referred to—and the practical need to rebuild. The period when the site was being cleared provided a kind of space for working through the catastrophe and for appropriate mourning. While people still searched for their lost ones, and for evidence of a loved one's death with the finding of some remains, the focus was on coming to terms with the events. As Ulrich Baer puts it in an introduction to his 2002 edited collection, *110 Stories: New York Writes after September 11,* "The stories address the need for narrative in the wake of a disaster . . . with *110 Stories,* poets, novelists, short story writers, script authors, playwrights, and artists enter terrain that needs not only remediation by engineers and clean-up crews but integration into the city beyond zoning and construction. Their stories explore the possibilities of language in the face of gaping loss, and register that words might be all that's left for the task of finding meaning in—and beyond—the silent, howling void" (Baer 1). But Baer does not have in mind easy or sentimental attempts at closure so hard to resist in times like these, especially given our culture's investment in sentiment—an investment bred in United States citizens through addiction to Hollywood. Rather, Baer explains, "Instead of providing solace, the work of fiction cauterizes the wound with uncomfortable questions and unflinching reflection. It sears the event into the collective imagination by embedding the initial shock in narratives, poems, theater, and tales" (3). Baer argues that as against political explanations, which aim for closure in the manner of Hollywood cinema, "literature resists the call for closure." The stories he has collected eschew orthodox genres since these would just reinscribe norms unable to deal with the unique new catastrophe. His volume fully recognizes that there can be no single story to contain the event (5). He also writes that "the political discourses on both the

33. A piece of paper on the park pavement on which many different messages are scrawled (Courtesy of the author)

left and the right seemed irreconcilable with what had happened" (5). "To declare surrender," he remarks, "seemed as incommensurate with the experience as the call for revenge" (6). Literature seemed the only mode to Baer through which he could regain "a foothold on reality from which [he] had slipped momentarily" (7).

In what follows, I will limit my comments about memorializing 9/11 to select media coverage.[2] Studying how debates over rebuilding were represented in select articles reveals unconscious residues of the traumatic situation and the unique challenge of designing an appropriate commemorative site for 9/11.[3] For while debates about designs for Ground Zero have something in common with similar debates about other memorials (such as those commemorating victims of the Holocaust, Hiroshima, the Vietnam War, or of catastrophes in Latin America), there are also major differences that make memorializing 9/11 unique. Basic questions facing the building of memorials include the following: Should a memorial remind viewers of the terribleness of the catastrophe? Should it deliberately reevoke the horror, emphasizing aspects of human nature that cannot be denied? Or should it focus on the individuals lost, and what they contributed to society, in which case the memorial's main aim is to remember the victims, mourn their loss? Could a memorial be structured so as to enable a kind of national (or even international) "working through" of the trauma? Who is the memorial for? Is it for people living now and within whose memory the catastrophe took place? Or should it be thought of as a pedagogical tool, providing knowledge about and experience of the tragedy for generations to follow in the hopes of preventing future occurrences of violence and hatred?

If those constructing commemorative sites all have to face these general questions, each specific instance raises its own complex political, ideological, and architectural issues. In some cases, the responsibility of the nation itself for the catastrophe is a burning issue, and here the most obvious case is the Holocaust. For example, a Holocaust memorial in Germany cannot avoid recalling the complicity of ordinary Germans in the annihilation of the Jews, making a commemorative site in the heart of the German capital an extremely sensitive project. Much has been written especially about the commemorative site now being built in Berlin.[4] Some articles focus on how to avoid a monumentality linked to the Nazi and Fascist architecture that would undercut the purposes of the site.[5] In her essay "'Aesthetic Pollution': The Paradox of Remembering and Forgetting in Three Holocaust Commemorative Sites," Brett Kaplan reviews these debates and correctly argues "that the connection between particular aesthetic choices and particular ideologies cannot be maintained, and that, therefore, commemorative sites to the Nazi genocide should maintain their pedagogical aims over and above fears of aesthetic pollution" (13).

Kaplan is right to stress pedagogical issues in the case of the Holocaust since it took more than fifty years before the United States, Germany, and Poland were ready to honor that trauma. Many of the survivors had already died by that time, and many Jews and non-Jews alive had only passing knowledge of the crimes committed by the Nazis. Memorials in this case have to be organized to present information about the Holocaust and indeed about the history of Jewish life and traditions, as well as conveying something of the horror of the experience. Similar issues in regard to pedagogy and commemorative sites have arisen with catastrophes engineered by national leaderships in Latin American nations (see Andreas Huyssen,"Memory Practices in Sculpture").

War memorials per se offer a different case. Regardless of whether a particular war was justified or not, many innocent navy and military personnel died, and their service to the nation has to be remembered. Here, the overall issue of mourning those who served is relatively straightforward, and the site is usually in a nation's capital city.

Such discussions of debates about commemorative sites throw into relief the uniqueness of creating a New York memorial to 9/11. Unlike most of the memorials to catastrophe, this one is to be built on the very site of the catastrophic event—a site where ashes of those who perished remain. Usually, the catastrophe being remembered pulls together tragic losses from an entire nation (memorials at Auschwitz and Dachau come closest to the situation of the Twin Towers). For some weeks, there was a question of whether it was appropriate, sensible, or safe to rebuild at all. At this stage, the issue of the memorial had nothing to do with what Kaplan has called possible "aesthetic pollution" but rather with what turned out to be the extreme vulnerability of the Twin Towers, the tallest buildings in the world for many years, now seen open to airplane attack by terrorists.[6] In addition to issues regarding vulnerability, debates about putting the towers back, as many immediately wanted to do, included the pride on the part of some (leading to replacing the Towers) pitted against the feelings of many relatives of victims that any rebuilding, even of a commemorative monument, would be desecration of the place, a crematorium, where the ashes of loved ones lay.

Ellsworth Kelly, it later turned out, had thought, along with two other artists, that no building should be put on the site. Writing later to Herbert Muschamp at the *New York Times,* he said, "At that time [October 2001] my idea for the World Trade Center was a large green mound of grass" (quoted by Muschamp, *New York Times,* September 11, 2003: E1, 4). Kelly believed "that what is needed is a 'visual experience,' not additional buildings, a museum, a list of names or proposals for a 'freedom monument.' These . . . are distractions from a spiritual vision for the site: a vision for the future" (E1).[7] For those arguing for pride and revenge, however, new towers would evoke a sense of America's strength, and imply that we are strong as a nation, and we will resist aggression. Rebuilding copies of the Twin Towers would be an act of defiance, throwing down the gantlet to the terrorists to try again.[8]

Eventually, as the process of clearing the site advanced, so it became clear that something had to be done with this gaping hole. Even if many would have wanted it to be left as exactly that, a gaping void with ashes of the dead to forever recall the devastation, practically, with a city the size of New York and space at a premium, a decision to rebuild in some fashion had to be made.

Like the tragedy of the Oklahoma City bombing (although involving far more victims), 9/11 is unique, as noted, in that there is just one specific site where the catastrophe took place, suggesting that the memorial should be built on the site of the violence and destruction. But the politics of each case is quite different. In Oklahoma, the catastrophe was engineered by a small group of disaffected Americans with whom very few people in the nation could identify. The federal building that was destroyed has become a museum, and the site commemorating the 161 victims is just outside the reconstructed walls of the building. It's an elegant, simple design—a lake with arches at each end noting the time of the explosion and the duration of the destruction, and a glass chair for each victim placed on grass by the lake. In no public discourse was there support for those who carried out the bombing.

The case of 9/11 is different because almost at once voices were heard, if not supporting the attacks at least proclaiming that America's international behavior had produced the extreme hatred on the part of many around the world that could have led to the catastrophe. These voices, however, while free to circulate in the United States and internationally, could not play a part in the question of the memorial as such. But Herbert Muschamp, in discussing one of the many fantasies that emerged as ideas "to fill the void" left by 9/11, discussed a proposed Museum of Freedom. After describing the aims of the project, Muschamp makes this comment: "Not everyone in the United States is ideally poised at this moment to point fingers at 'places that lack basic human freedom.'" He notes that the museum would be linked to the International Coalition of Historic Site Museums of Conscience, but he sees "scant evidence of conscience in the brochure." He objects to an underlying assumption in the brochure, which is that "freedom has been assaulted; therefore retaliation is legitimate—even more, is part of the heroic struggle that includes the cause of civil rights" (*New York Times,* August 31, 2003).

In addition to 9/11 involving one specific site for a catastrophe where as many as three thousand people lost their lives all at once and where their ashes lie buried, equally unusual is the fact that the site was a bustling, postmodern area, a center for international business and communications, as well as a thriving commercial, art, and entertainment space, full of shops, restaurants, and game centers, to say nothing of the extensive network of subway systems and tunnels beneath the complex, connecting city workers to the surrounding suburban areas. Once rebuilding was seen as inevitable, a clash between relatives of the victims and commercial interests was destined to happen. The deep conflict was that between Larry A. Silverstein, the developer who holds the lease rights to the World Trade Center's commercial space, and the relatives of the victims who wanted to keep the space free from commercialism as an arena for mourning. City and state officials, mainly Governor George Pataki and Mayor Michael Bloomberg, have been intermediaries between these interests. The more appropriate agency, namely the Lower Manhattan Development Corporation, was often outraged at being upstaged by Pataki and Bloomberg.

The family members of those killed in the 9/11 attacks did not speak with one voice, but they were listened to. A major debate emerged over the winners of the second design contest for the rebuilding of the site (the first had been voided because none of the designs was acceptable). Six finalists' designs were put on display in the Winter Garden—the splendid glass structure that overlooks Ground Zero. The public was encouraged to view and submit comments to the Lower Manhattan Development Corporation, which promised to take them into consideration. As a New Yorker, I too participated in the process, and submitted comments. I surveyed the model designs in the Winter Garden and on the Lower Manhattan Development Corporation's Web site, where all seven designs could be studied in the quiet of one's home. It seemed to me that Libeskind's unique Jewish Museum in Berlin already showed his ability to make architecture "feel" and "speak," that is, to convey emotions as well as ideas. His design for Ground Zero similarly addressed the horror that happened there, New Yorkers' complex feelings about it, and it honored the need for mourning. The horror was addressed through the destabilized, jagged, and sharp forms of the buildings. The glass was to be crinkly and torn; there were no smooth, easy lines; all was awry. In fact, some of the buildings in Libeskind's design reminded me of the way the site looked in the days following the attacks—the buildings torn, with jagged steel hanging loosely from the sides.[9] One building looked a bit like the shard that remained for so long, haunting the space with traces of the Towers. One was reminded of Libeskind's Jewish Museum where the very outside walls of the building are scarred, large wounds piercing the surfaces at angles, while the jagged forms of the sides pierce the skies like huge pieces of cut glass. Inside, as would also happen in the 9/11 project, Libeskind offers visitors disturbing experiences, such as being enclosed in a cell for a moment or being unable to walk without stumbling.[10]

But the design also suggested the need to think about a new future. There was to be a thin spire-like building that reaches up to the sky, and which would have gardens in it, conveying the idea of hope and the future (fig. 34). Other buildings had sloping roofs, conveying the natural idea of the crystal shape, comforting in its sense of history and predating mankind (fig. 35).

I liked the Meier et al. design as well. Quite unlike the Libeskind, this one had clear firm lines, reminding one of the Twin Towers, but then, instead of offices and restaurants, there were only empty spaces, symbolizing all the absences,

34. Daniel Libeskind's original Master Plan for Ground Zero (Millerhare)

35. Libeskind Master Plan: View of street (Millerhare)

and the loss that had taken place. Loss and strength were amazingly combined in this proposal. Once again, there were gardens and spaces below for reflection and quietness. I liked the fact that the traffic would move below the structures, not around them. This structure made a striking impression in the cityscape—completely different from the Twin Towers, but similar in making a strong statement. The fact that it would generate solar power during the day to shine at night was a great idea. The building would enhance the nightscape of the city and provide the sort of comfort that light always provides in the most dire circumstances.

The United group's THINK design differed from both the first two but had perhaps something in common with the Libeskind in that the stress was on misshapen forms; in this case, the buildings bulged out in places, again giving a sense of things awry. However, the Libeskind project managed to convey this same sense while also offering aesthetic satisfaction, which was not so much the case in THINK's design.

The Lower Manhattan Development Corporation chose the THINK design. Conflict emerged again when this choice was overridden by Pataki and Bloomberg, who preferred Daniel Libeskind's design. In justifying this, Pataki noted that he had listened to the family members of victims, some of whom said that "the Libeskind memorial sent the message that those victims would be remembered by a symbol of strength—the slurry wall—rather than by what they characterized as a pair of skeletal towers that recalled how their loved ones had died" (*New York Times,* September 28, 2003).[11] In his summary of events surrounding the decision about which model to adopt, Herbert Muschamp noted the benefits that had emerged from the design process, the most important of which was "that public building is itself an educational process. Far more than a set of designs, images, or blueprints for the physical objects that will be realized in urban space, architecture is also the art of mapping changing relationships between social and artistic values" (*New York Times,* February 28, 2004: A25). Muschamp argued that the design process for 9/11 had usefully opened up "a promising way out of the creative impasse" of the past when "getting it done" (appealing to the lowest denominator) conflicted with the vision, integrity, and brains of the best architects.

But the city's decision to go with Libeskind's design ushered in the next serious rounds of debate and conflict, this time between Silverstein and his designer, David Childs, and Daniel Libeskind, in danger of being sidelined by Childs, who wanted to alter the original agreed upon design.[12] Robert Ivy, editor in chief of *Architectural Record,* is quoted in the *New York Times* urging that Libeskind be allowed to take the lead in the next stage of the process because "Daniel Libeskind's plan had a vertiginous, dizzying quality that captured something of New York and that it would be a shame to lose" (Iovine,"The Invisible Architect"). From all accounts, Libeskind has tried to accommodate new ideas put forward by Silverstein and Childs while working with community groups to keep the basic ideas of his plan. David Childs will be the primary architect for the so-called Freedom Tower (which will be higher than the original towers but have no office or other space on the higher levels) since he designed 7 World Trade Center, but in addition park land and other open spaces have been taken over by bus routes and shops in Child's design.

By the time of the second anniversary of the attacks, New Yorkers were becoming restless and disturbed by the secretive nature of revision of Libeskind's plan. In his *New York Times* piece on September 13, 2003, "Ground Zero Plan Seems to Circle Back," Edward Wyatt noted that "the secretive evolution of the plan contrasts sharply with the continuing portrayal of the rebuilding process as one of the most open and inclusive of civic building in memory. Government officials, architects, and civic groups and developers still speak in awestruck tones about the town hall meeting in the summer of 2002 when more than 4,500 New Yorkers spent hours discussing, of all things urban planning" (*New York Times,* September 13, 2003: B1). Wyatt argues that elements of one of the rejected designs are creeping back into the final plans.

While Libeskind and Childs were working out an accommodation about the overall rebuilding of the site, New York City was ready to move onto the next series of discussions and debates, this time about the memorial to the victims to be built within the site, and for which each designer had provided a specific space. Over the months after the open call for designs had been issued, 5,200 submissions had been received, creating a massive job for the jurors and the Lower Manhattan Development Corporation, which ran the competition. All was done with utmost secrecy and anonymity for all entrants. On November 19, 2003, after a preview by the relatives of victims, the eight memorial designs were unveiled. Once again, the models were displayed in the Winter Garden for all to see, although this time comments were not solicited. Thirteen jurors were chosen to select the final design, including Maya Lin, James E. Young, and Vartan Gregorian. Once again, I went to the Winter Garden to see the models, and was struck, like others, by the resemblances among the winners—a resemblance that was evident in their somewhat similar titles (for example, "Garden of Lights," "Inversion of Light," and "Passages of Light" on the one hand; "Suspending Memory," "Reflecting Absence," and "Dual Memory" on the other) embodying the similarity of themes. Decorative lights, pools of water, waterfalls, names, symbols, or places for each victim could be found in most of the chosen entries.

Some critics attacked all of the chosen entries for being "pastiches of different media and styles—the definition of postmodern, in keeping with so much contemporary mixed-media art," instead of a memorial that would exist outside of time, slowing things down, giving us "a larger sense of history" (*New York Times,* December 7, 2003: AR 1, 37). This same critic condemned the process for its appeal to "populism," claiming that the democratic process was a sop to expediency and politics and that, as the article's title put it, "The Ground Zero's Memorial's Only Hope: Elitism" should have been the governing principle.

In fact several designs were tasteful and thoughtful. Again, I picked the winner, "Reflecting Absence" by Michael Arad. This design is simple and elegant, featuring two pools in the footprints of the Towers, thirty feet below street level. Visitors would descend down to the pools, seeing victims' names on the walls. There would be a chamber with unidentified remains accessible only to relatives of the victims, and a cultural building on street level would shelter the site from the highway. Obviously, as with Libeskind's design, the winning memorial design will be revised according to the needs of safety and other practical issues that will intervene.

As 2003 drew to a close, the final piece of the process fell into place. For months, New Yorkers had known of an impasse between Childs and Libeskind over the Freedom Tower being designed by Childs within Libeskind's project.[13] The compromise required Childs to reduce the height of his tower by 276 feet (*New York Times,* December 17, 2003: B10).[14] So by the time of New Year's Day 2004, it seemed as though New York had arrived at a sort of closure as far as rebuilding and the memorial were concerned. It also seems that some of the unique needs for this, as against other memorials, have been attended to. Elements of the site as it was before the attacks have been retained in the slurry wall and in creating pools out of the original footprints of the Twin Towers. Attention to the unique aspect of the site as a crematorium remain in creating a chamber with unidentified remains (and I assume vessels with "ashes") accessible only to the families of victims. The movement of people down into the site respects the nearness of death on the site, and the lighting will be appropriate to mourning. But people will in turn emerge back into the light with the Freedom Tower offering a symbol of hope.

Perhaps lacking (as far as I can tell) is a properly pedagogical aspect to the memorial. If this is lacking, most likely it is because New Yorkers may not agree about the political message to be learned, as indicated above. In the case of most memorials, there is public agreement about the politics of the event being commemorated. Here again, 9/11 is different putting particular stress on how to provide a "lesson" to upcoming generations. It is perhaps for this very reason that so much of the writing about 9/11 has focused on individuals and on personal loss—a focus that many object to and describe as "sentimental." It would be better to leave aside attributions of sentimentality (who is one to say how loss should be handled?) and rather address the differing politics surrounding the attacks together with the natural defense nations construct against remembering what is humiliating.[15]

At any rate, having the contentious issues about rebuilding partially decided is a relief to many and a sign that a certain process of working through, of providing a fitting "witness" to the tragedy, has taken place. This is not to say that there is not continuing discussion about the rebuilding. New York will be forever "wounded." How can it be otherwise? But at least the residues of the trauma that perhaps lay beneath the conflicts and tensions of rebuilding may be lessening. We have begun to translate the trauma into a language of acceptance while deliberately keeping the wound open; we are learning to mourn what happened, bear witness to it, and yet move forward.

NOTES

INTRODUCTION 9/11 AND "DISTURBING REMAINS"

"Disturbing Remains" is the title of a book coedited by Michael Roth and Charles Salas and published in 2001.

1. I should note here, parenthetically, that while the data I rely on mainly establishes the impact of catastrophe in American culture, it seems logical (given the information provided by Joseph LeDoux, Martin Hoffman, and others about changes in the brain produced by trauma, which I address below) to deduce its pervasiveness across cultures, wherever humans are abused or made to suffer untold catastrophe.
2. Interviewers of Holocaust victims, who engaged in this work as part of the Yale Fortunoff Archive Project, offer an example of a rare way of encountering trauma. The impact on such interviewers has been detailed by Dori Laub in essays in his volume, *Testimony*, coauthored with Shoshana Felman.
3. I say "paradoxically" because art is usually thought of as something passively consumed rather than, as I view it, an *activity*. Art is not just receiving, but involves active participation. The meaning of art is created in between the space of the work and the spectator/reader/listener.
4. Luhrman points out, "The word 'trauma'. . . refers to singular or repeated events which injure. Some injuring events are dramatic and soul-destroying. Some are quiet and humiliating" (158). Luhrman goes on to describe a quiet trauma and its impact several generations later in his essay "The Traumatized Social Self: The Parsis Predicament in Modern Bombay," in *Cultures under Siege: Collective Violence and Trauma*, edited by Antonius C.G.M. Robben and Marcelo M. Suárez-Orozco. Meanwhile, Deidre Barrett, in her edited collection *Trauma and Dreams,* points out that some writers object to using the word "trauma" for events that are potentially or inevitably encountered in the course of a normal life. While she sees some logic to this view, as I do as well, she argues that the similar experiences of shock, grief, destruction of security, and the induction of disturbing dreams is the reason the term "trauma" can be applied to such common or quiet events (5).
5. Writing about the Holocaust is in part an exception. Certainly attention has been given in memoirs and film to the plight of children and women, and female survivors have written powerfully about their experiences. Yet the issue of gender per se perhaps still needs more attention.
6. As Martin Hoffman notes, quoting Veroff et al., there has been a dramatic shift in acceptance of seeking counseling. See J. Veroff, R. Kulka, and E. Donovan, *Mental Health in America.*

CHAPTER I "WHY TRAUMA NOW?"

1. This was a situation that Freud confronted but was unable to address adequately given the ideological constraints of his historical moment.

2. I am not alone in thinking that Freud indeed had anticipated much that is being "discovered" by neuroscientists today. See Fred Guteril's essay, "What Freud Got Right," *Newsweek,* November 11, 2002: 50–52. The subheading reads: "His theories, long discredited, are finding support from neurologists using modern brain imaging," and an insert reads: "Unconscious drives, similar to libido and aggression, have now been located in the most primitive parts of the brain" (50). There is even a journal, *Neuropsychoanalysis,* and in Guteril's essay Antonio Damasio is quoted as saying that "Freud's insights on the nature of consciousness are consonant with the most advanced contemporary neuroscience views."
3. Freud developed his theories of trauma from studying female hysteria and then the impact of train accidents and wars. Late in life, he also hypothesized that a violent historical act can remain in cultural consciousness and continue to have a traumatic impact, as I go on to show in some detail. For more discussion of the history and development of the concept of trauma by Freud, see Cathy Caruth, *Unclaimed Experience: Trauma, Narrative, and History* (Baltimore: The Johns Hopkins University Press, 1986). See also essays in Cathy Caruth, ed., *Trauma and Experience: Explorations in Trauma and Memory* (Ithaca, NY: Cornell University Press, 1985). In chapter 2, I discuss Freud's *Moses and Monotheism* as a traumatic text, and as it theorizes a collective or cultural historical trauma.
4. This volume, published only in German in 1895, was later translated by James Strachey and published in volume 2 of the Standard Edition in 1955. A separate English volume, *Studies in Hysteria,* of the SE section, was published in 1957.
5. As the editors of the Standard Edition point out, Freud mentioned in a letter to Fliess at the time that he had omitted reference to the father's abuse of the women in his and Breuer's *Studies in Hysteria.*
6. After stating his notion that all major neuroses "have as their common source the subject's sexual life," he comments: "I am quite sure that this theory will call up a storm of contradictions from contemporary physicians" (Freud, "Heredity" 151).
7. In his essay on "Heredity and the Aetiology of the Neuroses," Freud mentions siblings, other children, and nannies as the figures involved in genital activity with small children. However, this does not prove, as Richard McNally (2000) suggests, that Freud was *not* protecting his colleagues in his later abandoning of the seduction theory, for in a letter to Fleiss discussing his patients at the same time, as the editors of the Standard Edition point out, Freud noted that "in every case it was the father who had to be held responsible (for perverse acts with children)" (SE 1: 160. Freud later admitted to suppressing the father's abuse in cases in *Studies in Hysteria* (see SE 1: 164).
8. As most readers will know, a huge bibliography surrounds this move by Freud—a bibliography that reentered public consciousness when issues relating to child abuse surfaced in the United States around highly visible cases in the late 1980s. Trauma theory and PTSD were central to these debates, since the cases relied on traumatic phenomena as evidence of abuse. My case studies take up other kinds of family traumas, but readers can find a thorough survey of Freud's theories and writings, as well as discussion of the recent so-called "false memory syndrome" in Richard J. McNally's *Remembering Trauma* (Cambridge, MA: Harvard University Press, 2003).
9. War trauma greatly stimulated medical doctors and those interested in psychoanalysis in World War I. While concepts of trauma were first investigated in regard to industrial agents and accidents, it was the research opportunity afforded by traumatized soldiers that impelled work on trauma forward. Indeed, the work done in regard to World War I set the stage for concern about traumatic reactions in World War II, and then most recently and in its most elaborated form, in relation to the Vietnam War, as noted earlier.

   See articles dealing with war trauma in the *Lancet,* such as Dr. David Forsyth's essay reviewing ongoing debates, i.e., "Functional Nerve Disease and the Shock of

Battle: The So-Called Traumatic Neuroses Arising in Connexion with the War" (*Lancet* 2 [December 25, 1915]: 1399).

10. Since *Studies in Hysteria* was published in 1909 in English, the doctors writing in the *Lancet* were no doubt drawing on Freud and Breuer's ideas (significantly, the English edition, translated by A. A. Brill, omitted the case histories of Anna O, Emmy Von N., and Katharina, as well as Breuer's theoretical chapter). But they were also drawing on much earlier research on railway and industrial accidents, such as 1864 research by J. Eric Erichsen, "On the Concussion of the Spine," mentioned in an article by Thomas R. Glynn, "The Traumatic Neuroses" in the *Lancet* 2 (November 5, 1910): 1332). Glynn awards to two American physicians the insight that since the symptoms of railway spine were cerebral more than spinal disturbances, the term "railway brain" would be more appropriate.
11. In a series of novels, Pat Barker (1991, 1995, 1996) has written convincing fictional accounts of Rivers's psychotherapy with soldiers suffering what was then called "shell shock" in the military hospital in Craiglockhart, Scotland. Doctors were supposed to get these men ready to return to the battlefront, and the soldiers knew this, but Barker shows the very difficult position doctors found themselves in, since their empathy for the men went deep, and they did not necessarily believe in the war. No man wanted to be accused of "malingering." Freud found himself having to judge just such a case, as I go on to show.
12. Pat Barker's novels are interesting in light of this. More than one of Barker's major characters describe sexual arousal in moving out to a dangerous confrontation with German troops in trenches across from the British ones. Some characters are gay, others bisexual. While Rivers appears to leave such sexual themes unexplored in his therapy sessions, the "data" is there for readers to see.
13. Pat Barker's novels, again, dramatize clearly the ways in which traumatic battle events haunt the soldiers in dreams and hallucinations. While sometimes the men can recall the dreams and precipitating events, they prefer not to. Others suffer from total amnesia as a symptom. Partial dissociation, then, is observed in Barker's representing of Rivers's cases in her fiction.
14. For full details of this investigation, see Kurt. R. Eissler, *Freud as an Expert Witness: The Discussion of War Neuroses Between Freud and Wagner-Jauregg* (Madison, WI.: International University Press, 1986).
15. One of the problems with *Beyond the Pleasure Principle* is that Freud is trying to do too many things. The entire discussion involves Freud's working out of differences among anxiety, fear, and fright (something he will take up later on) and he is also continuing an earlier discussion of the compulsion to repeat. Most significantly, *Beyond* is also where Freud begins to theorize the death drive. However, his introduction of the traumatic war neuroses, when these neuroses are not the main discussion, highlights how bothered Freud was about the challenge to his prior theories that the existence of war neuroses had produced.
16. Juliet Mitchell makes a similar point, perhaps expanding on Freud's insight. Focusing on trauma from the perspective of the person who experiences it, she says: "This means both that the same event will not always be traumatic for different people, and that the experience of different events, if they are experienced as trauma, will be the same whatever the event and whoever the sufferer." Mitchell also seems to agree with Freud's later ideas about trauma when she says that trauma represents a breach in consciousness: "A trauma, whether physical or psychical, must create a breach in a protective covering of such severity that it cannot be coped with by the usual mechanisms by which we deal with pain or loss. . . . In trauma, we are untimely ripped" (121). See her "Trauma, Recognition, and the Place of Language," in *Diacritics* 28, no. 4 (Winter 1998): 121–133.
17. Fictional psychotherapy interviews in Pat Barker's novels between a character modeled

on William H. Rivers, the British World War I analyst who treated traumatized soldiers including the poet Siegfried Sassoon, demonstrate precisely this intermixture of fantasy with the traumatic battle happening. Her characters suffer PTSD, and again Barker is able to represent the flashbacks and intrusive memories brilliantly. See, for example, *The Eye in the Door* (Penguin, 1993): 67–76, for an example of such an interview. Following pages provide for examples of PTSD, as does also the earlier novel, *Regeneration* (Viking, 1991), where much of the action takes place in Craiglockhart, the military hospital to which soldiers suffering from war neurosis were sent to be treated by Rivers.

18. See for instance the drawn out libel suit between Jeffrey Masson and Janet Malcolm resulting from Malcolm's *New Yorker* essays on Masson's theories about Freud's rejection of his seduction theory. Masson's views can be found in his *The Assault on Truth* (1984). See also Allen Esterson and others on Masson and Freud's seduction theory in *History of the Human Sciences* 11, no. 1 (February 1998): 1–21. See also the detailed research studies by Elizabeth Loftus in her influential *Eyewitness Testimony* (reprint. Cambridge, MA: Harvard University Press, 1996). Loftus shows how inaccurate recollections combined with inappropriate police photo and lineup presentations can cause a witness to create false recollections. Loftus also provides proof that eyewitness testimony is not superior to circumstantial evidence. In addition, the book shows how fallible juries can be. The case histories for the most part describe trials in which eyewitness testimony resulted in the conviction of an innocent person.
19. Courses, like that Ban Wang and I taught in 1997 at Stony Brook (and subsequent ones I taught on trauma and aging), encouraged students to write dissertations using trauma theory. Indeed, our edited collection, *Trauma and Cinema: Cross-Cultural Explorations* (2004) grew out of our 1997 course and includes essays students wrote for the course.
20. See Freud and Breuer, *Studies in Hysteria* (1895) and Freud and Breuer, "On the Theory of Hysterical Attacks" (1892). This latter essay was not published until 1940.
21. See William Connolly, *Neuropolitics: Thinking, Culture, Speed* (2002) in which he details a view of the amygdala as giving certain kinds of meanings. Connolly argues that "meaning" has to be dealt with in a series of increasing levels, rather than as in a binary of thought/no-thought.
22. In his unpublished paper, "Why Trauma Now?" Michael Roth makes several interesting arguments. Most compelling, perhaps, is his noting the intersection of identity politics and literary theory, as these two engage trauma. For Roth, the reason several literary theorists turned to trauma was the increasing concern that deconstruction "was a way of thinking compatible with just about any politics" (16). However, "the traumatized subject . . . was something that theory could connect to" (17). While some of my views differ widely from Roth's (he does not mention possible personal experiences of theorists with trauma itself such as their being involved in ways beyond theory, for instance), his paper is provocative in useful ways.
23. Roth goes on to argue, "Rather than suggesting alternative perspectives in aesthetics, politics or ethics, those inspired by deconstruction were able to show that our habitual perspectives were without foundation, that they deconstructed themselves when looked at intently. . . . For those now *trained* in this area, the question became how to connect a critique of representation and subjectivity with things that happen in the world. How to make it real?" (17).
24. Roth points out that deconstruction is perfectly compatible with "the view that we are not fully present to ourselves and that we represent all our experiences in highly mediated forms" (18).
25. For a thoughtful and astute review of Leys's volume, see Dorian Stuber's essay on the book, in *Bryn Mawr Review of Comparative Literature* 3, no. 2 (Fall 2002). Stuber surveys briefly, like Roth, the interest in trauma arising out of poststructuralism, within

and not necessarily against the linguistic turn, and yet importantly opening up attention to affective states of various kinds. She understands what irritated Leys about Caruth's project—the historian's rigor as against the humanist's logical sloppiness—yet points out, "Ultimately Leys finds herself caught in a contradiction between the ways things are and the way things ought to be; she confused the normal with the normative. Her scrupulously exacting historical examination rests upon ultimately untenable theoretical premises" (2).

26. See, for example, my 1997 monograph *Looking for the Other: Feminism, Film, and the Imperial Gaze* (London and New York: Routledge, 1997).
27. See E. Ann Kaplan and Ban Wang, "Introduction," to our coedited volume, *Trauma and Cinema: Cross-Cultural Explorations* (Hong Kong: Hong Kong University Press, 2003), where we argue this case in some detail.
28. See for example Marianne Hirsch, *Family Frames: Photography, Narrative, and Postmemory* (Cambridge, MA: Harvard University Press, 1997), Dori Laub (1992; 1995) and the work of clinicians such as Ira Brenner in his *Dissociation of Trauma: Theory, Phenomenology, and Technique* (2001). Films like Rea Tajiri's *History and Memory: For Akiko and Takeshi* (1991) or Melissa Hacker's *My Knees Were Jumping: Remembering the Kindertransports* (1997) also testify to children's uncanny awareness of their parents' past traumatic experiences. See chapter 5 for discussion of transgenerational trauma, and my work in progress on this topic.
29. Ruth Leys's careful historical overview, meanwhile, leaves us with a kind of "so what?" response. Her genealogy does not move us forward, but rather puts us into an intellectual paralysis. Her concluding comments can only suggest that if we are suffering from trauma, we should get clinical help—a point unrelated to anything she's argued in the book.
30. While McNally's is a reasoned, careful, and useful survey of studies about trauma within the historical framework of work by Freud and Janet among others, unfortunately his book offers opportunities for die-hard opponents of psychoanalysis, like Frederick Crews, to rehearse their tired, decades long polemics. See Frederick Crews, "The Trauma Trap," *New York Review of Books,* March 11, 2004: 37–40. See also *New York Times* article, "Defying Psychiatric Wisdom: These Skeptics Say 'Prove It,'" March 9, 2004: F1, F6.
31. The issue of whether or not there can be art after Auschwitz has, of course, been one huge, ongoing, debate within Holocaust studies.
32. As will become clear, a few psychologists studying stress have tried to garner evidence about the impact of films about shocking events. But clearly much more research is needed to study such reactions. The problem is the difficulty of undertaking these kinds of study. A vast interview project, such as that undertaken by Professor Martin Hoffman, and discussed below, might contribute something to such understandings. The kind of experimental studies that have been done require a great deal of funding and highly specialized equipment. This however should not deter scholars from attempting to find out more about reactions to media images of extreme suffering, when we know the victims are real people. That is, studying the horror film, as Adam Lowenstein has done, might provide useful information, since one still "knows" somewhere that the images are fictional. In documentary or live television coverage, no matter how mediated, how sensationalized through editing and other visual techniques, we know only too well that the people suffering are living beings like oneself. See Adam Lowenstein, *Shocking Representation: Historical Trauma, National Cinema and the Modern Horror Film* (forthcoming).
33. The psychologist Martin Hoffman early on recognized a phenomenon he called at the time "empathic overarousal" (Hoffman, "Empathy, its Development and Prosocial Implications"). Much later, Charles Figley, as a result of his work with Vietnam veterans, coined the term "secondary traumatization" (see "Catastrophe: An Overview

of Family Reaction," in Figley and McCubbin) to describe the signs and symptoms of traumatization he noticed in the relatives of victims he was working with. Later, he renamed this phenomenon "compassion fatigue" (1995). Subsequently, psychologists coined several different terms for the phenomenon, such a "vicarious traumatization" (the term being used here) (McCann and Pearlman, "Vicarious Traumatization"); secondary traumatic stress (Davies and Frawley, *Training the Adult Survivor of Childhood Sexual Abuse*); secondary wounding or event countertransference (Danieli, "Countertransference, Trauma and Training"; "Countertransference and Trauma: Self-healing and Training Issues"), countertransference reactions and empathic strain (Wilson and Lindy, "Theoretical and Conceptual Foundations of Counter-Transference in Post-Traumatic Therapies"); finally, burnout (Ackerley et al., "Burnout Among Licensed Psychologists"). (List compiled by Tatiana Friedman, working with Martin L. Hoffman.) See for summary of their research over several years, Laura Pearlman and Saakvitne, *Trauma and the Therapist.*

34. See Martin L. Hoffman, "Empathy and the Origins of Vicarious Traumatization in Clinicians," currently being reviewed for publication; and Tatiana Friedman's Ph.D. dissertation, titled "The Role of Empathy in Vicarious Traumatization," and submitted to the Department of Psychology at New York University in May 2001.
35. It is interesting in this context to study the portrayal of the therapist, played by Lorraine Bracco in the successful HBO series *The Sopranos*. Increasingly, as the therapist comes to understand the full extent of Tony Soprano's involvement with murder, so her task becomes more and more difficult. In the 2003 series, the therapist is seen severely traumatized by dealing with Tony. In sessions with her supervising therapist, she confesses to being terrified, to taking to drink and finally to the unprofessional behavior of "judging" Soprano, taking a stand on his kind of work, his kind of life.
36. See also in this connection discussions throughout Pearlman and Saakvitne's *Trauma and the Therapist*, but especially chapters 16–18.
37. An exception, discussed in chapter 4, is Joshua Hirsch, whose paper, "Posttraumatic Cinema and the Holocaust Documentary," I read when considering it for a coedited volume as I was myself researching vicarious traumatization. See Hirsch.

Chapter 2 Memory as Testimony in World War II

1. See Janet Walker's essay, "The Vicissitudes of Traumatic Memory and the Postmodern History Film," in *Trauma and Cinema: Cross-Cultural Explorations,* ed. E. Ann Kaplan and Ban Wang (Hong Kong: Hong Kong University Press, 2004): 125–144. Talking of the film *Saving Private Ryan,* Walker notes, "Memory is inherently unstable. Moreover, the film is a fictionalization. . . . [T]he particular incidents depicted do not reflect on any one real incident nor do the bit players on the beach correspond to certain individuals. The distance between past actions and present memory widens" (134). Walker goes on to ask what are the implications of understanding memory as reconstructive and variable? "If our purchase on traumatic memory owes more to the apt rendition of its altered state than to its literal correspondence to the past, how far does the film takes its project to render the traumatic mindscape?" (134). Walker quotes Ian Hacking, saying that even when past actions are remembered, they may be remembered differently, i.e., "Old action under new descriptions may be re-experienced in memory. When we remember what we did, or what other people did, we may also rethink, redescribe, and refeel the past. . . . As we change our understanding and sensibility, the past becomes filled with intentional actions that, in a certain sense, were not there when they were performed" (133).
2. Gobodo-Madikizela also quotes Primo Levi noting that "human memory is a marvelous but deceptive tool" (86). She also notes that Eli Wiesel too "speaks about the chasm between what is remembered and how it is retold" (n.164).

3. Acknowledging that the "vicissitudes of memory" is now *de rigueur* in trauma studies. Leigh Gilmore quotes Janice Haaken, *Pillar of Salt: Gender, Memory and the Perils of Looking Back* (New Brunswick, NJ: Rutgers University Press, 1998) cautioning against literalizing every aspect of a report of sexual violence, since such a report "necessarily and appropriately combines fantasy with memory. . . . Haaken is less concerned with whether any particular memory is true or false than with the way that memory functions in a therapeutic narrative about sexuality" (Gilmore 26).
4. While Walker here is concerned with pitting realistic character stories against those using other than realist cinematic modes, such issues are not central to my discussion. I will address the different kinds of linguistic and narrational strategies used by my three authors, but the binarism that Walker sets up actually does not work for my texts. Kofman's text offers as powerful an emotional rendering of trauma as anything I have read, and yet the style is clear, simple, "realist" narration. It's possible that Freud's *Moses* and Duras's *The War* (*La Douleur*) do provide examples of the fragmentation and certainly of the influence of fantasy, but this does not make their representation of traumatic memory more powerful than Kofman's. It is rather that the authors find varying strategies through which to communicate what the traumatic events mean to them emotionally.
5. I am reminded of the "shattered subjects" whom Suzette Henke (1998) studied: These were all women writers who, in their sixties or so began to recall sexual traumas that had marked them for life but that had been "forgotten" until the women's middle-age. Freud too had "forgotten" the humiliations that Nazi anti-Semitism reevoked but that somehow remained, waiting to be written about, searching for a witness, where (as Dori Laub argues) there had been none before (Laub, "Truth and Testimony" 65–67).
6. I had likewise apparently "forgotten" about my war experiences that in fact remained marked on my body into adulthood.
7. I use the term in Dominick LaCapra's sense, as he develops it (in opposition to "acting out") in his *Writing History, Writing Trauma* (2001). LaCapra uses Freud's concepts of mourning and melancholia together with Walter Benjamin's *Erlebnis* and *Erfahrung* to construct his own concepts. See chapter 1: 1–42.
8. I will deal with the crucial topic of giving testimony, seeking a witness and being a witness in a later chapter. But for now, let me note Dori Laub's important contributions to theorizing witnessing in the senses I am working with in this book. See Laub, "Truth and Testimony," in *Trauma: Explorations in Memory,* ed. Cathy Caruth (Baltimore: The Johns Hopkins University Press, 1995): 61–75. Laub talks of a "degree of unconscious witnessing that would not find its voice or its expression during the event," and of how essential it is "for this narrative that *could not be articulated* to be *told,* to be *transmitted,* to be *heard*" (68–69). His interviews with Holocaust survivors enable the survivors to bear witness. Trauma victims like Kofman, who also had no witness to her wartime suffering, seek such witnesses through writing.
9. At the start of the section for 1934 in *The Diary of Sigmund Freud: 1929–1939 (A Record of the Final Decade)* (1992), there is a quotation from a letter by Freud to Arnold Zweig. "Faced with the new persecution, one asks oneself again how the Jews have come to be what they are and why they have attracted this undying hatred. I soon discovered the formula: Moses created the Jews" (165). Freud was finishing what he called in 1934 a historical *novel, The Man Moses.* This title is significant for the text that he continued to work on and that we know as *Moses and Monotheism* in regard to any claims for historical veracity. While this level of things does not concern me here, it is important to distinguish psychic from factual "truth." See on this point A. L. Kroeber's contemporary reviews of *Moses* (1920, 1939) reprinted in *Sigmund Freud: Critical Assessments,* ed. Laurence Spurling (1989).
10. Page numbers are taken from the following edition: *Moses and Monotheism,* trans.

Katherine Jones (New York: Vintage Books, 1939). At the start, Freud is anxious about denying a people "the man whom it praises as the greatest of his sons," and sees this as even worse if one is a Jew. He begins part 2 with the same hesitations, doubting his qualifications for his task. He hints that he's only solved part of the whole and not the most important part, and attributes this to "conflict of motives," without spelling these out. Can we infer rising Nazism, increasing anti-Semitism, unconscious wish to escape from being a Jew in this context? Soon he has to agree that his first argument "has failed again." After more text, he seems to gain headway, but then pulls back and thinks he needs more proof. At the start of part 4, again he worries about the validity of his argument, he's uncertain again. At the end of part 4, claims he is vanquished, the thread is broken off, the leads go nowhere. By part 6, he agrees that his argument is open to criticism but he goes on nevertheless. On page 63, he says he would be left uncertain, but now feels better having some expert observers to rely on. He thinks he has come to an end, on p. 65, but we know he will not have in fact. Indeed, we come upon the third and final part of the book, begun tentatively in March 1938 while the family was still tenuously in Vienna, and then taken up again in the safer climate of London in June 1938. And here it is that Freud introduces his theories of trauma, as if unconsciously recognizing his traumatized state.

11. See *The Diary of Sigmund Freud* (1992), which details the movements of Freud and his family from 1934 to 1939, with excerpts from letters and commentary situating Freud's writings.
12. See *Diary of Sigmund Freud.*
13. See discussion of Freud's *Moses and Monotheism* in Cathy Caruth, *Unclaimed Experience: Trauma, Narrative, and History* (New Haven: Yale University Press, 1986): 67–71. Caruth makes some similar arguments, if with different ends in mind. I use *Moses* to suggest a theory of genre as traumatic cultural symptom. In chapter 3, I will argue that Hollywood melodramas may function like a traumatic symptom, reflecting cultural crisis in their anxious repetition, their obsessive return to the same themes, as happens also in individual trauma.
14. The volume called *La Douleur* contains three narratives, the last one having two separate parts. In what follows, I only discuss the first text, with the title of the volume, that is "The War," because that text alone is the one that Duras's claims not to have recalled writing and that seems to me interesting precisely because of that, and because of its style, which is that of being inside a panic attack. The others have short notes before them that show that Duras recalls writing them, and has chosen for various reasons not to publish them before 1985.
15. It is well known that Robert L. stands for Robert Antelme, Duras's first husband. D. is Dionys Mascolo, who was a friend of Antelme.
16. I should note here that this theme of Duras's face "falling apart" recurs in her later work, at least twice that I know of. At the beginning of *L'Amant*, Duras mentions seeing her face change and age, becoming Other; and in *C'est Tout,* her last text, there is a powerful passage rather like this one, of Duras's face "falling apart," she has no face, etc. Obviously, these passages describe a dissolution of the subject into fear; the face is perhaps the part of the body we most often look at in the mirror; it thus symbolizes (or can symbolize) one's identity. Passages about the face falling apart then suggest Duras's attempt to express the collapse of identity into fear, her being becoming just fear, and nothing else.
17. Reading these words, it's hard not to think of 9/11. I do not intend to equate 9/11 and the Holocaust—far from it. But the structure of the horrors appears parallel as one reads Duras's powerful account. The crashing into the Twin Towers known to be full of people using a plane full of people as the weapon parallels in terms of the thought of the perpetrators the deliberate and immediate annihilation of innocent humans by

fire. And the production of a crematorium of huge dimensions, such as the Nazis daily produced over years.

18. It is interesting that Duras uses the word "share" here in relation to a crime. Since, in a way, I am also asking that we find modalities for sharing the results of a crime—results that appear in the form of trauma.
19. Once having written the book, Antelme evidently never again wanted to speak about what he suffered and saw in the camps. As we'll see below, Antelme provides a link between Duras and Kofman, in that Kofman is powerfully affected by Antelme's book.
20. The preoccupation with humanity's capacity for evil opens up a can of worms beyond my specific concerns. Claude Lanzmann, for instance, scorns this kind of concern as avoiding fully confronting the abyss between a search for causes for events like the Holocaust (such as humanity's evil) and the events themselves. This kind of thinking amounts for Lanzmann to an "obscenity of understanding." See his essay, "The Obscenity of Understanding," in Caruth, *Trauma* 200–220.
21. As her powerful text *Paroles Suffoquées* shows, Kofman was profoundly affected by Antelme's *L'Espèce humaine*, so much so that it probably inspired her to write *Rue Ordener, Rue Labat*, chapter 5 of *Paroles* (43–75). Earlier in the text, Kofman explicitly mentions Duras's text, *La Maladie de la Mort* (36). Clearly, Duras's mental landscape must have resonated with Kofman, despite different concerns, as I note below.
22. As Steve Edwin notes in his unpublished manuscript, "Cultural Healing: Gender, Race, and Trauma in Literatures of the Americas," in her *Smothered Words* (the translation of *Paroles Suffoquées*), Kofman remarks how Antelme's *L'Espèce Humaine* "can make us hear the silence of those who could not speak."
23. In his essay "'Impossible' Professions: Sarah Kofman, Witnessing, and the Social Depth of Trauma," Steve Edwin makes a similar point. He argues (from perusing the fragmentary autobiographical notes in Kofman's work over the years) that "Kofman was yearning to tell her life story while hesitating at the edge of a chasm, writing, it would seem, without being able to write." See Edwin in *Between the Psyche and the Social*, coedited with Kelly Oliver (Lanham, MD: Rowman and Littlefield, 2002): 123–148.
24. White was suffering from terminal cancer when he sat down to write his extraordinary memoir, "Too Close to the Bone." It was only as he felt himself close to death that he could begin to work through the trauma of the accidental death of one of his twin sisters—a death for which he (in his child's mind and without reason) felt guilty. Unfortunately, he was unable to complete the work before his illness tragically took him away in the prime of life. Extreme illness in a young person, it seems, can produce the same impetus to work a trauma through as does arriving at middle or old age.
25. Steve Edwin points to a moment in Kofman's *Paroles Suffoquées (Smothered Words)* where Kofman says one must speak "without power," that is, she says, "without allowing language, too powerful, sovereign, to master the most aporetic situation, absolute powerlessness and utter distress, to enclose it in the clarity and happiness of daylight (English translation 10). This suggests something of what I am trying to say about the way trauma emerges in this text's clear language.
26. Kelly Oliver offers a different and interesting alternate interpretation in her essay, "Sarah Kofman's Queasy Stomach and the Riddle of the Paternal Law," in Deutscher and Oliver. In reflecting on the apparent paradox in the text—Kofman's dependency and need for her mother, and yet her identification with her rabbi father, and her ongoing search for philosophical fathers perhaps to replace her lost birth-father—Oliver makes an interesting suggestion, namely that instead of reading the memoir as a struggle between two mothers, we should read it as the two mothers representing the maternal and the paternal axes—that is, Kofman's mother comes to represent and

uphold the paternal Judaic law, while Mémé, the substitute mother, represents the maternal for Kofman. She enigmatically mixes maternal and paternal functions (Oliver 188).

27. I want to thank Steve Edwin, whose paper on Kofman I have referred to above, for first reminding me of this section of *Rue Ordener, Rue Labat* in a presentation in a class on "The Politics and Aesthetics of Trauma" that I taught at Stony Brook.
28. Kelly Oliver, one of the authors who sees what Kofman's work can bring to life, argues persuasively, I think, that through her identification with Nietzsche (Oliver reminds us that Kofman wrote several books on Nietzsche) and with her philosophical fathers, Kofman created "her own fantastic genealogy, her own family romance, through which she attempts to give birth to herself" (Deutscher and Oliver 183).
29. Edwin also discusses the possible and complicated reasons for Kofman's suicide so soon after finally giving voice to her painful wartime experiences. See essay referred to above.
30. This is a point I will return to later in discussing the varied impacts of testimony and witnessing.

Chapter 3 Melodrama and Trauma

1. See Abraham and Torok. I return in chapter 5 to essays in Rand's translation and edited collection of Abraham and Torok's innovative research.
2. This is taken from a summary of the paper provided for the conference. Many other papers addressed issues having to do with collective trauma and cultural context, especially in the working group on "Individual and Collective Trauma: Reality, Myth, Metaphor?" Dori Laub organized a Working Group on "From Genocide to Terrorism: The Outcome of Collective Grandiose Omnipotence." Several speakers were concerned with the phenomenon of the transmission of trauma across generations; Ira Brenner, for example, talked on "Trauma, Transmission and Time," and Annette Streeck-Fischer, in her paper "What is Transmission of Trauma?" discussed a case history that involved a young girl with inexplicable symptoms. Streeck-Fischer concludes, "In the case of the young woman A, not only the ghosts of the familial past [her parents suffered anti-Semitism in the Soviet Union, wanted to emigrate to Israel but ended up in Germany, ed.], but also the past history of Jewish persecution and the Holocaust was involved. Thus it was almost impossible to find any space beyond this entanglement."
3. In chapter 5, where the focus is different, I address a related theory regarding transmission of catastrophes, developed by Nicholas Abraham and Maria Torok building on Freud's metapsychology and his ideas in *Moses*. Abraham discusses ways in which the falsification and disregard of the past breeds the phantomatic return of shameful secrets not only in individuals but also for entire nations.
4. In his *Representing the Holocaust: History, Theory, Trauma* (Ithaca, NY: Cornell University Press, 1994), Dominick La Capra quotes Eric Santer in *Probing the Limits of Representation: Nazism and the "Final Solution,"* ed. Saul Friedlander (Cambridge, MA: Harvard University Press, 1992) developing a point similar to mine: "By narrative fetishism I mean the construction and deployment of a narrative consciously or unconsciously designed to expunge the traces of the trauma or loss that called that narrative into being in the first place. . . . [It] is the way an inability or refusal to mourn employs traumatic events; it is a strategy of undoing, in fantasy, the need for mourning by simulating a condition of intactness, typically by situating the site and origin of loss elsewhere" (Santner, "History beyond the Pleasure Principle: Some Thoughts on the Representation of Trauma" in Friedlander 143–154; here cited from 144).
5. This seems an exaggerated fear, and was perhaps meant only polemically. At the most recent Society for Cinema and Media Studies conference, there was not one panel on

trauma. While it's true that a couple of books on trauma and cinema have appeared or are in process, far more books on other topics in screen studies are being published. But Radstone's other worries that I address in what follows are valuable.

6. Radstone's in-progress book, *On Memory and Confession,* explores these very questions.
7. See Lauren Berlant's "Poor Eliza" essay, in *American Literature* 70, no. 3 (September 1998): 635–668. Berlant argues that the "ravenous yearning for social change" has installed the pleasures of entertainment instead of politics. Sentimental structures, she argues, have been "deployed mainly by the culturally privileged to humanize those very subjects who are also, and at the same time, reduced to cliché within the reigning regimes of entitlement or value" (636).
8. For detailed discussion of traumatic memory and scientific experiments designed to test psychoanalytic theories about dissociation and forgetting, see Richard J. McNally, *Remembering Trauma* (2003). McNally is mainly concerned to examine psychobiological claims for recovered memories, especially regarding sexual child abuse, and to critique the concept of dissociation or "splitting," which many trauma theorists accept without question. Since the model I am using relegates pure splitting to the very rare case, McNally's persuasive arguments need not be rehearsed here. My model involves a process of forgetting rather than dissociation. This forgetting means that the traumatic event is relegated to a part of consciousness but is not readily available to cognition. It therefore may be worked on by fantasies and at an appropriate time, recalled in its mixture of reality and fantasy.
9. See films such as *Memento, The Eternal Sunshine of the Spotless Mind,* and *Paycheck.* I return to the issue of "forgetting" in these films in the epilogue.
10. See McNally, chapter 7 for full discussion of, and debates about, traumatic amnesia in current psychological and psychoanalytic research.
11. Leff does not explain, so I can only infer that psychoanalysis still carried the stigma of prying into sexuality, and of the improper investigation of people's most intimate spheres.
12. Leff quotes Selznick in a note to Karl Menninger saying that *Since You Went Away* contained "a sequence that I personally conceived and wrote in the hope that it would have a value in making the American public aware of the work being done by psychiatrists to rebuild men shaken by their war experiences" (116).
13. Interestingly, Selznick at this point added two Americans to the team: his own psychiatrist, May Romm, and Eileen Johnston, a college graduate in psychology. Romm cut the dream sequence because of its sexual aspects, and Hitchcock would not meet with her, perhaps because he was afraid that she would "read" some of his neuroses! Studio notes show that there were worries from the psychoanalytic community. Karl Menninger, director of the now famous Menninger Institute, had helped Selznick with *Since You Went Away,* but worried about the image of psychoanalysts in the asylum in the film—and especially the image of the director Dr. Murchison as maladjusted if not mad—this despite the fact that Dr. Petersen's (Ingrid Bergman) own psychiatrist, Dr. Brulov, ends up doing a "successful" dream analysis and ultimately helps cure the hero.
14. This is *not* to deny a close link between dreams and trauma. Indeed, nightmares replaying a traumatic situation often offer insights into an event that the dreamer may have repressed, or that may never have fully entered into consciousness. For interesting discussion of trauma and dreams, and observations about the lack of attention to dreams in much trauma theory, see Deidre Barrett, ed., *Trauma and Dreams.*
15. In chapter 6 of the *Interpretation,* Freud says: "Suppose I have a picture-puzzle, a rebus, in front of me. It depicts a house with a boat on its roof, a single letter of the alphabet, the figure of a running man whose head has been conjured away . . . obviously, we can only form a proper judgement of the rebus if we put aside criticisms such as these of the whole composition and its parts and if, instead, we try to replace

each separate element by a syllable or word that can be represented by that element in some way or other" (Avon Books, 312). That Selznick/Hitchcock had this very page in mind is clear in the following dream analysis in which Dr. Brulov indeed assigns to each separate dream element a particular meaning.

16. Very interesting here is the similarity of this freezing of the traumatic image to the routine Hollywood "freezing" of woman's image. Women too according to feminist film theorists function as castrated (traumatic) object in the male unconscious, as Laura Mulvey argued (see "Visual Pleasure and Narrative Cinema"). In such moments, then, woman evokes trauma. I'll return to this in discussing gender relations in regard to the hero's traumatic attacks in the film.
17. Visuality is closely linked to trauma. The more visually alert a person happens to be, the greater likelihood of overwhelming events being registered in visual terms and the person susceptible to triggering visual elements in the world.

Chapter 4 Vicarious Trauma and "Empty" Empathy

1. It is interesting to note, as I write in 2003 and 2004, how much attention is now being given to the horrors of war and role of photography in this, the most recent of which are the already notorious photographs from Abu Ghraib prison. Chris Hedges, a newspaper reporter, has written a book, *What Every Person Should Know about War* (London and New York: Free Press, 2003), that basically details the pain, suffering, and traumatic impact of war on individual soldiers. He intends it to turn young people away from signing up for the military but he got into trouble when voicing such sentiments at a graduation ceremony. Meanwhile, numerous books criticizing the Bush administration's handling of the war have appeared or are about to appear.
2. Many, like Richard McNally (2000), consider dissociation unproven, but I view it as a possible if rare occurrence. The problem with discussions of dissociation, including those in McNally's thorough review of psychological experiments testing the phenomenon, is the lack of clarity about what exactly has been dissociated and what cannot be recalled.
3. In regard to one trauma situation triggering a prior one, see article, "The Quest to Forget" by Robin Marantz Henig (*New York Times Magazine,* April 4, 2004: 32–37). This article raises interesting and complex questions about trauma and subjectivity that seem related to an April 2004 film, *Eternal Sunshine of the Spotless Mind,* but for my purposes here it is the trauma victim's thoughts at the moment of her accident that is pertinent. The article describes three thoughts the victim reported, of which the third was "of a different trauma, eight years earlier; when driving home one night, she was sitting at a red light and found herself confronted by an armed drug addict, who forced his way into her car." (32). Significant as well is the victim's ready knowledge about trauma and its workings, supporting views that discussions of trauma are prevalent in United States culture today. I return to these thoughts in the epilogue.
4. Martin Hoffman mentions that the degree of vividness does indeed contribute to the therapist's response. See his unpublished paper (11–12).
5. Actual accounts would be extremely difficult to obtain (clinicians would have had to tape-record sessions, highly unusual if not unethical).
6. It would make sense that some ways of telling would evoke for the clinician a voyeuristic position, which would make the clinician uncomfortable and could, almost in an effort to reduce the voyeurism, produce more secondary symptoms. By voyeuristic position, I mean a position that suggests looking in on the events as the patient speaks with some sort of pleasure. An account of sexual abuse, for instance, if told in a certain way, might evoke unwanted sexual feelings in the clinician; an account of war atrocities might evoke aggressive impulses. Certainly, the Abu Ghraib prison

photographs offer an excellent example of voyeuristic war images. But I am not addressing voyeurism as such here.

7. In my piece "Melodrama, Cinema, and Trauma" (*Screen* 2001), I briefly listed these positions, without going into detail. Unfortunately, I may have left the impression that there was an implicit value judgment, such that the sensational or voyeuristic positions were "lower" on some scale in which "witnessing" came out on top. This sort of judgment sounds unhappily like screen studies' 1970s "grading" of films according to their ideological complicity, resistances, or outright revolutionary appeal. In our old model, the avant-garde, experimental film was often valued over classical commercial cinema. Such a "grading" is too simplistic and conceals the benefits that can accrue from various kinds of films. While feminists and others have abandoned such valuations in our work on melodrama, horror, and other genres, it can seem to return in this trauma study. Most often, in practice the borders between the types of film are blurred. Directors do not usually stay within one category. I set up the distinctions for purposes of clarity and argument, rather than to make a rigid taxonomy. While my choice of films for the "witnessing" category might appear to repeat the old high/low binary, in fact the films I choose respect and work out from classical Hollywood genres, as will be clear. And while I showed how Hitchcock's *Spellbound* indeed ended with closure, I tried to indicate the value of the film's dealing with psychoanalysis and presenting it to the American public and the value of recognizing the horror of war beneath the film's surface.
8. See also Patrick Gannon (1979) for summary of research on stress in the laboratory.
9. Hirsch also found, and discussed, Lazarus's and Horowitz's research in his essay referred to.
10. Those of us born just before or during World War II are most likely all similarly marked by such images of the camp victims. I know I was. My mother evidently hurried her children out of movie theaters in postwar England when newsreel footage of the camps was shown, but once I saw Resnais's *Night and Fog* (1955), I have ever since been haunted by the heaps of bodies made into objects, the skeletal figures that barely seemed human anymore, that Hirsch goes on to detail as part of what creates the vicarious traumatic impact. Resnais's *Night and Fog* for me as for Hirsch was and still is almost unbearable to watch. It brought back my childhood shock at what people could do to people—a shock that shattered forever my faith in a secure world in which one could count on kindness. Even now, my stomach wretches at the thought of what the camp victims endured, and which, as we saw earlier, Marguerite Duras so vividly details in describing her husband's return from a camp barely more than a corpse.
11. As this book goes to press, Susan Sontag has published a new book on photography, *Regarding the Pain of Others* (New York: Farrar, Straus and Giroux, 2003), in which she partly revises arguments in her 1977 *On Photography* in regard to the proliferation of images in modernity having a deadening effect. See my later discussion about war photography. I return to Sontag at the end of the chapter.
12. See debates about Claude Lanzmann's film *Shoah*, often compared to Steven Spielberg's *Schindler's List* by, for example Dominck LaCapra, Miriam Hansen, and Shoshana Felman. Joshua Hirsch, in "Post-Traumatic Cinema," also has much to say about Holocaust films, and especially interesting is his discussion of *Night and Fog*.
13. Especially in Holocaust studies, debates have raged about whether or not the holocaust can be represented, with Adorno's famous statement that there could be no poetry after Auschwitz (later modified) at the center of discussions. Cf. Theodor Adorno, *Negative Dialectics*, trans. E. B. Ashton (New York: Continuum, 1973): 360–370. Adorno later qualified his famous dictum in this volume, namely that "after Auschwitz, it is no longer possible to write poems," by noting that "literature must

resist this verdict." See *The Essential Frankfurt School Reader* (New York: Continuum, 1982): 312, 318. Shoshana Felman's discussion, "Education and Crisis" in her volume coedited with Dori Laub, *Testimony* (1992), usefully analyzes issues relating to the holocaust and representation. See also Michael Rothberg's excellent discussion of Adorno, "Modernism 'After Auschwitz,'" in his *Traumatic Realism: The Demands of Holocaust Representation* (Minneapolis: University of Minnesota Press, 2000): 25–58.

14. Here I have in mind not only that my location made it difficult to videotape CNN coverage, but also the difficulty of being able to focus on images in detail since there were so many. Here I agree with Susan Sontag's implied suggestion (*Regarding the Pain* 104–106) that the still photograph can accrue more power than the rapidly changing moving images on television. However that may be, it seemed more productive for me to work with the also highly mediated and selected *New York Times* images, many of which were ones I had seen on CNN.
15. The Lynch case provoked discussion of so-called "war spin." See BBC News report, "War Spin: Saving Private Lynch Story 'Flawed,'" by John Kampfner, broadcast on BBC Two, Sunday, May 18, 2003, at 1915 BST. It can be found online at *http://news.bbc.co.uk*. Kampfner notes, "The American strategy was to ensure the right television footage by using embedded reporters and images from their own cameras, editing the film themselves. The Pentagon had been influenced by Hollywood producers of reality television and action movies, notably the man behind *Black Hawk Down*, Jerry Bruckheimer."
16. As readers know, the situation in Iraq in the year following the coverage discussed here continued to deteriorate. By March 2004, guerilla attacks on American soldiers had become increasingly routine and sophisticated. But April 1 saw perhaps the most shocking of attacks in that perpetrators were not content just to kill the Americans, but proceeded to mutilate the bodies, burn them, and then hang them up on telephone poles for all to see. Further, Iraqis in the area celebrated these deaths and mutilations in front of the bodies. Once again, I withdrew from the pictures I saw, since the juxtaposition of horrible treatment of corpses and enthusiastic celebration was too much to bear, regardless of fault or blame. The horror was of such a magnitude that journalists evidently debated which images to show, much as they had debated showing people jumping from the Twin Towers on 9/11. An article by Bill Carter and Jacques Steinberg, "To Portray the Horror, News Media Agonize," accompanied the images. See the *New York Times*, Thursday, April 1, 2002: A12. The article notes that "CNN, Fox News, and NBC News decided to avoid the most graphic images. 'I think we can convey the horror of this despicable act while being sensitive to our viewers,' said Steve Capus, the executive vice president of NBC's 'Nightly News.'"
17. See "Death on the Front Page," by Martha A. Sandweiss, *New York Times*, April 4, 2004, "Week In Review." Weiss is partly responding to the media choosing not to show graphic images of the mutilation of Americans referred to earlier. She says, "So it is a bit of a paradox that while photographers can now finally capture the fury and pace of warfare, few are getting the chance to do so. The news media has been reluctant to publish images of death in Iraq and the Bush administration has done its best to hamper photographers, even banning photographs of body bags and coffins." This is why the 2004 shocking images of soldiers' sexually and in other ways abusing Iraqi prisoners in Abu Ghraib created such a strong reaction. The easy release of these images was enabled by new digital technologies. Soldiers regularly sent the images to one another via the computer, until one soldier forwarded them to a commander.

CHAPTER 5 "TRANSLATING" TRAUMA IN POSTCOLONIAL CONTEXTS

1. Ching-Ling Wo, a comparative literature graduate student at Stony Brook who briefly joined the HISB ongoing Seminar on Transmission of Cultures, pointed out the hitherto exploitative role of "embodied translators" who proliferated in the eighteenth century, and "who might include Defoe's *Consolidator* (1705) and Eliza Haywood's *Adventures of Evoaai* (1736)—a tale that pretends to be translated from the Adamic language by a Chinese translator." Wo also mentioned the many Oriental Observer figures in epistolary satires by European authors "pretending to be foreign who compare Western customs to their native customs . . . , e.g. a Turk in Marana's *Turkish Spy* (1684), a Persian in *Lettres Persanes* (1721), and a Chinese in Goldsmith's *The Citizen of the World* (1762)." Wo notes how "some versions of hybridity are erased from public memory while others participate in the formation of capitalist modernity by becoming part of a situation that coordinates differences" (Wo, e-mail memo to me, April 23, 2002).
2. Nichols here references Trinh T. Minh-ha's title to her influential volume, *Woman, Native, Other* (Bloomington: Indiana University Press, 1989).
3. What Bill Nichols has to say about the anthropological unconscious may apply equally to scholars and critics. Regarding anthropology, Nichols notes, "Among other things, this anthropological unconscious might contain: whiteness, maleness, and . . . the body of the observer; the experiential; the narrative conventions and forms of other cultures; the canonical conventions of western narrative; the full indexical particularity of the image and its emotional impact; the erotics of the gaze . . . etc." (Nichols, "The Ethnographer's Tale" 32).
4. For more details about experiences in World War II England, see my "Performing Trauma: On the Border of Fiction and Autobiography," *Women and Performance,* nos. 19–20 (April 1998): 33–55. See also my essay on "Transgenerational 'Haunting' and Trauma: Culture and the Unconscious in Two Case Studies," presented in London at the "Culture and the Unconscious 2" Conference, July 2004.
5. Indeed, more than one scholar referred to Western criticism of Chinese films as yet another example of "colonizing"—a view that was then actively debated.
6. See research by Daniel Stern in his *The Interpersonal World of the Infant* (New York: Basic Books, 1985), and Jessica Benjamin, *The Bonds of Love* (New York: Pantheon, 1988).
7. Indeed, reactions to a film that I showed at a conference in Bellagio (August 2003) provided an excellent example of such a dialogue. While I had chosen the film because of its interesting issues about translation on many levels, one First Nations conference member found the film extremely offensive to her and her people. I had been totally unaware that the film could be so offensive before I got this response. It changed my view of the film, it has made me uncertain as to whether I should show the film in the future, and it has resulted in my leaving that film out of this version of my paper.
8. One may well ask in whose interest is it to dwell on traumatic residues of cross-cultural trauma. Sneja Gunew once pointed out an interesting juxtaposition of styles and themes in transcultural work. She alluded to the varying kinds of "performance" that scholars and artists adopt at academic conferences, and referred to one case where "a theoretical paper that looked at 'mourning' and 'melancholia' in psychoanalytical analyses of trauma associated with First Nations and colonialist encounters, was followed by a First Nations Artist and playwright." He spoke about his postmodern encounters with a theater group based in Venice, who staged his play set on a First Nations reservation (Gunew, Transculturalisms Web site, at http://transculturalisms.arts.ubc.ca).
9. See Mary Louise Pratt, *Imperial Eyes: Travel Writing and Transculturation* (London and New York: Routledge, 1992), especially 6–7.

10. The Revolutionary War provides examples of both kinds of contact. See Mary Jemison's eighteenth-century account of her experiences, and Susan Scheckel's *The Insistence of the Indian* (1998).
11. There is a good deal of psychoanalytic research on this phenomenon of transgenerational trauma. But see, for example, Ira Brenner, "Intergenerational Transmission of Trauma," in his *Dissociation of Trauma* (2001): 91–104; and Annette Streeck-Fischer, "What Is Transmission of Trauma?," paper read at the Trauma Research Networking Conference, Wiesbaden, Germany, June 2002.
12. Phantoms appear in films about indigenous conflict and suffering. See the mysterious ways in which the young girls, almost dying of thirst in the Australian desert during their escape from a government school in *Rabbit-Proof Fence,* are revived by indigenous revenants. More recently, in *Hidalgo,* the protagonist, once again dying in the desert, is saved by phantoms who silently appear to him.
13. In 1983, Eddie Mabo filed a groundbreaking land rights claim. After years of litigation, his claim was honored by the highest court in 1992, and in 1993 the groundbreaking Native Title Act was passed. Subsequent legislation sought to mitigate the gains, but nevertheless the case set an irrevocable precedent that Aborigines can claim land in certain contexts.
14. Anthropologists have sometimes theorized the impossibility of knowing the Other, as well as the phenomenon of succumbing to indigenization. Readings (1992) made the most dramatic argument yet about the impossibility of knowing the other in regard to Herzog's film. He reads *Where the Green Ants Dream* as illustrating the incommensurable difference between the Aborigines and white Australians. Using Jean-François Lyotard's concept of *le différend* to make his point, Readings argues that, from this extreme philosophical position, it is impossible for white Westerners to "know" the Aborigines. An implacable, impenetrable Otherness pertains to them, and Readings claims it would be desecration even to term the Aborigines "human," since this concept is flooded with harmful Western Enlightenment concepts.
15. Herzog was lucky to get Wandjuk Marika and Roy Marika, who are Aboriginal artists, to play the roles of Miliritbi and Dayipu, Aboriginal leaders of the sit-in in his film. These indigenous people bring a dignity and grace to the film that could not have been achieved any other way. Indeed, they make the film worth watching, both because of their superb acting, but also because of the irony and subtle humor they communicate. It is to Herzog's credit that he could get the cooperation of these men and their group for his film. It would seem that they contributed to the script, but I have been unable to date to find much documentation about the film.
16. Another artist of Herzog's generation, Lothar Baumgarten, has likewise been for years haunted by the violence of what Western civilization has done to indigenous cultures. A former student of Joseph Beuys, Baumgarten represented Germany at the 1984 Venice Bienale and "has been known since the late 1970s for scarring the names of vanished or vanishing North and South American tribes across the walls, and occasionally the floors, of museums and galleries" (Roberta Smith, *New York Times,* Friday, September 5, 2003: E29). In 1977, Baumgarten's film *Origin of the Night: Amazon Cosmos,* appeared, but significantly, this was not filmed in the Amazon but near the artist's home in the Rhein-Walder (forests along the Rhine). Baumgarten was perhaps seeking to "purify" his homeland, and its destruction of nature through recreating the Amazon and the Tupi Indians on the Rhine.
17. Perhaps Herzog was unconsciously influenced by Leni Riefenstahl's famous photos of the Nuba people, whom Riefenstahl similarly exoticizes. But Herzog's larger interest is far different from what I understand Riefenstahl's to be; that is, Herzog was, in a sense, "going native" in his own culture by finding himself the "Other" of at least his parents' Germany. As Ban Wang commented, radical and reflective intellectuals (like Herzog) may be seen as the "Other" of dominant Western culture.

18. As readers will know, *Broken Arrow* (1950), starring James Stewart, introduced less ugly images of Native Americans, and included a rare romance between the white hero and a young Native American woman (she has to die, however, before the film ends). *Little Big Man* later for the first time showed Custer's Last Stand from the Native American point of view. *Dances with Wolves* builds on this more progressive tradition.
19. Costner and Mary McDonnell, who plays Stands with Fist, learned to speak Lakota, one of several Sioux dialects, and so did many of the Indian actors who belonged to tribes other than the Sioux. See Kelvin Caddies, *Kevin Costner: Prince of Hollywood* (London: Plexus, 1992): 81.
20. It's significant that the woman turns out to really be white—as if Costner unconsciously fears that it would be too much for the United States audience to encounter an actual love affair between a genuine Native American and a white man. We see here why the film is still very much bound by Hollywood codes, however progressive.
21. So while it is true, in Ebert's words again, that "by allowing the Sioux to speak in their own tongue, by entering their villages and observing their ways, the film sees them as people, not as whooping savages in the sights of an Army rifle," yet it offers no hope of white Americans and Native Americans living together within the geographic space we know as the United States.
22. See Clifford Geertz, *Local Knowledges: Further Essays in Interpretive Anthropology* (New York: Basic Books, 1983); and James Clifford, *The Predicament of Culture: Twentieth-Century Ethnography, Literature, and Art* (Cambridge, MA: Harvard University Press, 1988).
23. It's yet another version of the eighteenth-century "noble savage" idea seen in Herzog's and Costner's images of indigenous peoples, in which they bemoan the loss of "purity" that would redeem white people and that in fact is not of much use to the peoples themselves.
24. See Robert C. Young, *Postcolonialism: An Introduction* (New York and London: Routledge, 2001). And see also his earlier *Colonial Desire: Hybridity in Theory, Culture, and Race* (New York and London: Routledge, 1995).
25. In June 2003, according to a *New York Times* article, people gathered in New Town, North Dakota, to celebrate the day Custer "was whipped at Little Big Horn . . . and where a Nez Percé guide who led Lewis and Clark over the Bitterroot Mountains is remembered by his native name, which means "Furnishes White Men with Brains" (*New York Times,* Sunday, June 15, 2003: 1–16). The article discusses the ways in which Indian tribes, like the Mandans, helped Lewis and Clark survive only later to have white Americans return to drown their "old" town and flood their land by building a dam. "It is time, the Indians say, to tell their own story of Lewis and Clark, an epic about Indians bailing out whites, showing them where to go, what to eat, whom to avoid along the way, and how to get back home in one piece" (16).
26. Obviously, arguments have gotten to a very complex stage. But from what knowledge I have from seeing indigenous films and reading Native American novels (such as those by Louise Erdrich), it seems to me that people are deeply embedded in their cultures while simultaneously making a living within inevitable "Western" frames. And this is not really a "choice." Elements of their histories, ways of knowing and being, of stories passed along, are simply there. People differ broadly, as in any culture, in terms of their receptivity to traditional ways of knowing and being, but there is no sense of such ways being "lost" or of the people mourning for some Golden Age.
27. Among the many themes (multiple life roles people have; special skills and crafts they strive to keep alive; life-ways in different geographical locations; tensions between modernity and tradition; abuse of children in welfare systems, and the like) taken up in the by now fairly large number of Aboriginal films being made in several nations

(Canada, the United States, and Australia, for example) since the 1970s, the theme of struggles to regain land rights or over abuse to sacred Aboriginal sites looms large. Representing such struggles is of paramount importance to indigenous peoples, both as a way to express their rage at past and present injustices done and as a way to communicate abuses to a wider public—that is, to translate their experience to nonindigenous peoples or to record it for indigenous peoples.

28. See Web site, *www.bloorstreet.com/300block/ablawleg.htm* for details of Australian legislation and specific cases vis-à-vis Australian Aborigines.
29. As Australian scholars note, it is dangerous to talk about any monolithic collective trauma to the Australian nation as a whole. The nation is made up of many different groups, each of which deals with Australia's past in its own ways. The national leadership may well be perfectly aware of the crimes committed against the Aborigines, and in no way feel a need for reparation or reconciliation. Many followers of such leadership would take up the same position. While this stance might be seen as a form of denial—as really representing repressed guilt—one cannot be sure. Meanwhile, many in Australia are in denial because the past is simply too painful to remember. Others actively seek reparation and healing. But these are issues too complex to address fully in this context.
30. See pamphlet, *Link Up*, and Peter Read's volume, *A Rape of the Soul So Profound* (Australia: Allen and Unwin, 1999).
31. See the following sites: *http://www.geocities.com/CapitalHill/7124/english.html.* You can click on any item and the entire document will come up. Try also in regard to Canadian Government and Native Sovereignty, *www.sisis.nativeweb.org/clark/cangovt.html.* For details about the vagaries and complex arguments about the so-called Indian Act, see *www.bloorstreet.com/200black/sindact.htm.* See also Vine Deloria Jr. and David E. Wilkins, *Tribes Treaties and Constitutional Tribulations* (Austin: University of Texas Press, 1999); and Peter Nabokov, *Native American Testimony: A Chronicle of Indian-White Relations from Prophecy to the Present, 1492–2000* (New York and London: Penguin Books, 1991/1999).

Chapter 6 The Ethics of Witnessing

1. Daughter of Russian Jewish immigrants, Maya Deren came to the United States in 1922, living first with her parents in Adams, New York, then Columbus, Ohio, and finally in Syracuse, where she studied journalism and began to be interested in Socialism. Married to Gregory Bardacke, also from Russia, who was a union organizer, Deren became active in the Young People's Socialist League, a Trotskyite group. While at Smith College, now divorced from Bardacke, Deren studied French symbolist poetry, but did not show any particular interest in French surrealism. Soon after this, she worked for dance choreographer Katherine Dunham and began to be interested not only in dance but also in "primitive peoples" and their rituals, including voodoo. Her meeting with Alexander Hammid, a filmmaker with skills in editing, lighting, and photography, inspired Deren to turn her multiple artistic talents to film and it was with Hammid and Teiji Ito that she made *Meshes of an Afternoon* in 1947.
2. See the excellent study of this film by Lauren Rabinovitz in her *Points of Resistance: Women, Power, and Politics in the New York Avant-Garde Cinema in New York, 1943–1971* (Champaign, IL: University of Illinois Press, 1991).
3. I am aware of the dangers of too readily collapsing Western theories and non-Western contexts. Questions still remain about the applicability of psychoanalysis to contemporary Western, let alone non-Western, cultures. But that problem, while one I have thought about a good deal, is not part of this project. See my *Looking for the Other: Feminism, Film, and the Imperial Gaze* (New York and London: Routledge, 1997).

4. A personal note: As a visiting fellow at the Humanities Research Center, Australian National University, about ten years ago, I wanted to find out about multicultural Australian women's films, and managed to contact Tracey Moffatt. She agreed to an interview, and I found her just completing a first cut of *Night Cries*. I was able to ask her a few questions about the film. I subsequently wrote informally about my impressions of Moffatt's work, its relation to Chauvel's film *Jedda*, for the *Olive Pink Society Journal* and talked about the need for cross-cultural film analysis, since I was then working on Chinese film. My short Moffatt essay had its impact and was reprinted in a volume edited by Julie Marcus aimed at university media students (see *Picturing the "Primitif,"* edited by Julie Marcus [61–72]). When I later I wanted to work on aging, Moffatt's *Night Cries* immediately occurred to me. The images of the white mother in *Night Cries* were etched on my mind. Seeing the film again, I was impressed by the daughter's trauma as a "stolen" child. I return to the film again now through the lens of trauma studies.
5. Moffatt was born in Brisbane, and was brought up by a white Australian woman. She studied filmmaking at Queensland College of the Arts in Brisbane, and is recognized as a still photographer. She graduated in 1982, moved to Sydney, and started to make documentaries and short films. For more details see interviews such as that on her film *Bedevil* by John Conomos and Raffaele Caputo, in *Cinema Papers* 93 (1993), and those in the impressive volumes on her work, linked to exhibitions in New York and Germany, such as *Free Falling,* published by the Dia Center for the Arts (New York: Arts Publishers, 1998); or *Tracey Moffatt,* ed. Martin Hentschel and Gerald Matt (Stuttgart: Dr. Cantz'sche Drukerei, 1998). In a personal communication with me, Moffatt told me that she "couldn't bear to be written about as a 'minority.' I see myself [she continues] as an artist who happens to cast black people (and other races—for various reasons) in my movies. I think my films break rules" (1993). Moffatt's declared influences are often from Western literature and drama: she says that writers like Garcia Lorca, Eugene O'Neill, and Tennessee Williams have influenced her, but also Japanese films by Ozu and Kobayashi, Italian ones by Fellini, and American cinema too (as she notes in several interviews). For these reasons, as I will argue, there is certainly a deliberate universal cast to *Night Cries*. However, the relationship between the white and Aborigine characters is specific to Australia, including the policy of forced adoption of light-skinned Aboriginal children by white families. The landscape in the film is also specifically Australian and this setting is important in carrying out the troubled family theme. In a brochure about Moffatt's 1998 show at the Dia Center for the Arts, it is stated that Moffatt's "trademark synthetic approach" is evident in *Night Cries,* "typified here in the fusion of stenographic compositional modes with the forms and palette characteristic of postwar Australian landscape painting from Arthur Boyd and Russell Drysdale to Albert Namatjira, the latter a highly successful and popular Aboriginal painter whose work has never, however, been sanctioned within the fine art canon."
6. Let me just note that while Moffatt eschews being identified as an Aboriginal artist, this does not mean that there are not obvious Aboriginal themes in her work.
7. Interestingly, their book focuses on the traumas of the children being stolen. But in some ways, I imagine the traumas of the mothers to be even worse. The children clearly did not know what was happening, or it only slowly dawned on them. The mothers knew at once, in an instant, and react powerfully if without impact. In a pamphlet by Peter Read on "The Stolen Generations," Read does imagine the mother's trauma: "The mother, suddenly deprived of her family, went into a state of shock from which she never really recovered. For months, not a word was heard of her children" (6).
8. In 2002, Philip Noyce produced a film, *Rabbit-Proof Fence,* based on Molly Kelly's story about her mother Doris Pilkington Garimara's forced removal in 1931 from her

mother (Kelly's grandmother). She was sent to a government institution, as happened to many Aborigines. This moving and vivid portrayal brought Australia's cruel policies (only abandoned in 1971) to wide public notice.

9. Laleen Jayamanne also discusses this scene in her "'Love me tender, love me true, never let me go . . .': A Sri Lankan reading of Tracey Moffatt's *Night Cries—A Rural Tragedy*," in *Feminism and the Politics of Difference*, ed. Sneja Gunew and Anna Yeatman (London: Allen and Unwin, 1993): 73–84. Jayamanne notes that the song being sung silently by Jimmy Little here is Elvis Presley's "Love me tender, lover me true." See note, p. 82.
10. Artists and scholars have begun to explore links between comedy and trauma, some of the work inspired by Robert Benigni's film, *Life Is Beautiful* (1999), about a father's using humor to protect his son from knowledge about what was really going on in the Nazi concentration camps. Two students in a class I taught wrote interesting essays about ways in which humor might be one way to work trauma through.
11. I have developed this difficult argument in my paper, "Trauma, Aging, and Melodrama (with Reference to Tracey Moffatt's *Night Cries*)," in *Feminist Locations*, ed. Marianne DeKoven (New Brunswick, NJ: Rutgers University Press, 2001): 304–328.
12. Since cinema melodrama continues the function that theatrical melodramas had already been filling as traumatic cultural symptom, Moffatt's reference acknowledges the way that traces of historical violence (like white Australian colonialism) irrupt in repeated narratives of suffering and loss.
13. See Ken Gelder and Jane Jacobs, *Uncanny Australia; Sacredness and Identity in a Postcolonial Nation* (Melbourne: University of Melbourne Press, 1999).
14. Freud's theories in *Moses* about the violence of historical events leaving traces for the generations that follow are obviously relevant, along with those of later theorists like Bakhtin, Peter Brooks, and Kaja Silverman.
15. See Dominick LaCapra, "Consciousness and Working-Through," in his *Representing the Holocaust: History, Theory, Trauma* (Ithaca, NY: Cornell University Press, 1996).

EPILOGUE "WOUNDED NEW YORK"

Judith Greenberg used this phrase in the title to her essay for her edited volume, *Trauma at Home: After 9/11* (Lincoln: University of Nebraska Press, 2003): 21–38.

1. This quotation is from Thomas W. Laqueur's review of Schivelbusch's 2003 book, *The Culture of Defeat: On National Trauma, Mourning, and Recovery*. Wolfgang Schivulbusch asks, in this book, might "the destruction of September 11 [have] uncovered the suppressed remains of Vietnam," making a second humiliation even more unbearable? And therefore the trauma of defeat even more unbearable?
2. The flurry of books, plays, documentaries, and fiction about 9/11 abated a bit as 2003 drew to a close, but nevertheless, hardly a day went by in 2003 without an article on 9/11 in the *New York Times*—an activity that continues in 2004. As with coverage of the early days of the attacks and then of the war in Iraq, I have obsessively clipped stories about 9/11, partly out of an attempt to fully come to terms with what has happened, partly because of interest in the social and psychological processes of rebuilding, and for what I could learn about behavior in such a situation. Coverage of each anniversary provided a kind of gauge of how the city as a whole was coping with the personal and public losses, while other incidental stories revealed unexpected aspects to the catastrophe. In what follows, I draw on select clippings, and tease out unconscious cultural legacies of the violence, evident, perhaps, in the reporting in the one newspaper seen to be the public "voice" of the city if not the nation.
3. Articles that I collected fall into four main categories, excluding the continuing coverage of the war on Iraq seen (rightly or wrongly) as a direct consequence of 9/11,

and of the new provocative legislation authorized by the Bush regime to protect American citizens from terrorism. This includes the notorious and controversial so-called Patriot Act. The four main categories, then, are articles surrounding the anniversaries, which in themselves take varied forms; those dealing with psychological issues, and with the related art works about 9/11, some of which I have discussed earlier; a miscellaneous group into which I put articles about what to do with artifacts from Ground Zero, recurring stories about firefighters and others who worked for months cleaning up Ground Zero, and health effects of the attacks, especially in lower Manhattan; stories about the government subsidies for relatives of victims and who has and has not applied for them, and other incidental stories; and finally, those (by far the most frequent in 2003) that I will focus on here covering debates about the rebuilding of Ground Zero and about designs for the memorial. Most of the political analyses from both liberal and right positions have not focused specifically on 9/11 but on the rightness or not of the Iraq war and the United States' handling of postwar Iraq (or as some would say, the continuing war-torn Iraq), and thus I did not include them per se in these files.

4. An image of the first stages of the project was printed in the *New York Times* on August 17, 2003, close to the second anniversary of 9/11. The monument, designed by the American architect, Peter Eisenman, will consist of 2,700 concrete slabs of varying heights meant to leave visitors disoriented. The first slabs were erected on August 16, 2003, according to the *Times*.
5. See, for example, James E. Young, *At Memory's Edge: After-Images of the Holocaust in Contemporary Art and Architecture* (New Haven and London: Yale University Press, 2000); and his *Texture of Memory: Holocaust Memorials and Meaning* (New Haven and London: Yale University Press, reprint edition, 1994). In this latter book, Young explores in depth how different nations remember the Holocaust in varied ways depending on their traditions, ideals, and experiences. He also takes into account aesthetic and architectural movements that pertain to building memorials. Many of the issues at stake in these different forms of Holocaust memorial are pertinent to other kinds of memorial building.
6. Debates about vulnerability continued in 2004 in regard to the so-called Freedom Tower, at this point the project of David M. Childs. See the *New York Times* article by James Glanz, "High Anxiety: Designing the Safest Building in History for the Scariest Address on Earth," Sunday, March 14, 2004, section 2: 25, 28.
7. Other voices have said similar things. Leon Wieseltier is quoted by David W. Dunlap in the *New York Times* saying that "nothing could more faithfully represent the loss we suffered on Sept. 11 2001 than a big, terrifying, unhelpful void. . . . There should be a substantial patch of ground that one is almost afraid to approach, but that one must. There should be something frightening about it" (*New York Times,* November 13, 2003). Tadao Ando, like Kelly, has "proposed a 'memorial tomb' in the form of a spherical mound 90 feet high" and argued that "if we are to fill the void at the site of the lost World Trade Center, it should not be with architecture but with a 'place' to remember and reflect" (ibid.). Dr. Sherwin B. Nuland reminds us that "one of the things Americans do least well . . . is to contemplate, meditate and be alone with themselves and with their thoughts" (ibid.).
8. Of course, even without this gauntlet, the terrorists are apparently striving for another catastrophic attack.
9. Libeskind's involvement with the Twin Towers' rebuilding adds another link to the Holocaust. While not conflating these catastrophes, whose relative scale and context and so on are vastly different, small echoes continue to emerge. In addition to the space being referred to as a "crematorium," in 2004 Art Spiegelman, known for this graphic novels (*Maus I* and *Maus II*) about how his Jewish parents survived the Holocaust, talked about his forthcoming book, *In the Shadow of No Towers* (Pantheon

Books). See interview with Claudia Dreifus, "A Comic-Book Response to 9/11 and Its Aftermath," *New York Times,* Saturday, August 9, 2004: B9, 11.

10. A new Holocaust Museum in Farmington Hills, Michigan, designed by Neuman/Smith and Associates, also aims to provide visitors with some experience of the holocaust by making the building evoke a concentration camp, including narrow ramps where only one person can pass at a time, and a dark room where disturbing clips from films taken during the liberation of the camps are shown. See the *New York Times* article, "In Suburbs, Reminder of Horror," March 16, 2004: E1.
11. In light of my own ways of reading Libeskind's design, this is ironic, but it just goes to show that there are a myriad ways of interpreting what one sees.
12. In a long *New York Times* article (August 31, 2003: Arts in Review 17), Julie V. Iovine surveys David Child's other three-high profile New York City projects, and outlines the characteristics of his designs.
13. As this book goes to press, however, it seems that there is to be yet one more round of competition in the space, this time for buildings in a museum complex. Libeskind, not deterred by his previous experiences, will evidently submit a design. See David W. Dunlap, "Cultural Centers Fill Out Latest Ground Zero Picture," *New York Times,* Saturday, August 7, 2004: B3.
14. See David W. Dunlap, "1,766-Foot Design Is Unveiled for World Trade Center Tower: Architects United on Plan for Tallest Building," *New York Times,* December 20, 2003, where more about the process by which the two came to agreement is detailed.
15. For example, in 2003 and 2004, when Americans should have been dealing with 9/11 and America's resulting global actions, we find a whole batch of films either imagining an inability to remember (*Memento)* or fantasizing finding ways to eliminate memory, to help people to forget (as in *Eternal Sunshine* or *Paycheck*). In other words, what cannot be addressed surfaces in symptoms like the films about memory today. Interestingly, according to a *New York Times* article, scientists have joined the effort to act out in seeking to discover a pill that would help people forget trauma. The article details an experiment in which research subjects who had taken the drug propranolol showed no physiological signs of stress when listening to a tape to reexperience their trauma (see "The Quest to Forget," *New York Times,* April 4, 2004: 35).

Works Cited

Abraham, Nicolas, and Maria Torok. *The Shell and the Kernel: Renewals of Psychoanalysis.* Edited and translated by Nicholas T. Rand. Chicago: University of Chicago Press, 1994.

Ackerley, G. D., J. Burnell, D. D. Holder, and L. A. Kurdek. "Burnout among Licensed Psychologists." *Professional Psychology: Research and Practice* 19, no. 6 (1996): 624–631.

Adorno, Theodor. *Negative Dialectics.* Translated by E. B. Ashton. New York: Continuum, 1973.

Ahmed, Sara. *Strange Encounters: Embodied Others in Postcoloniality.* New York and London: Routledge, 1999.

American Psychiatric Association. "Post-Traumatic Stress Disorder." *Diagnostic and Statistical Manual of Mental Disorders: III-R.* Washington, DC: American Psychiatric Association, 1987: 247–251. *DSM IV* (1994): 424–429.

Antelme, Robert. *L'Espèce humaine.* Paris: Éditions Gallimard, 1957. Translated by Jeffrey Haight and Annie Mahler as *The Human Race.* Marlboro, VT: Marlboro Press, 1992.

Argenti-Pillen, Alex. *Masking Terror: How Women Contain Violence in Southern Sri Lanka.* Philadelphia: University of Pennsylvania Press, 2003.

Baer, Ulrich. *110 Stories New York Writes After September 11.* New York: New York University Press, 2002.

Barker, Pat. *The Eye in the Door.* New York: Penguin, 1996.

———. *The Ghost Road.* New York: Viking, 1995.

———. *Regeneration.* New York: Viking, 1991.

Barrett, Deidre. *Trauma and Dreams.* Cambridge, MA: Harvard University Press, 1996.

Becker, David. "Dealing with the Consequences of Organized Violence in Trauma Work." In *Berghof Handbook for Conflict Transformation.* Berlin: Berghof Research Center for Constructive Conflict Management, 2001: 1–21.

———, and Brandon Hammer. "Trauma Work in Crisis Regions—Developing and Assessing Quality." Paper read at the Trauma Research Networking Conference, Wiesbaden-Naurod, June 30, 2002.

Berger, John. "Photographs of Agony." In *About Looking.* New York: Vintage Books, 1980: 41–44.

Berlant, Lauren. "Poor Eliza." *American Literature* 70, no. 3 (September 1998): 635–668.

Blake, Michael. *Dances with Wolves.* New York: Ballantine Books, 1997.

Bourke, Joanna. *Dismembering the Male: Men's Bodies, Britain, and the Great War.* London: Reaktion Books, 1996.

Bremner, J. Douglas. *Does Stress Damage the Brain? Understanding Trauma-Related Disorders from a Mind-Body Perspective.* New York: W. W. Norton, 2002.

Brenner, Ira. *Dissociation of Trauma: Theory, Phenomenology, and Technique.* Madison, WI: International Universities Press, 2001.

Breton, André. "Manifesto of Surrealism" (1924). In *Manifestoes of Surrealism.* Translated by Richard Seaver and Helen R. Lane. Ann Arbor: University of Michigan Press, 1969: 3–47.

Bringing Them Home: Report of the National Inquiry into the Separation of Aboriginal and Torres Strait Islander Children from Their Families. Canberra, April 1997.

Brooks, Peter. *The Melodramatic Imagination.* New Haven: Yale University Press, 1976.

Brown, Laura S. "Not Outside the Range: One Feminist Perspective on Psychic Trauma." In Caruth, *Trauma* 100–112.

Brown, Wendy. "Wounded Attachments." In *States of Injury: Power and Freedom in Late Modernity.* Princeton, NJ: Princeton University Press, 1995: 52–76.

Burgoyne, Robert. *Film Nation: Hollywood Looks at U.S. History.* Minneapolis: University of Minnesota Press, 1997.

Caddies, Kelvin. *Kevin Costner: Prince of Hollywood.* London: Plexus, 1992.

Caruth, Cathy. "The Claims of the Past." Lecture at the Humanities Institute, State University of New York at Stony Brook, November 1998.

———. *Unclaimed Experience: Trauma, Narrative, and History.* Baltimore: The Johns Hopkins University Press, 1996.

———, ed. *Trauma: Explorations in Memory.* Baltimore: The Johns Hopkins University Press, 1995.

Cheng, Anne Anlin. *The Melancholy of Race: Psychoanalysis, Assimilation, and Hidden Grief.* Oxford: Oxford University Press, 2001.

Clark, Vé Vé, Millicent Hodson, and Catrina Neiman. *The Legend of Maya Deren: A Documentary Biography and Collected Works.* New York: Anthology Film Archives/Film Culture, 1984.

Coates, Susan W., Jane L. Rosenthal, and Daniel S. Schechter, eds. *September 11: Trauma and Human Bonds.* New York: Analytic Press, 2003.

Collin, Françoise, and Françoise Proust, eds. *Sarah Kofman: Les Cahiers du Grif.* Paris: Descartes et Cie, 1997.

Connolly, William E. *Neuropolitics: Thinking, Culture, Speed.* Theory Out of Bounds, no. 23. Minneapolis: University of Minneapolis Press, 2002.

Costner, Kevin, Michael Blake, and Jim Wilson. *Dances With Wolves: The Illustrated Story of the Epic Film.* New York: Newmarket Press, 1991.

Crews, Frederick. "Defying Psychiatric Wisdom: These Skeptics Say 'Prove It.'" *New York Times* March 9, 2004: F1, F6.

———. "The Trauma Trap." *New York Review of Books* March 11, 2004: 37–40.

Cvetkovich, Ann. *An Archive of Feelings: Trauma, Sexuality, and Lesbian Public Cultures.* Durham, NC: Duke University Press, 2003.

Dalenberg, C. J. "Counter-Transference and the Treatment of Trauma." Washington, DC: American Psychological Association, 2000.

Danieli, Y. "Countertransference, Trauma and Training." In *Countertransference in the Treatment of PTSD.* Edited by J. P. Wilson and J. D. Lindy. New York: The Guilford Press, 1994: 368–388.

———. "Countertransference and Trauma: Self-Healing and Training Issues." In *Handbook of Post-Traumatic Therapy.* Edited by M. B. Wilson and J. F. Sommer. Westport, CT: Greenwood Press, 1994: 540–563.

Davies, J. M., and M. G. Frawley. *Training the Adult Survivor of Childhood Sexual Abuse: A Psychoanalytic Perspective.* New York: Basic Books, 1994.

De Certeau, Michel. "The Fiction of History: The Writing of *Moses and Monotheism.*" In *The Writing of History.* Translated by Tom Conley. New York: Columbia University Press, 1988: 310–350.

Dean, Tim, and Christopher Lane, eds. *Homosexuality and Psychoanalysis.* Chicago: University of Chicago Press, 2001.

Deloria, Vine Jr., and David E. Wilkins. *Tribes, Treaties, and Constitutional Tribulations.* Austin: University of Texas Press, 1999.

Deutscher, Penelope, and Kelly Oliver, eds. *Enigmas: Essays on Sarah Kofman.* Ithaca, NY: Cornell University Press, 1999.

Dreifus, Claudia. "A Comic-Book Response to 9/11 and Its Aftermath." *New York Times* August 9, 2004: B9, 11.
Dunlap, David W. "1,766-foot Design is Unveiled for World Trade Center Tower." *New York Times* December 20, 2003: A1, B4.
———. "A 16-Acre Memorial That'll Never Be." *New York Times* November 13, 2003, Metro sec.: 2.
———. "Cultural Centers Fill Out Latest Ground Zero Picture." *New York Times* August 7, 2004: B3.
Duras, Marguerite. *C'est Tout.* Paris: P.O.L., 1995.
———. *La Douleur.* Paris: P.O.L., 1985
———. *The War: A Memoir.* Translated by Barbara Bray. New York: Pantheon, 1986.
Early, Emmett. *The Raven's Return: The Influence of Psychological Trauma on Individuals and Culture.* Wilmette, IL: Chiron Publications, 1993.
Edwards, Coral, and Peter Read, eds. *The Lost Children.* Sydney and New York: Doubleday, 1997.
Edwin, Steve. "'Impossible' Professions: Sarah Kofman, Witnessing, and the Social Depth of Trauma." In *Between the Psyche and the Social,* edited by Kelly Oliver and Steve Edwin. Lanham, MD: Rowman and Littlefield, 2002: 123–148.
Eissler, Kurt Robert. *Freud as an Expert Witness: The Discussion of War Neuroses between Freud and Wagner-Jauregg.* Translated by Christine Trollop. Madison, WI: International Universities Press, 1986.
Elsaesser, Thomas. "Postmodernism as Mourning Work." In "Trauma and Screen Studies: Opening the Debate." *Screen* 42, no. 2 (Summer 2001): 193–201.
———. "Tales of Sound and Fury: Observations on the Family Melodrama." In Gledhill 43–69. (Originally published in 1972.)
Eng, David, and David Kazajian, eds. *Loss.* Berkeley: University of California Press, 2002.
Erdrich, Louise. *The Antelope Wife.* New York: HarperCollins, 1998.
Erikson, Kai. "Notes on Trauma and Community." In Caruth, *Trauma* 183–199.
Essed, Philomena, and David Theo Goldberg, eds. *Race Critical Theories: Text and Context.* Oxford and Malden, MA: Blackwell, 2002.
Esterson, Allen. "Jeffrey Masson and Freud's Seduction Theory: A New Fable Based on Old Myths." *History of the Human Sciences* 11, no. 2 (February 1998): 1–21.
Fanon, Frantz. "Colonial Wars and Mental Disorders." In *The Wretched of the Earth.* Translated by Constance Farrington. New York: Grove Press, 1963: 201–251.
Farquhar, Dion. "Reading Crises of the 'Real': A Cross-Talk Essay." In Hesford and Kozol 262–275.
Felman, Shoshana. "Education and Crisis, or the Vicissitudes of Teaching." In Caruth, *Trauma* 13–60.
———, and Dori Laub. *Testimony: Crises of Witnessing in Literature, Psychoanalysis, and History.* New York and London: Routledge, 1992.
Figley, Charles R. *Coping with Secondary Traumatic Distress Disorder in Those Who Treat the Traumatized.* New York: Brunner/Mazel, 1995.
———. "Catastrophe: An Overview of Family Reaction." In *Stress and the Family: Coping with Catastrophe,* vol. 2. Edited by Charles R. Figley and H. I. McCubbin. New York: Brunner/Mazel, 1983: 3–20.
Forsyth, Dr. David. "Functional Nerve Disease and the Shock of Battle: A Study of the So-Called Traumatic Neuroses Arising in Connexion with the War." *Lancet* 2 (December 25, 1915): 1399–1405.
Freud, Sigmund. *Beyond the Pleasure Principle.* 1920. Translated by James Strachey. New York and London: W. W. Norton, 1961.
———. *The Diary of Sigmund Freud: 1929–1939 (A Record of the Final Decade).* Translated and with an introduction by Michael Molnar. London: Freud Museum Publications, 1992.

———. "Heredity and the Aetiology of the Neuroses." In Standard Edition, vol. 3. Translated by James Strachey. London: The Hogarth Press, 1962: 143–156.

———. *Interpretation of Dreams.* Translated and edited by James Strachey. New York: Avon Books, 1955. Also: Standard Edition, vol. 4 (1953).

———. Introduction to Psycho-Analysis and the War Neuroses." In Standard Edition, vol. 17. Translated by James Strachey. London: The Hogarth Press, 1955: 205–210.

———. *Moses and Monotheism.* 1939. New York: Vintage, 1955.

———. "On the Psychical Mechanisms of Hysterical Phenomena." 1893. In *Collected Papers,* vol. 1. Translated by Joan Riviere. London: The Hogarth Press, 1949: 24–41.

———. "On the Theory of Hysterical Attacks." 1892/1940. In *Collected Papers,* vol. 5. Translated Joan Riviere. London: The Hogarth Press, 1949: 27–30.

———. "Thoughts for the Times on War and Death." 1915. In *Collected Papers,* vol. 4. Edited by Joan Riviere. London: The Hogarth Press, 1949: 288–317. Also Standard Edition, vol. 14: 273–289.

———, with Josef Breuer. "Charcot." 1893. In *Collected Papers,* vol. 1. Translated by Joan Riviere. London: The Hogarth Press, 1949: 1–24.

Freyd, Jennifer J. *Betrayal Trauma: The Logic of Forgetting Childhood Abuse.* Cambridge, MA: Harvard University Press, 1996.

Friedlander, Saul, ed. *Probing the Limits of Representation: Nazism and the "Final Solution."* Cambridge, MA: Harvard University Press, 1992.

Fussell, Paul. *The Great War and Modern Memory.* New York and London: Oxford University Press, 1975.

Gannon, Patrick J. "The Traumatic Commercial Film Experience: An Extension of Laboratory Findings on Stress in a Naturalistic Setting." Ph.D. dissertation, California School of Psychology, 1979: 8–14.

Gelder, Ken, and Jane Jacobs. *Uncanny Australia: Sacredness and Identity in a Post-Colonial Nation.* Melbourne: University of Melbourne Press, 1999.

Gilmore, Leigh. *The Limits of Autobiography: Trauma and Testimony.* Ithaca, NY: Cornell University Press, 2001.

Gilroy, Paul. *Against Race: Imagining Political Culture Beyond the Color Line.* Cambridge, MA: Belknap Press/Harvard University Press, 2000.

Glanz, James. "High Anxiety: Designing the Safest Building in History for the Scariest Address on Earth." *New York Times* Sunday, March 14, 2004, sec. 2: 25, 28.

Gledhill, Christine. *Home Is Where the Heart Is: Studies in Melodrama and the Woman's Film.* London: The British Film Institute, 1987.

Glynn, Thomas R. "The Traumatic Neuroses." *Lancet* 2 (November 5, 1910): 1332.

Gobodo-Madikizela, Pumla. *A Human Being Died That Night: A South African Story of Forgiveness.* Boston and New York: Houghton Mifflin, 2003.

Grady, Denise. "War Memories May Harm Health." *New York Times* December 16, 1997: F9.

Greenberg, Judith, ed. *Trauma at Home: After 9/11.* Lincoln: University of Nebraska Press, 2003.

Gunning, Tom. "The Cinema of Attraction: Early Film, Its Spectator, and the Avant-Garde." *Wide Angle* (Fall 1986): 63–70.

———. "An Aesthetic of Astonishment: Early Film and its (In)credulous Spectator." *Art & Text* 34 (Spring 1989): 31–45.

Guteril, Fred. "What Freud Got Right." *Newsweek* November 11, 2003: 50–52.

Haaken, Janice. *Pillar of Salt: Gender, Memory, and the Perils of Looking Back.* New Brunswick, NJ: Rutgers University Press, 1998.

Hacking, Ian. *Rewriting the Soul: Multiple Personality and the Sciences of Memory.* Princeton: Princeton University Press, 1996.

Hallward, Peter. *Absolutely Postcolonial: Writing between the Singular and the Specific.* Manchester: Manchester University Press, 2001.

Hansen, Miriam. "Introduction." In *Theory of Film* by Siegfried Kracauer. Reprint edition. Princeton: Princeton University Press, 1997: vii–xiv.

———. "*Schindler's List* is Not *Shoah*: The Second Commandment, Popular Modernism, and Public Memory." *Critical Inquiry* 22 (Winter 1996): 292–312.

Hardt, Michael, and Antonio Negri. *Empire*. Cambridge, MA: Harvard University Press, 2000.

Hedges, Chris. *What Every Person Should Know about War*. New York and London: Free Press, 2003.

Henig, Robin Marantz. "The Quest to Forget." *New York Times Magazine* April 4, 2004: 32–37.

Henke, Suzette A. *Shattered Subjects: Trauma and Testimony in Women's Life-Writing*. New York: St. Martin's Press, 1998.

Herman, Judith. *Trauma and Recovery: The Aftermath of Violence—from Domestic Abuse to Political Terror*. New York: Basic Books, 1992, 1997.

Hesford, Wendy S., and Wendy Kozol, eds. *Haunting Violations: Feminist Criticism and the Crisis of the Real*. Urbana and Chicago: University of Illinois Press, 2001.

Hirsch, Joshua. "Post-Traumatic Cinema and the Holocaust Documentary." In Kaplan and Wang 95–123.

Hirsch, Marianne. *Family Frames: Photography, Narrative and Postmemory*. Cambridge, MA: Harvard University Press, 1997.

———, and Leo Spitzer. "'We Would Not Have Come Without You': Generations of Nostalgia." *American Imago* 59, no. 3 (Fall 2002): 253–276.

Hoffman, Eva. *After Such Knowledge: Memory, History, and the Legacy of the Holocaust*. New York: Public Affairs, 2004.

———. *Lost in Translation: A Life in New Language*. New York: Penguin Books, 1989.

Hoffman, Martin L. *Empathy and Moral Development: Implications for Caring and Justice*. New York: Cambridge University Press, 2000.

———. "Empathy and Vicarious Traumatization." Unpublished manuscript, 2003.

———. "Empathy, its Development and Prosocial Implications." In C. B. Keasey, ed., *Nebraska Symposium on Motivation*, no. 25 (1978): 169–218.

Horowitz, Mardi Jan. "Psychic Trauma: Return of Images after a Stress Film." *Archives of General Psychiatry* 20 (1969): 552–559.

Huyssen, Andreas. "Memory Practices in Sculpture, Architecture, and Monuments." Lecture at the Humanities Institute, Stony Brook, February 20, 2001.

Ifekwunigwe, Jayne O. *Scattered Belongings: Cultural Paradoxes of "Race," Nation, and Gender*. London and New York: Routledge, 1999.

Iovine, Julie V. "The Invisible Architect." *New York Times* August 31, 2003: Arts Review 17.

Jameson, Fredric. *The Political Unconscious: Narrative as a Socially Symbolic Act*. Ithaca, NY: Cornell University Press, 1981.

Jayamanne, Laleen. "'Love me tender, love me true, never let me go . . . ': A Sri Lankan Reading of Tracey Moffatt's *Night Cries—A Rural Tragedy*." In *Feminism and the Politics of Difference*, ed. Sneja Gunew and Anna Yeatman. London: Allen and Unwin, 1993: 73–84.

Joseph, Betty. "Globalization and Feminist Accumulation: The Time and Space of Gendered Work." Paper read at Global Feminisms Conference, State University of New York at Stony Brook, March 2002.

Kampfner, John. "War Spin: Saving Private Story 'Flawed.'" BBC News Report (May 18, 2003). See http://news.bbc.co.uk.

Kaplan, Brett Ashley. "'Aesthetic Pollution': The Paradox of Remembering and Forgetting in Three Holocaust Commemorative Sites." *Journal of Modern Jewish Studies* 2, no. 1 (2003): 1–18.

Kaplan, E. Ann. *Looking for the Other: Feminism, Film, and the Imperial Gaze*. New York and London: Routledge, 1997.

———. "Melodrama, Cinema, and Trauma." *Screen* 42, no. 2 (Summer 2001): 201–205.
———. "Problematizing Cross-Cultural Analysis: The Case of Women in the Recent Chinese Cinema." *Wide Angle* 2, no. 11 (Spring 1989): 40–50.
———. "Trauma, Aging, and Melodrama (with Reference to Tracey Moffatt's *Night Cries*)." In *Feminist Locations,* ed. Marianne DeKoven. New Brunswick, NJ: Rutgers University Press, 2001: 304–328.
———, and Ban Wang. "Introduction." In Kaplan and Wang 1–22.
———, eds. *Trauma and Cinema: Cross-Cultural Explorations.* Hong Kong: Hong Kong University Press; Seattle: University of Washington Press, 2004.
Kaplan, Gary B., and Ronald P. Hammer. *Brain Circuitry and Signaling in Psychiatry: Basic Science and Clinical Implications.* Washington, DC: American Psychiatric Pub., 2002.
Kennedy, Rosanne, and Tikka Jan Wilson. "Constructing Shared Histories: Stolen Generations—Testimony, Narrative Therapy and Address." In *World Memory: Personal Trajectories in Global Time,* edited by Jill Bennett and Rosanne Kennedy. York: Palgrave Macmillan, 2003: 119–140.
Kirby, Lynne. *Parallel Tracks: The Railroad and Silent Cinema.* Durham, NC: Duke University Press, 1997.
Klein, Melanie. "A Contribution to the Psychogenesis of Manic-Depressive States (1935)," and "Mourning and Manic-Depressive States (1938)." In *The Selected Melanie Klein,* ed. Juliet Mitchell. New York: The Free Press, 1986: 115–174.
Kofman, Sarah. *Paroles Suffoquées.* Paris: Editions Galilée, 1987. Translated by Madeleine Dobie as *Smothered Words.* Chicago: Northwestern University Press, 1998.
———. *Rue Ordener, Rue Labat.* Translated by Ann Smock. Lincoln: University of Nebraska Press, 1996.
Kristeva, Julia. "The Malady of Grief: Duras." In *Black Sun: Depression and Melancholia.* Translated by Leon S. Roudiez. New York: Columbia University Press, 1989: 219–260.
Kroeber, A. L. "Totem and Taboo: An Ethnologic Psychoanalysis" (1920) and "Totem and Taboo in Retrospect." In Spurling 33–46.
Krystal, Henry. *Integration and Self-Healing: Affect—Trauma—Alexithymia.* New York: Analytic Press, 1988.
LaCapra, Dominick. *Representing the Holocaust: History, Theory, Trauma.* Ithaca, NY: Cornell University Press, 1994.
———. *Writing History, Writing Trauma.* Baltimore: The Johns Hopkins University Press, 2001.
Langton, Marcia. "*Well, I Heard It on the Radio and I Saw It on TV.*" Sydney: Australian Film Commission, 1993.
Lanzmann, Claude. "The Obscenity of Understanding." In Caruth, *Trauma* 200–220.
Laqueur, Thomas. "Lost Causes: Review of Wolfgang Schivulbusch's *The Culture of Defeat.*" *Nation* November 24, 2003: 25–29.
Laub, Dori. "Bearing Witness, or the Vicissitudes of Listening." In Felman and Laub 57–74.
———. "An Event without a Witness: Truth, Testimony, and Survival." In Felman and Laub 75–92.
———. "Truth and Testimony: The Process and the Struggle." In Caruth, *Trauma* 61–75.
Lazarus, R. S. et al. "A Laboratory Study of Psychological Stress Produced by a Motion Picture Film." *Psychological Monographs* 76 (1962).
LeDoux, Joseph. *The Emotional Brain.* New York: Simon and Schuster, 1996.
Leff, Leonard J. *Hitchcock and Selznick: The Rich and Strange Collaboration of Alfred Hitchcock and David O. Selznick in Hollywood.* New York: Weidenfeld and Nicolson, 1987.
Leonard, John. "Not What Happened But Why." Review of Susan Sontag's *Regarding the Pain of Others. New York Review of Books* February 2004: 11–12.
Lifton, Robert Jay. *The Broken Connection: On Death and the Continuity of Life.* Washington, DC: Analytic Press, 1979.
Lincoln, Sarah. "This Is My History: Trauma, Testimony, and Nation-Building in the 'New' South Africa." In Kaplan and Wang 27–46.

Leys, Ruth. *Trauma: A Genealogy*. Chicago: University of Chicago Press, 2000.
Loftus, Elizabeth. *Eyewitness Testimony*. Reprint. Cambridge, MA: Harvard University Press, 1996.
———. *The Myth of Repressed Memory: False Memories and Allegations of Sexual Abuse*. New York: St. Martin's Press, 1994.
Lowenstein, Adam. *Shocking Representation: Historical Trauma, National Cinema and the Modern Horror Film*. Forthcoming.
Luhrmann, T. M. "The Traumatized Social Self: The Parsi Predicament in Modern Bombay." In Robben and Suárez-Orozco 158–194.
Marcus, Julie. *Picturing the "Primitif": Images of Race in Daily Life*. Canada Bay: lhR Press, 2000.
Markus, Maria R. "Cultural Pluralism and the Subversion of the 'Taken-for-Granted' World." In Essed and Goldberg 392–408.
Masson, Jeffrey Moussaieff. *The Assault on Truth: Freud's Repression of the Seduction Theory*. New York: Ballantine Books, 1984/2003.
McCann, I. L., and L. A. Pearlman. "Vicarious Traumatization: A Framework for Understanding the Psychological Effects of Working with Victims." *Journal of Traumatic Stress* 3, no. 1 (1990): 131–149.
McNally, Richard J. *Remembering Trauma*. Cambridge, MA: Belknap Press/Harvard University Press, 2003.
Mitchell, Juliet. "Trauma, Recognition, and the Place of Language." *Diacritics* 28, no. 4 (Winter 1998): 121–133.
Mulvey, Laura. "Notes on Sirk and Melodrama." 1977. Reprinted in *Visual and Other Pleasures*. London: Macmillan, 1989: 39–44.
———. "Visual Pleasure and Narrative Cinema." In *Visual and Other Pleasures*, edited by Laura Mulvey. Bloomington: Indiana University Press, 1989: 14–26. (Originally published 1975.)
Muñoz, José. "Feeling Brown: Ethnicity and Affect in Ricardo Bracho's *The Sweetest Hangover (and other STD's)*." *Theater Journal* 52 (2000): 67–79.
Muschamp, Herbert. "One Vision: A Green Hill at Ground Zero." *New York Times* September 11, 2003: E1, 4.
Nabokov, Peter. *Native American Testimony: A Chronicle of Indian-White Relations from Prophecy to the Present, 1492–2000*. New York and London: Penguin Books, 1991/1999.
Nancy, Jean-Luc. "Forward: Run, Sarah!" In Deutscher and Oliver viii–xvi. Originally in *Les Cahiers du Grif* (new series), 3 (1997): 29–32.
Newmark, Kevin. "Traumatic Poetry: Charles Baudelaire and the Shock of Laughter." In Caruth, *Trauma* 236–255.
Nichols, Bill. *Blurred Boundaries*. Bloomington: Indiana University Press, 1994.
———. "The Ethnographer's Tale." *Visual Anthropology Review* 7, no. 2 (Fall 1991): 31–47.
———. *Introduction to Documentary*. Bloomington: Indiana University Press, 2001.
Nowell-Smith, Geoffrey. "Minnelli and Melodrama." Reprinted in *Home Is Where the Heart Is:Studies in Melodrama and the Woman's Film*, edited by Christine Gledhill. London: The British Film Institute (BFI), 1987: 70–74.
Oliver, Kelly. "Sarah Kofman's Queasy Stomach and the Riddle of the Paternal Law." In Deutscher and Oliver 174–188.
———. *Witnessing: Beyond Recognition*. Minneapolis: University of Minnesota Press, 2001.
Oram, Gerard. *Worthless Men: Race, Eugenics and the Death Penalty in the British Army during the First World War*. London: Francis Boute Publishers, 1998.
Pearlman, L. A., and P. S. MacIan. "Vicarious Traumatization among Trauma Therapists: Empirical Findings on Self-Care: Traumatic Stress Points." *Traumatic Stress Points: News for the International Society for Traumatic Stress Studies* 7, no. 3 (1993): 5.
———, and K. W. Saakvitne. *Trauma and the Therapist*. New York: W. W. Norton, 1995.
Povinelli, Elizabeth A. "Settler Modernity and the Quest for an Indigenous Tradition." *Public Culture* 11, no. 1 (1999): 19–48.

Pratt, Mary Louise. *Imperial Eyes: Travel Writing and Transculturation.* London and New York: Routledge, 1992.

Rabinovitz, Lauren. *Points of Resistance: Women, Power and Politics.* Urbana: University of Illinois Press, 1991.

Radstone, Susannah. "Introduction" to "Trauma and Screen Studies: Opening the Debate." *Screen* 42, no. 2 (Summer 2001): 188–193.

———. "Screening Trauma: *Forrest Gump.*" In *Memory and Methodology*, edited by Susannah Radstone. Oxford and New York: Berg, 2000: 79–110.

Read, Peter. *A Rape of the Soul So Profound.* Sydney: Allen and Unwin, 2000.

Readings, Bill. "Pagans, Perverts or Primitives? Experimental Justice in the Empire of Capital." In *Judging Lyotard,* edited by Andrew Benjamin. London and New York: Routledge, 1992: 168–191.

Resick, Patricia A. *Stress and Trauma.* Philadelphia, PA: Psychology Press, 2001.

Robben, Antonius C.G.M., and Marcelo M. Suárez-Orozco. *Cultures under Siege: Collective Violence and Trauma.* Cambridge: Cambridge University Press, 2000.

Root, Maria P. P. "A Bill of Rights for Racially Mixed People." In Essed and Goldberg 355–368.

Rosenstone, Robert A. "The Future of the Past: Film and the Beginnings of Postmodern History." In *The Persistence of History: Cinema, Television and the Modern Event,* edited by Vivian Sobchack. New York and London: Routledge, 1996: 201–218.

Roth, Michael. "Why Trauma Now?" Unpublished paper delivered at the Humanities Institute at Stony Brook, 1998.

———, and Charles G. Salas, eds. *Disturbing Remains: Memory, History and Crisis in the Twentieth Century.* Los Angeles: Getty Research Institute, 2001.

Rothberg, Michael. *Traumatic Realism: The Demands of Holocaust Representation.* Minneapolis: University of Minnesota Press, 2000.

Sandweiss, Martha A. "Death on the Front Page." *New York Times* April 4, 2004: 13.

Scheckel, Susan. *The Insistence of the Indian: Race and Nationalism in Nineteenth-Century American Culture.* Princeton, NJ: Princeton University Press, 1998.

Schivelbusch, Wolfgang. *The Culture of Defeat: On National Trauma, Mourning, and Recovery.* New York: Metropolitan Press, 2003.

———. *The Railway Journey: Trains and Travel in the Nineteenth Century.* Translated by Anselm Hollo. New York: Urizen Books, 1979.

Sedgwick, Eve Kosofsky. *Shame and Its Sisters: A Silvan Tompkins Reader.* Durham, NC: Duke University Press, 1995.

———. *Touching Feeling: Affect, Pedagogy, Performativity.* Durham, NC: Duke University Press, 2003.

Seltzer, Mark. "Wound Culture: Trauma in the Pathological Public Sphere." *October* 80 (Spring 1997): 3–26.

Showalter, Elaine. *The Female Malady: Women, Madness and English Culture, 1930–1980.* London: Virago, 1987.

———. *Hystories: Hysterical Epidemics and Modern Culture.* New York: Columbia University Press, 1997.

Silverman, Kaja. "Male Subjectivity and the Celestial Suture: *It's a Wonderful Life.*" Reprinted in *Feminism and Film,* edited by E. Ann Kaplan. Oxford: Oxford University Press, 2000: 100–119.

———. *Male Subjectivity at the Margins.* New York and London: Routledge, 1992.

Simon, Sherry. *Gender in Translation: Cultural Identity and the Politics of Transmission.* London and New York: Routledge, 1996.

Slade, Andrew. "*Hiroshima, mon Amour,* Trauma, and the Sublime." In Kaplan and Wang 167–184.

Sobchack, Vivian, ed. *The Persistence of History: Cinema, Television, and the Modern Event.* New York: Routledge, 1996.

Sontag, Susan. *On Photography.* New York: Farrar, Straus and Giroux, 1977.

———. Editorial in "The Talk of the Town." *New Yorker* September 24, 2001: 32+.
———. *Regarding the Pain of Others*. New York: Farrar, Straus and Giroux, 2003.
Spiegelman, Art. *In the Shadow of No Towers*. New York: Pantheon, 2004.
Spurling, Laurence, ed. *Sigmund Freud: Critical Assessments*. Vol. 3, *Psychoanalysis of Culture*. London and New York: Routledge, 1989.
Streeck-Fischer, Annette. "What is Transmission of Trauma?" Paper peresented at the Trauma Research Networking Conference, Wiesbaden, Germany, June 2002.
Stow, Sara. "*To Live* and the Trauma of the Cultural Revolution." Paper presented at the "Trauma, Memory, and Cultural Politics" seminar, State University of New York at Stony Brook, 1997.
Truffaut, François, with the collaboration of Helen G. Scott. *Hitchcock*. New York: Simon and Schuster, 1967. Revised edition 1985.
van Alphen, Ernst. "Colonialism as Historical Trauma." In *Grey Areas: Representation, Identity, and Politics in Contemporary South African Art,* edited by Ernest van Alphen. Johannesburg: Chalkham Hill Press, 1999: 269–291.
van der Kolk, Bessel A. *Psychological Trauma*. New York: American Psychiatric Press, 1987.
———, and Onno van der Hart." The Intrusive Past: The Flexibility of Memory and the Engraving of Trauma." In Caruth, *Trauma* 158–182.
Veroff, J., R. Kulka, and E. Donovan. *Mental Health in America: Patterns of Help-Seeking from 1957–1976*. New York: Basic Books: 1981.
Walker, Janet. "The Traumatic Paradox: Documentary Films, Historical Fictions, and Cataclysmic Past Events." *Signs* 22, no. 4 (Summer 1997): 803–825.
———. "The Vicissitudes of Traumatic Memory and the Postmodern History Film." In Kaplan and Wang 125–146.
White, Allon. "Too Close to the Bone: Fragments of an Autobiography." In *Carnival, Hysteria, and Writing: Collected Essays and Autobiography*. Oxford: Clarendon Press, 1993: 26–58.
White, Hayden. "The Modernist Event." In Sobchack 17–38.
Williams, Linda. "'Something Else Besides a Mother': *Stella Dallas* and the Maternal Melodrama." *Cinema Journal* 24, no. 1 (1985): 2–27.
Wilson, J. P., and J. D. Lindy. "Theoretical and Conceptual Foundations of Counter-Transference in Post-Traumatic Therapies." In J. P. Wilson and J. D. Lindy, eds. *Countertransference in the Treatment of PTSD*. New York: Guilford Press, 1994: 1–82.
Wolf, Michael. "What, Us Worry? Yes, Us Worry." *New York* (February 24, 2003).
Wylie, Philip. *A Generation of Vipers*. New York: Farrar, 1942.
Young, James E. *At Memory's Edge: After-Images of the Holocaust in Contemporary Art and Architecture*. New Haven and London: Yale University Press, 2000.
———."A Prisoner of Memory." Review of Eva Hoffman's *After Such Knowledge*." *New York Times Book Review* (January 18, 2004): 13.
———. *Texture of Memory: Holocaust Memorials and Meaning*. Reprint. New Haven and London: Yale University Press, 1994.
Young, Robert J. C. *Colonial Desire: Hybridity in Theory, Culture and Race*. New York and London: Routledge, 1995.
———. *Postcolonialism: An Introduction*. New York and London: Routledge, 2001.

Index

About the Author

E. Ann Kaplan is a professor of English and comparative literary and cultural studies at the State University of New York at Stony Brook, where she also founded and directs the Humanities Institute. She was recently the president of the Society for Cinema and Media Studies.

Kaplan has written many books and articles on topics in cultural studies, media, and women's studies, from diverse theoretical perspectives including psychoanalysis, feminism, postmodernism, and postcolonialism. She has given lectures all over the world and her work has been translated into six languages. Her many books include, most recently, *Looking for the Other: Feminism, Film, and the Imperial Gaze* (1997), *Playing Dolly: Technocultural Formations, Fantasies, and Fictions of Assisted Reproduction* (1998, coedited with Susan Squier), and *Feminism and Film* (2000). Her volume *Trauma and Cinema: Cross-Cultural Explorations* (coedited with Ban Wang) appeared from Hong Kong University Press in 2004. She is working on two further book projects: *Found (and Lost) in Translation,* on images of bi- or multicultural encounters in film internationally; and *The New Cultural Obsession with Aging*, which looks at contemporary discourses about age and the elderly in science, literature, and the media in historical perspective.

Trauma Culture